"THE ORIGINAL X"

Created and Directed by Hans Höfer

INSIGHT GUIDES

aTLanTa

Edited and Produced by Martha Ellen Zenfell
Photography by Bob Krist

Editorial Director: Brian Bell

HOUGHTON MIFFLIN COMPANY

APA PUBLICATIONS

ABOUT THIS BOOK

Höfer

Ralph McGill, writing in the *Atlanta Journal and Constitution,* observed that "Atlanta was born with energy in her body. In her genes were transportation, movement, drive." A city with the aplomb of Atlanta lends itself especially well to the approach taken by the 190-title award-winning *Insight Guides* series, created in 1970 by **Hans Höfer**, founder of Apa Publications and still the company's driving force. Each book encourages readers to celebrate the essence of a place rather than try to tailor it to their expectations and is edited in the belief that, without insight into a people's character and culture, travel can narrow the mind rather than broaden it.

The books are carefully structured: the first section covers a destination's history, and then culture in a series of magazine-style essays. The main Places section provides a comprehensive run-down on the things worth seeing and doing, with a little bit of gossip thrown in for good measure. Finally, a fact-packed listings section contains all the information you'll need on travel, hotels, shops, restaurants and opening times. Complementing the text, remarkable photography sets out to communicate directly and provocatively life as it is lived by the locals.

Zenfell

Insight Guide: Atlanta was masterminded by **Martha Ellen Zenfell**, Apa's editor-in-chief for US titles. Having edited Insight Guides to New York, New Orleans, Los Angeles and Chicago, Zenfell was perfectly placed to realize one of the city's dreams. "Atlanta wants to be recognized as a city on an equal par with Paris, London and New York," she says. "So I deliberately set out to make an international book – authoritative, sassy and sophisticated." A Southerner by birth and now based in London, Zenfell feels the city might achieve its aims "when it grows up a little bit."

Krist

Zenfell's first job was to hire the photographer **Bob Krist**, winner of 1994's Travel Photographer of the Year award presented by the Society of American Travel Writers. Krist's work appears regularly in *National Geographic, Travel & Holiday* and many other publications. He began the daunting task of taking the 200-plus pictures which illustrate the book before Zenfell had even finished commissioning writers.

The first on board was **Tom Chaffin**, who wrote most of the history chapters. He has worked as a journalist in New York, San Francisco, and Paris. With a PhD in US history and two books under his belt, Atlanta-based Chaffin has strong views about the city. "It's a great place to do business – and the taxes that come from that business have allowed it to do many things. But I also think that certain dangers attend a blind worship of growth; both history and a sense of community get paved over. I worry that Atlanta could become Anyplace, North America."

Richard M. McMurry, who wrote "War Comes to Atlanta," is a Civil War specialist who also conducts guided tours to various battle sites.

For the past decade, **Ren** and **Helen Davis**, along with their son Nelson, have hiked hundreds of miles around the city researching and writing their popular guidebook *Atlanta Walks*. A perfect choice, then, to walk the streets again for most of this book's Places

Ren and Helen Davis

Schemmel

chapters. All three agree that the best way to sample the colorful tapestry of Atlanta – from the inner city to the distant suburbs – is on foot.

William Schemmel has done his share of traveling, too, but Georgia is his specialty. This native son's two books, *Georgia Off the Beaten Path* and *Country Towns of Georgia,* cover such distances that the research for this book's "The Antebellum Trail" could be conducted at a suitably rural snail's pace.

Byrd and Kerdasha

Our women in Savannah are **Georgia R. Byrd** and **Mary Beth Kerdasha.** Byrd is the editor of *Savannah Magazine* and a columnist for the *Savannah News-Press.* Mary Beth Kerdasha is managing editor of *Savannah Magazine.* "I hope the Savannah chapter captures the flavor of our historic city and compels readers to complete their journey south from Atlanta," says Kerdasha. "It will only take one visit for travelers to become intrigued with the gracious Southern style of my hometown."

Simmons

T he book's essays were written by a host of locals and experts. "Atlantans" was penned by **Vincent Coppola**, who has covered the South for many years for both *Newsweek* and *Atlanta* magazines. "Black Atlanta" was written by Tina Chism, associate editor of the *Atlanta Tribune*, an African-American business and lifestyle publication. Her colleague, **Carole R. Simmons**, the editor of the *Tribune*, contributed the "Sweet Auburn" chapter. Says Simmons: "Atlanta makes you think about who you are, why you are and how much more you could be – if only you could get off the interstates."

Tony Heffernan, who wrote "Atlanta Means Business," worked for Reuters, UPI and *Business Week* magazine, and is a regular contributor to Atlanta's business magazine, *Georgia Trend.* The two lifestyle and culture essays are the work of **Jane F. Schneider**, a native of Pennsylvania, but who has spent most of her life in Georgia. Co-author of a guidebook for residents, Schneider writes weekly about food and wine for the *Atlanta Journal and Constitution.*

'eman-Herring

Award-winning radio producer and reporter **Ed Hula** is the Olympics correspondent for News Radio WGST in Atlanta, and authoritative author of our piece on the games. **Louise Forrester Chase** is an Atlanta-based freelance writer and author of our two short pieces on the Atlanta Project and Buckhead's etiquette school. The former associate editor of *Charleston* magazine, she will soon be covering that city's charms in a forthcoming Insight Guide to the Southern States.

Another Insight stalwart is **Elizabeth Boleman-Herring**, compiler of the Travel Tips section. Author of the *Insight Pocket Guide to Atlanta* and numerous other books, Boleman-Herring's ideas, opinions, editing and, occasionally, actual words are liberally scattered throughout this book.

Thanks, finally, to our two Scarletts: **Mellie Meadows** (page 18) and **Talaxe Vasquez** (page 80), as well as **Kwa Hill** and **Jenny Stacy** of the Atlanta and Savannah Convention & Visitors Bureaus for smoothing our photographer's way. In Insight Guides' London editorial office, **Mary Morton** proofread and indexed the text.

—*Apa Publications*

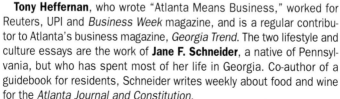

CONTENTS

CONTENTS

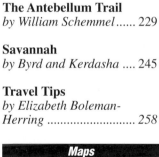

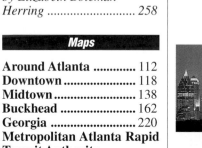

Atlanta – brave, bold, a cosmopolitan island surrounded by rural Georgia – has always been a city alert to opportunity. Many think this determination to succeed is a consequence of being burned during the Civil War. But in fact, as early as 1859, Greene B. Haygood was writing in *Sketch of Atlanta*: "the population of the city is remarkable for its activity and enterprise. Most of the inhabitants came here for the purpose of bettering their fortunes."

The "War of Northern Aggression" did indeed cripple the city, but at the same time strengthened its resolve to prevail. There is a definite note of satisfaction in the tone of Henry W. Grady, when in 1886 he penned the lines: "I want to say to General Sherman... that from the ashes he left us in 1864 we have raised a brave and beautiful city; that somehow or other we have caught the sunshine in the bricks and mortar of our homes." Grady, influential editor of the *Atlanta Constitution*, was an eloquent advocate of the new South, and it was due in no small measure to his efforts in wooing Northern investors that the city was soon on its feet again.

Atlanta hasn't looked back since. The undisputed capital of the Southeast, Atlanta leads the ranks in new jobs, new businesses, and new opportunities. The "sunshine in the bricks and mortar" is reflected in the graceful Victorian mansions of neighborhoods like Druid Hills and Inman Park, and it bounces, bright as a new penny, off the steel and chrome skyscrapers of Downtown, designed by internationally known native son John Portman in the brash, audacious manner that has contributed to the city's success.

Indeed, so accomplished has Atlanta become in rebuilding itself that, two decades ago, the *New York Times* was able to say: "Atlanta stands as the new American city in microcosm, still rising from the rubble of demolition and the dreams and determination of its business leaders. It is a 20th-century urban phenomenon."

Welcome, then, to a city of the future. This is evident, not just in Stone Mountain, which self-proclaimed New Agers have deemed a focal point of the world's upcoming "harmonic convergence," but in the attitude and outlook of Atlanta's residents. The city feels young. Its people look fresh. It has the prosperous, self-confident (and, it must be said, self-absorbed) air of a youthful town inventing itself.

John Portman, still actively involved in civic affairs, sums up the city's attitude this way: "Winning the Olympics is the latest example of our vision, our faith, and our cooperation. Clearly, we don't just let things happen – we make them happen. Therefore, we cannot just let the fact of our city change – we must direct the energy of these events and make it happen in the best manner possible."

Preceding pages: Dixie back in fashion; faces of Atlanta; wall of sound: practiced poise at L'Ecole des Ingenues etiquette school; sweet soul music; crinolines to go; a farmer's finest. Left, Scarlett goes shopping.

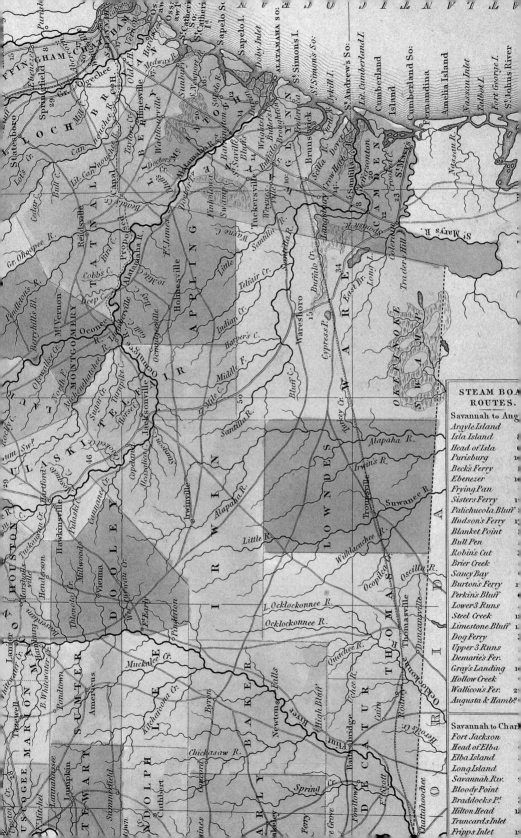

Tales of Atlanta's boosters – its incessant promoters of local business – are legion. The city that over the years has sold the world Coca-Cola, *Gone With The Wind*, CNN and the 1996 Olympics revels in its self-image as a good town for commerce – indeed, as a town whose business *is* business. What Atlanta lacks in seaports, navigable rivers, and mineral deposits, it more than makes up for with native pluck and a taste for somewhat over-blown sales rhetoric.

A scene a visitor stumbled upon in 1905 typified the spirit. In a hotel banqueting hall, "the cream of the business element in Atlanta," were gathered to plan the city's next "industrial exposition." Such fairs, designed to pitch the city to the world at large, were practically a growth industry unto themselves during Atlanta's first half-century.

But it wasn't the meeting's topic that left the strongest impression, more the assembly's almost religious fervor. "It was the one word – 'Atlanta' – that set the gathering to making a noise, a sort of talisman for a Babylonian confusion... To me it seemed that it was Atlanta alone every one in the banquet hall loved. For the time being at least every man present appeared to have forgotten his wife, his home, his father, his mother, his sweetheart. Atlanta was the all in all."

Capital city: The irony, of course, is that the tiny wilderness settlement that later grew into Atlanta began life, in 1837, as a place designed for the enrichment of capitalists in *other* American cities. A rail line, after all, has to end *somewhere*.

To understand Atlanta's rise from a desolate railroad stop to today's modern metropolis, it's necessary to ponder the dimensions of what one early settler called the "howling wilderness" from which the original settlement was carved. Four decades after independence from Great Britain, the United

States remained largely a seaboard civilization, a loosely connected chain of cities fronting the Atlantic Ocean and the Gulf of Mexico. Before rail lines pushed into the nation's interior, being located on a navigable river or coastline remained essential to the life of most cities. Indeed, as late as 1900, of all of the nation's cities with more than 100,000 residents, only two – Denver, Colorado and Indianapolis, Indiana – were not located on navigable waterways.

Away from the cities and towns that lined Georgia's coast during the early 19th century, Native American Indians still dominated much of the state. For the Indians of the rolling Piedmont, the piney foothills of the Appalachian Mountains, the beginning of the end came early in the century. For decades, white settlers from Savannah and Georgia's other coastal towns had been slowly pushing into the interior. Land was the main lure. After the War of 1812, cotton agriculture, once confined to the coast, spread rapidly into the interior.

By the 1820s, merchants in Georgia's

Preceding pages: map of Georgia, *circa* 1830. **Left**, *Yoholo-Micoco*, portrait of a Creek chief from the High Museum of Art. **Right**, Etowah Indian Mounds, Cartersville.

older towns like Savannah, Athens, and Macon increasingly pined for the chance to buy and sell that new inland cotton. Beyond that, the cotton boom increased the demand for meat and produce from other regions. In their rush to plant the cash crop, planters across Georgia had reduced their production of livestock and food crops to that which they needed for their own personal consumption. For everyone else in the state, that meant a growing dependence upon the "western produce" of the Ohio and Mississippi river valleys.

Eager to dominate the new interior cotton trade – and the market for western produce –

event, just three years later, sealed their fate. The discovery, in 1829, of gold in the state's northern mountains lured thousands of land-hungry prospectors onto lands occupied by the Cherokee and Creek Indian tribes. The former lived west of the Chattahoochee River, the latter to its east.

A treaty which had been more imposed than negotiated, and signed in 1825, had already forced most of the Creeks out of Georgia. Another imposed pact, in 1835, followed by a brutal, forced evacuation, dispatched the Cherokees. With the Indians gone, state officials completed the interior's division into counties and land parcels,

merchants in competing towns across Georgia began developing rival canal schemes. Each local group hoped, with the state government's financial assistance, to develop its own watery link to the interior and to the West. By the end of 1826, however, all the canal schemes had been abandoned. North Georgia's mountains, a state survey that year concluded, rendered all the canal plans impracticable: new rail lines would have to carry the freight.

Alone, the construction of rail lines into Georgia's interior spelled disaster for the region's Native Americans. But yet another

which white settlers acquired through a state-sponsored lottery.

Rival railroads: The removal of the tribes also hastened the coming of railroads into the interior. Georgia's government, in 1833, had licensed three private, rival, railroad companies. But while each sought to tap the inland cotton trade, none envisioned a connection with any of the westerly railroads. However, when out-of-state railroad companies began planning to bring in foodstuffs – in the process, bypassing Savannah in favor of Charleston – Georgia's three rival lines decided it was time to co-operate.

They asked the state to protect Savannah and other towns along Georgia's coast from commercial eclipse by Charleston. Responding to that request, Georgia's governor, Wilson Lumpkin, incorporated the Western & Atlantic Railroad in 1836. Designed to link with an existing east-west line north of Georgia, the new, state-sponsored line would run from a spot on the Tennessee River, near what is now Chattanooga, Tennessee, southward to a point on the southeastern bank of the Chattahoochee River. An amendment the next year stipulated that the line should run to the river's bank and beyond to "some point not exceeding eight

habited. There had once been a Cherokee village – Standing Peachtree, namesake of the modern thoroughfare – but it was long gone. There was a tavern 3 miles (5 km) to the west, and Decatur, 6 miles to the east.

What did impress the railroad officials, however, was the local topography: at a cool 1000 ft (300 meters) above sea-level, the site sat atop the intersection of three ridges – one reaching northwest, the other two southwards. It was, in other words, a natural setting for a junction of railroads.

Western & Atlantic officials had no great dreams about the little settlement, soon called Terminus, that began to grow around

miles as shall be most eligible for the running of branch roads to Athens, Madison, Milledgeville, Forsyth, and Columbus."

In 1837, Western & Atlantic officials decided to locate their railroad's southern terminus at a spot 7 miles (12 km) from the Chattahoochee River. To the untrained eye, it was an unremarkable locale. Three public roads intersected nearby (at today's Five Points, Atlanta's traditional center), but the surrounding wilderness lay virtually unin-

Left, streetscene, Terminus. **Above**, Stone Mountain, 1848.

the Zero Mile marker. It would, one predicted, "be a good location for one tavern, a blacksmith shop, and grocery store, and nothing else." Others, however, had higher hopes. At least a year before the site had been selected, local speculators had been buying and selling land in the area, anticipating a thriving new town.

With no local government to guide its design, Terminus grew haphazardly around the triangle of railroad tracks created by the Western & Atlantic and its two feeder lines. Property lots were drawn either perpendicular or parallel to the winding railroad tracks.

Adding to the confusion, property owners drew separate city grids and cut their own streets, with little regard for existing roads.

Even today, modern Atlanta attests to both the role of the railroad in the city's early development and to the laissez-faire entrepreneurship that animated its early growth. The orientation of the early settlement around railroad lines explains the curvilinear quality of the modern city's growth patterns. Likewise, on maps, note Downtown's various crunched-together grids. And when driving, note the odd angles at which streets often meet as they leave one grid for another.

Terminus had its amenities. But it remained a rough frontier town dominated by often out-of-work railroad hands. As a result of fits and starts in the national economy after a depression in 1837, it took more than a decade to complete work on the Western & Atlantic and its branch roads. Laid-off railroad workers in Terminus, meanwhile, idled away much of their time gambling and drinking. There was, one settler recalled, one saloon for every 50 inhabitants.

Terminus was renamed Marthasville in 1843, and Atlanta in 1847. The town continued to grow, but its rough edges remained. Indeed, one of Atlanta's first political controversies arose from a civic campaign to smooth out those edges.

Snake Nation: At the center of the dispute lay Snake Nation and Slab Town, two small villages on Atlanta's outskirts. It wasn't just that the drifters and railroad workers who inhabited both places were often noisy, drunk and violent. What *really* irritated was their refusal to pay taxes to the city's new municipal government, chartered in 1847. In 1850, determined to enforce the rule of law, a faction of local conservatives came together as the Moral, or Orderly, Party and offered their own candidate for mayor. The habitués of Snake Nation and Slab Town, meanwhile, countered with their own Rowdy, or Disorderly, Party.

Merchant Jonathan Norcross of the Moral Party won the mayoral race. But the battle wasn't over. Later, Rowdy thugs placed a cannon in front of his store, threatening to blow him out of business if he didn't promptly resign. But Norcross stood firm.

He gathered a posse of 100 men, surrounded the Rowdy Party's headquarters and arrested some 20 members. After promising to leave town, the arrested Rowdies were released. Norcross's posse, meanwhile, raided the Rowdies' old haunts – and Snake Nation and Slab Town were soon distant memories.

By 1855, Atlanta had taken on the trappings of a booming, even "respectable," commercial town: replete with thriving businesses, gas-lit streets, banks, churches, and theaters. Indeed, between 1850 and 1860, Atlanta's population jumped from 2,572 to 9,554 – a 271 percent increase.

Town of traders: Like the modern city of today, early Atlanta's economy was more commercial than industrial or agricultural. Reflecting that orientation, the 1860 population numbered 7,615 whites and 1,914 slaves. Despite images given by *Gone With The Wind*, Atlanta lay north of interior Georgia's main cotton belt: it sold but didn't grow the staple crop. Equally important for Atlanta's early growth, farmers from across the Upper Piedmont created a lively "wagon trade." They sold their crops in the city, then left with carts piled high with dry goods and groceries purchased during their stay.

The first Western & Atlantic train had run between Atlanta and the Tennessee River on May 9, 1850. Many had assumed that the straggly town which had grown around the new rail lines would not survive their completion. Perhaps a blacksmith shop or a crossroads store might survive, but little more. Instead, on the eve of the Civil War, the Rowdies had been sent packing, more rail lines had arrived, business was thriving, and Atlanta enjoyed the epithet "Gate City of the South."

Little wonder, then, that in the four-man presidential election of 1860, most of Atlanta's electorate turned their backs on secessionism and voted for Unionist candidates Stephen Douglas and John Bell. As one merchant summed up a shared skepticism: "the secessionists are chiefly professional men and young squirts who have little or nothing to lose."

Right, railroads have always played an important part in Atlanta's history.

Wilbur G. Kurtz
1963

In 1861 Atlanta was, by Southern standards, a bustling little city. Its 10,000 inhabitants worked in a variety of manufacturing, mercantile, and service businesses. Its four railroads connected it with the rest of the South, drew people to it, and gave it an importance far beyond its size. The "Gate City of the South", Atlanta boasted a zesty spirit that set it apart from older, even more urban areas.

Its population was far more diverse than would have been expected in such a small, inland place at that time. When 11 slave states withdrew from the Union in 1860–61 and established their own national government, Atlanta, after much debate, decided to abandon its anti-secessionist stance and throw in its lot with the rest of the South's native sons. Atlanta's voters supported secession by almost two-to-one. After their state had declared itself out of the old Union, most of them enthusiastically threw themselves into preparations for the war that all knew might come soon. There was even a brash bid to become the capital of the new Confederate States of America.

Gate City Guards: Local "volunteer companies" hastened to offer their services in defense of "Southern rights." These organizations, which before the war had been as much social groups as military units, each numbered about 100 men. They sported names like the "Atlanta Rifles," the "Gate City Guards," and the "Steuben Yagers." This last company was made up of German immigrants and its roll-call included such unGeorgian names as Lichtstenstedt, Heinz, and Geutebruck.

Each day in the spring and early summer of 1861 these uniformed companies marched through Atlanta's streets and practiced their maneuvers in the city park.

Preceding pages: the exodus of the Confederates, 1864. Left, a window from Atlanta's Rhodes Hall depicting the swearing in of Jefferson Davis. Right, General John Bell Hood was appointed to defend Atlanta from attack.

Then, one by one, they were ordered off to "camps of instruction" and afterward sent on to what one soldier called the "sean of action." The folks at home tried to resume their normal life and kept in touch with their men at the front by letter. Through "soldiers' relief organizations" the citizens held benefit dances to raise money and purchased clothes and other supplies to send to the men in the army.

Many of Atlanta's women spent long

hours sewing for the soldiers; others volunteered to serve as nurses in the hospitals that soon sprang up in the city. Still more went to work in newly-opened government offices or labored in one or another of the area's textile mills. Some took employment in manufacturing establishments that had previously had all-male workforces.

The railroads made Atlanta a major wartime transportation center, and early in 1862 events at several points on the distant frontiers of the Confederacy combined to increase the city's importance. Union forces captured New Orleans, Louisiana, and

Memphis and Nashville, Tennessee, three of the Confederacy's most valuable urban industrial centers.

Once these places were lost to the South, Atlanta's importance increased. The city soon became the chief center of Confederate government activities in the West. (At that time, "the West" was the region between the Appalachian Mountains and the Mississippi River, the states of Kentucky, Tennessee, Georgia, Alabama, and Mississippi.)

Georgia officials also established a number of state offices in Atlanta, through which they struggled to provide services to the area's civilians. For example, the state

plates for gunboats could be manufactured.

From Atlanta's factories and shops came swords, cannon, rifles, pistols, and shoes for the Southern armies. Distilleries produced tens of thousands of gallons of whiskey for the government (theoretically at least for medicinal purposes).

The area's textile and flour mills and its bakeries and meat packing plants sent off train after train loaded with uniforms and food for Rebel soldiers. Those same trains returned from the war zone bringing back what seemed an endless stream of sick and wounded men.

The more seriously ill and injured were

purchased salt (necessary for the preservation of meat) and distributed it to the families of soldiers. The Western & Atlantic Railroad connecting Atlanta with Tennessee was also owned and operated by the state; the city government likewise provided help to the poor in the form of food, clothing, firewood, and medical care.

War production: Existing industries in and around Atlanta increasingly turned to war production, and new manufacturing facilities quickly came into operation. The city was one of the few places in the Confederacy where heavy railroad equipment and iron

cared for in Atlanta's own hospitals and often buried in her cemeteries. Those able to bear more travel were sent on to the military hospitals that quickly sprang up in almost every town along the railroads to the east, south, and southwest.

Several thousand employees of the government – state and Confederate, civilian and military – poured into the city to work in the newly-established postal, quartermaster, commissary, engineer, paymaster, and naval offices. Beginning in early 1862, hordes of refugees fleeing triumphant Yankee armies on the coast or in Kentucky, Tennessee, and

Mississippi flocked into Atlanta. Runaway slaves, deserters from the army, assorted criminals, gamblers, thieves, relatives of hospitalized soldiers, and others joined the throngs in Atlanta.

Even pro-Confederate newspapers from such Tennessee cities as Memphis, Knoxville, and Chattanooga relocated to Atlanta where they resumed publication and added their editorial voices to the clamor raised by the city's own press. The Memphis *Appeal*, for example, went through several earlier stops before alighting in Atlanta. It became known as the "moving *Appeal*" and later it would travel on south to Alabama where it

sional fighting in the outlying parts of the state, but the war did not really touch the area until the spring of 1864. Then a Yankee army based at Chattanooga, Tennessee, just outside Georgia's northwestern corner, pushed into the state.

This massive Union force was commanded by Major General William Tecumseh Sherman and numbered some 110,000 men. General Joseph E. Johnston, with a Confederate army of about 75,000 men, met the invaders near Dalton some 85 miles (136 km) northwest of Atlanta.

Johnston believed that Sherman's army was so much stronger than his own that his

was being published when the war ended.

Hotels, restaurants, bars, brothels, banks, dentists' offices, and dozens of other businesses sprang up or expanded to provide goods and services to this growing population. By the middle of the war, more than 20,000 people lived in Atlanta and every week thousands more moved through the city *en route* to other destinations.

In the first years of the war there were some raids along the Georgia coast and occa-

Above, the 14th and 20th Corps move out as Atlanta burns in the distance.

best chance was to wait for the opposing general to make a tactical mistake – such as an unwise division of his force – which would give the Rebels an advantage. Only then, Johnston thought, could he strike. While awaiting such an opportunity General Johnston fortified a strong position in the hope that the Federal Army would make a suicidal attack upon it.

But Sherman was too smart to be drawn into such a trap. Throughout May and June and into July, he moved forward, encountering Johnston's strong fortifications, and then detaching part of his army to work its way around Johnston's position and threaten the railroad that brought the Confederates' supplies from Atlanta. Johnston was not alert enough to detect the mistakes that Sherman made. He was unwilling to come out of his trenches and fight a pitched battle, and he was unable to devise any way to counter Sherman's moves. The Confederate commander, therefore, saw no alternative but to retreat south to a new position, whereupon the whole ballet would be repeated.

By early July, Johnston had fallen back across the Chattahoochee River and almost into the outskirts of Atlanta. His long retreat had opened many areas of the Confederacy

defeated and driven back, or even just kept out of Atlanta, Northern voters might well lose heart. In the summer of 1864 it seemed certain that, if there were no great military successes, the Lincoln government would be turned out of office and replaced by a new president and a new administration that would be willing to negotiate peace and Confederate independence.

Enter Hood: On July 17, President Jefferson Davis made a momentous decision. He had long distrusted Johnston, and he had been very disappointed with the general's inability to hold North Georgia. Davis was unable to learn from Johnston about any plans he

to invasion, demoralized a large number of his own troops, encouraged the Yankees, and thrown many Southern politicians and civilians into a panic. If he were to abandon Atlanta as he had North Georgia, he would plunge the Confederacy into despair.

Even worse, he would hand the Yankees a military success that would assure the re-election that fall of Abraham Lincoln as President of the United States and guarantee that the Federal government would continue the war until it entirely destroyed the Confederacy.

On the other hand, if Sherman could be

might have had to defend Atlanta, and he had received information indicating that Johnston was preparing to abandon the city without making any serious effort to hold it. Faced with this great crisis, Davis promptly removed Johnston from command of the army and named General John Bell Hood to take his place.

Hood found himself in desperate straits when he assumed command. Sherman was south of the Chattahoochee, closing in on Atlanta from the north and east. If the city is thought of as the center of a clock, the Yankees were stretched around the top of the dial from the figures 11 to 3 and were moving directly toward the center. Quickly Hood organized a strike against the Federals between 11 and 12 on the clock, and two days later he made a furious attack on those at position 3. These engagements, known as the Battles of Peachtree Creek (July 20) and Atlanta (July 22), were brutal struggles in which the Southerners launched heroic – but uncoordinated, mismanaged, and unsuccessful – attacks on the Federals. (It is this latter fight that is depicted in the famous Atlanta Cyclorama – *see page 182*.)

Since his move to the 3 o'clock position had cut the railroad east of Atlanta, Sherman

managed their efforts and wasted the lives of many of their soldiers. After this attack on his army, however, Sherman did not make an aggressive push for the railroads.

During the next few weeks both armies concentrated on building massive fortified positions. Soon, two long parallel lines of trenches ran from the east of Atlanta, around the north and west of the city, and off to the southwest. Neither commander was foolish enough to make an attack on such strong earthworks. With his last railroads protected behind these fortifications, Hood, so far, was holding the city.

In late July and early August, Sherman

next shifted back around the top of the clock to get to the railroad lines running into the city from the southwest and south (7 and 6 on the clock). Hood sought to parry this movement at Ezra Church (the 9 o'clock position) on July 28.

In this battle, as in the earlier engagements, Hood was poorly supported by his subordinate generals, who once again mis-

The Civil War was one of the first wars to be documented by the camera. Left, Atlanta's railroad is left in ruins. Above, Union forces camp out in front of City Hall.

bombarded Atlanta with his artillery. He also tried to cut the Confederate rail lines by sending his cavalry to operate far to the south. Rebel horsemen defeated these efforts and chased Sherman's hapless raiders back to the safety of the main Yankee army.

With Sherman's cavalry crippled, Hood decided to retaliate. He ordered a major part of his own cavalry into North Georgia to break the railroad lines that transported supplies to Sherman's army. Unfortunately for the Confederates, the commander of this force ignored his instructions to operate against Sherman's rail line for only a few days. Instead, after doing minor damage to the railroad, he went off into East Tennessee, far from the beleaguered Atlanta army.

Once certain that many of the Southern horsemen had been removed from the picture, Sherman renewed his effort to cut Hood's last line of rail communication with the rest of the Confederacy. Drawing most of his army back, the Federal commander then moved it far around to the west and south of Atlanta. By the end of August Yankee troops were approaching the railroad in the area of Jonesboro, some 16 miles (25 km) below Atlanta (position 6 on the clock).

Although Hood was aware of the general munition and then marched away to the south. Mobs of civilians turned to looting and did further damage to the city until the Yankees came and restored order.

On September 2, Mayor James M. Calhoun surrendered Atlanta to Federal troops, and by noon that day the Stars and Stripes floated above the city for the first time in more than three years. Many of the civilian inhabitants had fled weeks earlier; many others left when, or soon after, Hood's army marched out.

Not all of those who remained were sad to see the Yankees come. Late on September 2, as General Alpheus S. Williams marched

nature and intent of Sherman's maneuvers, he did not have sufficiently detailed information quickly enough. When he did rush troops to the Jonesboro area, it was too late and they were too few to drive back the Yankees. A two-day battle at Jonesboro (August 31–September 1) sealed Atlanta's fate. With his last rail link cut, Hood had no choice but to destroy what he could not share out among the civilians or take away with him, and to flee the city.

During the night of September 1–2, Hood's men smashed, burned, gave away, or blew up buildings, supplies, and surplus am-

into Atlanta at the head of his troops, he heard a window open and from the darkness a female voice called "Welcome!"

Soon after his men occupied Atlanta, Sherman decided to make the city into a fortified military base. The remaining civilian inhabitants were given a choice of going north or south. Those electing to go south were escorted out under flag of truce and turned over to Confederate authorities.

In October most of Sherman's soldiers also left, for Hood had taken his entire army and marched northward, swinging east to get across the railroad to Chattanooga. The Federal commander set off in pursuit. For several weeks the two armies marched back across the fields where they had fought months earlier. Unable to do serious damage to the railroad, Hood moved west across Alabama and then north into Tennessee. Sherman decided not to follow his agile enemy. Instead, he detached a force sufficient to defend Tennessee, returned to Atlanta, and prepared his army to march across Georgia to Savannah on the Atlantic coast.

The burning of Atlanta: Before leaving Atlanta Sherman wanted to ensure that the city was no longer a factor in the war. For several days his troops were kept busy destroying

wrote later, did he hear that great chorus of "Glory, glory, Halleluiah!" sung with more spirit. Even as the last Northern soldiers left Atlanta, going off to the southeast, people began to filter back. Some were former inhabitants returning to claim their homes and businesses. Others were scavengers coming to salvage whatever they could find amid the rubble or to steal from the empty houses.

Once rebuilding got underway, it progressed rapidly. Before long the city had resumed many of its normal activities. Within a month there was an election to choose a new city government. A bar was among the earliest businesses to resume op-

Atlanta's remaining railroads, factories, and government offices. Inevitably much destruction that was not officially sanctioned also took place, and looters did even more damage. By mid-November, when Sherman marched out of the city, some 40 percent of Atlanta lay in smoldering wreckage.

As the Yankees left, they sang "The Battle Hymn of the Republic." Never, Sherman

Left, the Ephraim G. Ponder home was destroyed beyond repair. **Above**, Union officers pose for the camera in front of Confederate leader General Hood's former headquarters.

erations (a shot of bad whiskey cost $5, while good whiskey cost $10).

By the middle of December the Atlanta post office had reopened and one of the city's old newspapers, the *Daily Intelligencer*, was again publishing. Some of the railroads were even able to deliver Rebels to their homes after the surrender in the early spring of 1865. It was not long before Atlanta, its most traumatic moment behind it, was moving full tilt into the postwar development that was to make it the major city in the state, the state capital, and one of the great urban areas of the Southeast.

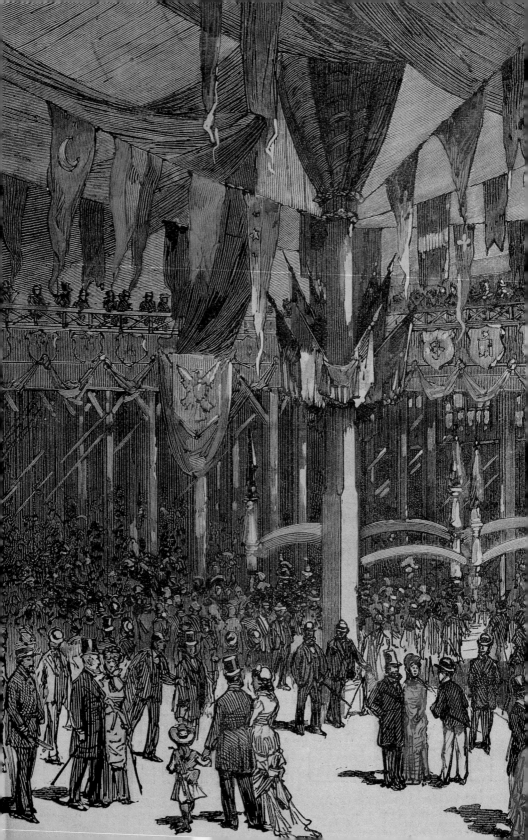

SOUVENIR
OF THE
INTERNATIONAL COTTON EXPOSITION,
1881.
ATLANTA,
GEORGIA.

WITH THE COMPLIMENTS OF THE
LOUISVILLE LITHOGRAPHIN

October 5, 1881, opening day for Atlanta's International Cotton Exposition, offered visitors a brass band, a noisy, flag-festooned parade and, inside the fair's 27 buildings, more than 1,000 exhibits gathered from around the world. To top it all off, a choir of 800 school children raised their voices in a rendition of Handel's "Hallelujah Chorus."

Brand-new suits: For all that, the promoters of the exposition would have been pleased if the half million visitors who toured the grounds over the next three months had seen just one activity: shortly after sunrise on October 27, fair employees gathered several bags of cotton grown on the fair grounds. The fiber was then taken to a model factory constructed for the exposition and, within hours, woven into cloth and clothes. By sunset, the state's Governor Alfred H. Colquitt and another visiting politician had each been presented with a brand-new suit – garments which they wore to several receptions that evening.

As theater, of course, new suits hardly competed with the "Hallelujah Chorus." But, then again, they did make the fair's point far better. For Atlanta, after all, such gatherings were never idle entertainments. And what was Atlanta's point? Simply that the city no longer just *sold* raw cotton. By then, it could produce finished products as well – a lesson that hardly went unnoticed among visiting textile industrialists from the North. Lured by cheap labor and cotton, New England's textile barons had already been moving their plants south for decades.

Such commercial stagecraft was hardly new for Atlanta; it had been organizing such shows since at least 1846. But the International Cotton Exposition was different: it not only dwarfed past fairs, its scope was world-wide. While past events had hawked Atlanta to the region, the Cotton Exposition sought to tell the entire *world* about what was already being called "the Atlanta spirit." In-

deed, between 1880 and 1890 alone, that spirit doubled the number of factories in Atlanta to 410.

Atlanta's grim face at the close of the Civil War hardly anticipated the optimistic city it would be a mere 16 years later. "A dirty, dusty ruin it is," one merchant had written in August 1865. Four years later, another visitor found neighborhoods where "the walls of houses alone remain, while a heap of charred rubbish occupies the interior."

Such images, however, failed to tell the entire story: in the commercial heart of the city, the clanking of hammers and the whining of saws had commenced as soon as the smoke of battle had cleared. Although the war had reduced most of Atlanta's commercial buildings to rubble, by the end of 1865, at least 150 businesses had reopened. Just two years later, the city boasted 250 commercial buildings. Equally important, all of the local railroad lines were operating again. As if to ratify the city's regeneration, in 1868 Atlanta became the new state capital. Further underscoring the rising economic tide, its 1870 population of 21,789 was double the 1860 figure.

Reconstruction: Resistance by Southern state governments to Federal efforts to guarantee former slaves their full rights as US citizens had, by 1866, resulted in the imposition of military rule over the region. In the end, however, that rule had achieved only limited progress. As Republican candidates for public office, Southern blacks achieved some ballot box victories. But stiffening white resistance soon rolled back most black advances. Finally, in 1876, collusion between conservative, white southern Democrats and their northern Republican counterparts resulted in the election of President Rutherford B. Hayes. Within months of taking office in 1877, Hayes had lifted all military rule in the South – thus ending the political transition called "Reconstruction."

The white, Democratic, so-called "Redeemer" governments that soon controlled the South's state governments knew that

Preceding pages and left, the International Cotton Exposition of 1881.

overtly strident racial repression risked triggering a Northern reaction. For that reason, they tolerated some black participation in the region's politics. By the 1880s, such pragmatism had produced a new vision of the South's place in the Union. Led by *Atlanta Constitution* editor Henry Grady, the "New South" movement stressed national reconciliation and what its followers considered a moderate approach to issues of race. To heal the region's economy, they prescribed diversification, industrialization, agricultural reform, and a search for new – even international – markets.

In Atlanta, and throughout the region, the

New South movement brought a renewed enthusiasm for industrial fairs. Indeed, the International Cotton Exposition of 1881 was followed in 1895 by the even larger Cotton States and International Exposition (held in what is now Piedmont Park).

Those keen to promote Atlanta's New South also wrote books and articles, lobbied, advertised, lectured and schemed. In the early 1870s, they even tried, unsuccessfully, to revive the long abandoned idea of building a canal from Atlanta to the Tennessee River – a scheme that eventually fell victim to the depression of 1873. Their efforts led, in

1888, to the founding of the Georgia Institute of Technology. Similar civic campaigns would result in the creation, in 1915, of the Atlanta campus of what is now Emory University and, in 1955, the founding of Georgia State University.

Followers of the New South movement also sought more local control over the railroads that passed through Atlanta. Since antebellum days, after all, the city's businesses had chafed under discriminatory freight rates imposed by railroad owners based in other cities. The region's large mining and timber companies had the clout to get fair rates, but the less established manufacturing industries of Atlanta and other Southern cities suffered rates higher than national norms.

To end such inequities, Atlanta businesses sought to increase local ownership of railroad lines. They encouraged the formation of new railroad companies as well as local investment in existing lines. They also lobbied the various government agencies that nominally oversaw freight rates. Those efforts, however, achieved little success. Atlanta's growth continued in spite of freight rates set to boost the fortunes of rival cities.

By the 1880s, Atlanta's business leaders had decided not to try to compete with the established iron and steel industries of nearby Chattanooga, Tennessee and Birmingham, Alabama. Instead, Atlanta concentrated on the production of food products, textiles, and other "articles of daily use." By 1886, the list of goods produced in the city included clothing, carriages, paper bags, lumber, watches, cologne, furniture – and, of course, Coca-Cola. Originally patented as a medical elixir, "French Wine Coca," on May 19, 1885, the beverage was invented by Confederate cavalry leader and pharmacist John Styth Pemberton.

Little wonder, then, that by 1886 New South booster Henry Grady could afford magnanimity – and even a little joke – concerning the fires that had engulfed his city in 1864. Speaking before the New England Society of New York, Grady turned toward fellow guest William Sherman and assured the general that he was "considered an able man in our parts, though some people think that he is a kind of careless man about fire." More seriously, Grady then assured his audience that from the ashes Sherman left behind, "we have raised a brave and beautiful city: that somehow or other we have caught the sunshine in the bricks and mortar of our homes, and builded [sic] therein not one ignoble prejudice or memory."

For many Atlantans, however, Henry Grady's rhetoric rang less than true. Indeed, for those who toiled in the New South's factories, Grady's vision meant long hours, low pay and poor working conditions. Promises of a cheap and pliant workforce, after all, were central to the New South's recruitment by northern reformers. The national Republican Party, increasingly more interested in business than social reform, had by 1877 largely withdrawn its reformist mandate in the South. While black Atlantans had obtained their political rights, their newfound liberty mostly entailed a freedom to fill the city's least desirable jobs and neighborhoods. In the end, even many unions excluded blacks from their ranks.

Outward Bound: The populace of any city built around a triangle of railroad tracks will inevitably yearn for greener – not to mention less smoky, oily and noisy – pastures. To understand that yearning, however, it's nec-

of northern capitalists to the region. Boosters, in turn, backed up those promises with an often virulent strain of anti-unionism.

Black Atlantans suffered even more. Paeans to rising prosperity, after all, could not mask the fact that, for most African-Americans, the New South, in many ways, differed little from the Old South. Few blacks enjoyed the bounties of New South prosperity. With the end of Reconstruction, southern blacks had been all but abandoned

Left, the first paid fire department, 1886. Above, Peachtree streetcars, 1898.

essary to imagine the city as it was before a series of viaducts, constructed during the 1920s, concealed the "gulch" of train tracks that once ran through downtown Atlanta. Once the viaducts were in place, some merchants erected new buildings. Most, however, stayed in their old quarters and simply moved their business operations up one floor. Their old storefronts suddenly became basements – and, much later, today's Underground Atlanta complex. The complex first opened during the 1960s and was rebuilt after a devastating fire in the 1980s.

For Atlanta's more prosperous, white citizens of the late 19th century, their coveted greener pastures increasingly lay north of the old "walking city." Real estate speculation and the opening of a series of horse-drawn trolley lines during the 1870s led many to move to the city's new suburb of West End. Others moved farther and farther up Peachtree Road, the city's main north-south thoroughfare. By the late 1880s, the introduction of the city's first electric streetcar line had also nurtured the Inman Park suburb, 2 miles east of Downtown.

White, working-class Atlantans, meanwhile, remained in downtown boarding houses or rough-and-tumble neighbor-

hoods, like Edgewood, Clarkston, and what is now called Cabbagetown, in the shadow of the city's growing number of factories. Working-class black Atlantans, meanwhile, clustered in Mechanicsville, Vine City, Pittsburg and similar neighborhoods near the city's railroad tracks. Employment patterns only deepened growing racial inequities. For whites of Atlanta, after all, the New South boom years increased demand for merchants and artisans – as well as for doctors, lawyers, journalists, and other professionals. For blacks, by contrast, the new prosperity primarily increased demand for

domestic servants and other jobs that offered little pay and less future.

For at least some of Atlanta's black population, however, new educational opportunities did ameliorate some of their difficulties. Thanks to northern philanthropists, five black colleges had opened in Atlanta by 1882: Atlanta University (1867), Clark College (1869), Morehouse College (1879), Spelman College (1881) and Morris Brown College (1881). Together, these institutions – which merged in 1929 to form today's Atlanta University Center – provided a much-needed pool of teachers, ministers, and other professionals for Atlanta's black community. Beyond that, its graduates, over the years, have provided much of the foundation for the entire South's black middle class.

Yet another factor helped cushion the lot of at least some blacks in late 19th-century Atlanta. Their very exclusion from white society, in the end, guaranteed that they would control the business life of the separate sphere to which they had been consigned. As a consequence, neighborhoods like Shermantown (now Sweet Auburn) and Jenningstown (near Atlanta University) offered both comfortable housing and varied employment opportunities for the growing number of professionals graduating from the city's black colleges. Indeed, such communities eventually supported independent, black-owned business – everything from doctors' and lawyers' offices to banks, barber-shops, insurance companies and tailors.

For most black Atlantans of that day, however, the odds of achieving any sort of prosperity were dwindling rapidly. The rise of the radical Populist Party across the United States during the 1890s divided the South's white vote and, briefly, gave black voters the balance of power in both state and local elections. In response, Democratic state legislatures across the region promptly rushed to circumvent federal guarantees of black voting rights.

By 1910, most blacks in the South had been effectively stripped of their right to vote. With the subsequent routing of Republicans and Populists throughout the region, "whites only" Democratic primaries rapidly monopolized the South's political life.

Beyond that, "Jim Crow" laws (named after a stock black character in antebellum minstrel shows) passed by the region's new "Lily White" Democratic legislatures and city councils gave the weight of law to what had been informal patterns of discrimination. By the end of the century, in Atlanta and throughout the South, all aspects of the region's life – including residential neighborhoods, schools, shops, hotels, theaters, and streetcars – bore Jim Crow's stamp. In 1896, even the US Supreme Court gave its seal of approval to the new order.

Running riot: It didn't take the newsboys long, on September 22, 1906, to get the word to warrant drastic action. By the evening, white rabble-rousers were calling for retaliatory lynch mobs. Rioting soon broke out. White mobs attacked blacks, and blacks responded in kind. As the fighting erupted, whites marauded through the pool rooms and saloons frequented by blacks along Downtown's Decatur Street. They pulled black people off streetcars and beat them. And as if to make clear their point about the kind of New South they wanted, several whites gathered up the corpses of two black victims and laid them at the base of a statue of Henry Grady, just west of Five Points, on Marietta Street.

around Atlanta that a black man had attempted to rape a white woman. It was hot that Saturday, and downtown was crowded with farmers come to market. As the afternoon wore on and extra editions of the newspaper appeared on the streets, three more assaults were reported.

The rape reports later proved to have been greatly exaggerated – or just plain wrong. But that afternoon they seemed real enough

By the end of the ensuing fracas, two whites and at least 25 blacks died. Such anti-black riots became all too commonplace in America's cities during the 20th century's first decade. In the South, anti-black sentiments were inflamed by the racist campaigns that accompanied the disenfranchisement movement. Above the Mason-Dixon line, meanwhile, white resentment had been stirred by a migration of southern blacks into northern cities. Even so, the Atlanta race riot of 1906 proved a deep embarrassment for the city's boosters, who had prided themselves on the city's ostensibly good racial relations.

Left, William E. B. Dubois was a hero to local blacks. **Above**, master and chain-gang on the job in rural Georgia.

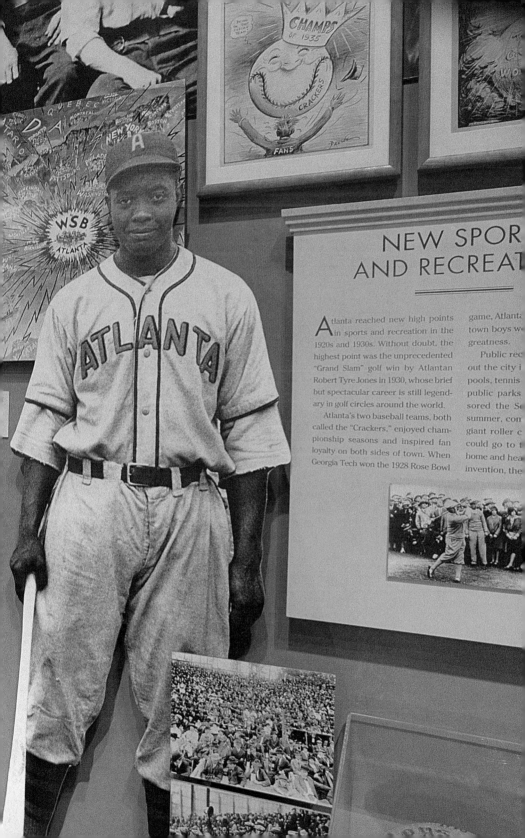

A national depression during the 1890s and, only a few years later, World War I, interrupted Atlanta's growth. But with the end of the war in 1918 and the boom years of the 1920s, the city enjoyed robust economic expansion. Aided by an ambitious "Forward Atlanta" national advertising campaign, designed to lure northern businesses southward, an unprecedented building boom soon began to reshape much of the city. In time, elegant, stone-sheathed, Chicago-style "skyscrapers" gave Downtown a fresh new look. During one four-year period alone, 762 new businesses opened in Atlanta. Indeed, business became so heady that one local wag suggested that as Grand Rapids was known for furniture making, and Detroit for automobiles, so Atlanta should be known as the city of office space.

Garden suburbs: The renewed economic bustle – along with a devastating fire in 1917 – also stimulated a brisk demand for new residential housing. In 1920, for instance, Atlantans erected 552 new, single-family dwellings – a figure they doubled the next year. By 1927, it had reached 1,387. As new streetcar lines came into operation, Atlanta's growing white middle-class stepped up their exodus from the city's center. With their gracefully curving roads and their elegant manses and bungalows, new sylvan landscapes like Druid Hills, Virginia-Highlands, and Ormewood Park attested to the growing enthusiasm for the "garden-suburbs" popularized by noted landscape architect Frederic Olmsted a generation earlier.

In the early 1890s, Olmsted himself had made the initial design for what became the east Atlanta neighborhood of Druid Hills. Owing to various financial problems, however, houses weren't constructed in the area until 1909.

In the weeks after Atlanta's 1906 race riot, streetcar companies were instructed to treat their black employees better. They were also told to arrange for a clearer division of the races in their cars, and black and white streetcar riders were kept more separate in the years ahead. But the larger impact of streetcars on the city's future lay less in how their seating was arranged, more in where they were going. For the most part, these streetcars were bound for newly-built, all-white suburbs north of the city.

Boundaries: Between 1917 and 1922, Atlanta's city officials passed ordinances designating racially exclusive neighborhoods. Each of the laws was struck down by Federal courts, but they were hardly necessary: streetcars and the popularity of the automobile were already hardening the boundaries of Atlanta's residential segregation.

Indeed, as Atlanta became a city of automobiles in the years after World War I, white commuters flocked to newer suburbs like Ansley Park, Brookwood Park, and Garden Hills that lay even farther north of the center. Black Atlantans, meanwhile, increasingly resided in the older neighborhoods that ringed the city. Other blacks – those who could could afford better – took up residence in new, middle-class black communities such as West View Park and Washington Park that were rising, in the shadow of Atlanta University, on the west side.

Atlanta's residential color line has bent over the years, retreated and advanced with the tides of economics, politics and urban migration. But for all that has changed, the essential contours of that line – established during the 1870s – have remained firm. Social, political and legal reforms since World War II have produced a relatively high level of integration in the city's public and commercial life. Beyond that, growing Asian and Latin American populations have carved out their own discrete neighborhoods. But at the end of the working day, Atlanta for the most part becomes two separate cities, one black, the other white.

Post-World War II: Atlanta suffered through the Great Depression of the 1930s and World

Preceding pages: the Atlanta History Center's 1920s and '30s exhibits. **Left,** the new spirit celebrated in song.

War II along with the rest of the country. And when recovery did come, it was transportation, once again, that lifted the city. Indeed, what railroads offered during the late 1800s – an economic edge over competitive cities – airplanes and freeways provided in the latter half of the 20th century. Only this time around, no discriminatory freight rates hamstrung Atlanta's ambitions. A decade-long effort by the South's governors culminated in 1945 in the US Supreme Court ordering railroad companies to end such unfair practices. The decision not only broke down much of the South's economic isolation, it also served as the legal foundation for the

only to the edges of the metropolitan region, it was nevertheless seen as a way of reinforcing Atlanta's growing status as a hub of regional commerce. Indeed, in case anyone should doubt that ambition, plans called for the three roads to merge just outside the central business district and then to flow as a single road – "a downtown connector" – through the heart of the city.

Those local ambitions got an added boost, in 1956, when the Federal government entered the freeway-building business. Uncle Sam's decision to construct what became the Interstate Highway system not only meant that new super-highways would run unbro-

region's post-World War II boom in new factories and skyscrapers.

Indeed, the bombs were still falling over Europe and Asia when Atlanta's business and political leaders sat down, in 1944, to map out the city they hoped to build in the anticipated post-war boom. The centerpiece of their plans, adopted two years later, was the construction of three "expressways" – all designed to improve traffic flow between Downtown and the various highways that linked Atlanta to the region's other cities.

Though the system, sponsored by the city of Atlanta and local counties, would extend

ken to all those other places whose business Atlanta sought, but it also meant that the federal government would be paying 90 percent of the costs for the new roads. By the end of the 1970s, the three highways that intersected Atlanta (I-75, I-20 and I-85) were joined by yet another: I-285, which encircled the city's growing metropolitan area.

Downtown Atlanta also grew with the post-war boom. By the 1960s, a skyline that had changed little during the past 30 years suddenly teemed with gleaming new steel-and-glass skyscrapers. Sadly, however, and far too often, many of those new skyscrapers rose at the expense of more attractive pre-World War II architecture, which fell to the wrecker's ball.

Beyond downtown Atlanta, much of the post-World War II growth bore an increasingly metropolitan cast. The original city had extended to a one-mile radius from its Zero Mile Post. A series of subsequent extensions culminated in the city more than doubling its size by annexing an additional 81 sq. miles (210 sq. km) – bringing its total to 118 sq. miles (305 sq. km).

As businesses and residences had once clustered along downtown railroad lines, so freeway off-ramps became the new foci for

Atlanta's freeways – as well as its baseball stadium and other post-war amenities – was that it forced the demolition of thousands of homes, and destroyed some of the city's oldest, mostly black, neighborhoods, which were replaced with bleak government housing projects. The freeways, in turn, became yawning concrete chasms that, even today, scar the central city.

Flights of fancy: In 1887, adopting a symbol long embraced by city boosters, Atlanta's local government dropped the locomotive that had adorned its official seal and replaced it with a phoenix, the bird that in Greek mythology rose from its own ashes. In com-

development. For all that was new, however, the modern commuter suburbs only reinforced old patterns of residential segregation. As the city's growing white population moved to ever-farther northern suburbs, black Atlantans, once again, filled the most recently abandoned "in-town" neighborhoods – at least those which had been spared by the freeways.

For the downside of the construction of

Left, masquerade ball, Piedmont Driving Club. **Above**, Margaret Mitchell and Clark Gable at the premiere of *Gone With The Wind*, 1939.

memorating Atlanta's post-Civil War rebuilding, the City Fathers could hardly have known how presciently this image had anticipated a boom in the city's life.

At the urging of Alderman William B. Hartsfield in 1929, the city purchased, for $94,000, an auto race-track on the city's south-side from Coca-Cola magnate Asa G. Candler, and converted it into a modest airport. Though a trickle of flights came in, the airport hardly boomed. Indeed, it wasn't until 1951 that regularly scheduled flights between Atlanta and New York began. In an Atlanta twist on an old ritual, Hartsfield, who by that time was mayor, christened the line by pouring the contents of a 2-ft (60-cm) high bottle of Coca-Cola over the nose of the departing four-engine propeller plane. (In 1971, the airport was renamed for Hartsfield, who, except for a brief period, was Atlanta's mayor from 1937 to 1961.)

Atlanta's air traffic grew steadily afterwards. Indeed, by the 1970s, the city had duplicated in the skies its earlier successes on the ground as a hub for railroads, and later, for cars and trucks. As the local joke soon went, "Whether you're going to heaven or hell, you have to change planes in Atlanta." In 1971, the airport added its first

Race reforms: Political changes also transformed Atlanta after World War II. Legal segregation had shown signs of morbidity as early as 1948 when Mayor Hartsfield hired Atlanta's first black policemen. But that, and most civil rights advances of that decade, tended to be token efforts. Not until the late 1950s and 1960s did more substantial reforms come: during that era, black civil rights activists and growing public indignation over Southern resistance to their efforts finally prodded the federal government into action: from restaurants to hotels, from buses to the ballot-box – the South's Jim Crow barriers, one by one, tumbled.

international flight. Today, Hartsfield International – which claims to be the world's fourth busiest in daily number of passengers – handles close to 1,000 flights each day, with direct connections to Europe, Latin America and Asia.

Reflecting those growing international ties, Atlanta embarked on an aggressive – and highly successful – campaign to recruit foreign investment to the city during the 1970s. By the 1980s, the once-upon-a-time "Gate City of the South" had adopted a new sales slogan: "Atlanta, The World's Next International City."

For Atlanta, the era's civil rights revolution left a special legacy. Black residents, of course, could exercise long-denied rights. Beyond that, however, the entire city basked in a reputation – not entirely undeserved – for racial moderation. Indeed, while Atlanta had its share of skirmishes, the era's major civil rights battles had been fought elsewhere. Thanks to a long-standing working relationship between Atlanta's pragmatic, white, political and business establishment and local black leaders, the city had been spared the sort of lurid headlines – and news photos – that so damaged other Southern cities: no images of police dogs or fire-hoses turned on civil rights demonstrators sullied Atlanta's reputation.

In fact, even before the dust had cleared, Atlanta's leaders – black and white – were burnishing the image of what they called "A City Too Busy to Hate." Soon, along with its excellent highway and air connections, Atlanta also boasted an atmosphere of racial toleration, plus big city amenities – everything from good restaurants to theaters, museums, and symphonies. By the mid-1970s, as high fuel and labor costs forced northern businesses to look south, Atlanta was poised for yet another boom.

Another particularly Atlantan legacy of the civil rights movement arose from its role as home-base for much of the movement's leadership. Dr Martin Luther King, Jr and his Southern Christian Leadership Conference were based in Atlanta, and so were many of King's associates – including Ralph Abernathy, John Lewis, Hosea Williams and Andrew Young. Accordingly, since the 1970s, those same leaders – and their successors – have worked to increase black participation in Atlanta's political life. In 1973, Maynard Jackson became the city's first black mayor. A year later, Andrew Young, representing Atlanta, became Georgia's first African-American Congressman since Reconstruction. (Young later also served as mayor.)

Trade-off: By the late 20th century, Atlanta's day-to-day politics consisted, in large part, of the trade-offs that arose – and still arise – from one central condition: while blacks hold most of the political power, whites control most of the money and – more critically – pay most of the taxes. Whatever racial tensions arise, each needs the other, and both, meanwhile, share the task of boosting the city's image. Indeed, Atlanta's growing black business establishment claims a facility for touting the city that would, no doubt, have pleased Henry Grady.

Modern Atlantans like to chart their city's rise by discrete junctures – the metropolitan

area's topping of the 1-million population mark (1960), the acquisition of the city's first major league sports team (the Atlanta Braves, 1966), the opening of its first subway line (1980), its first national political convention (the Democrats, 1988), its first World Series (1991) – and, most recently, the city's selection as the site of the 1996 International Olympics.

Such recitations, however, can mask serious problems. Atlanta's metropolitan area continues to grow: it now claims 2.9 million residents – almost one in every two Georgians. But the actual City of Atlanta has recently lost population; the 1990 census

counted 394,000 residents, a fall of about 10 percent from 1980. In a sense, then, the City of Atlanta, which is 67 percent black, is a small, shrinking island in an expanding metropolitan area which is 72 percent white.

Beyond that, growing problems of traffic, drugs, crime, and poverty dog the city; indeed, one in every four residents of the City of Atlanta lives in poverty. What will the future bring? Vast problems persist, but then so does the inherent optimism. Whatever the future brings, the themes of boosterism, race, and transportation will continue to animate Atlanta's life.

<u>Left</u>, Martin Luther King, Jr and Ralph Abernathy visit a local neighborhood in 1966. <u>Right</u>, Atlanta is encircled by freeways.

On the fringe of downtown Atlanta lies one prominent symbol of change brought by the 1996 Summer Olympics: the brick and steel of Centennial Olympic Stadium and lattice-work tower of the Olympic Cauldron. The stadium and other venues built by the games are changing the landscape of Atlanta, part of the new city visitors will see in 1996.

Other changes were promised by Atlanta mayor Bill Campbell: "Atlanta will be a radically different city by 1996. New parks, pedestrian corridors, infrastructure improvements like new water mains will transform the city for the Olympics."

Olympian task: But beyond the new Olympic venues, parks, and other improvements, some Atlantans say the city's real problems such as crime and poverty will be changed little. Some say the city waited too long to start its program of public works to prepare for the Olympics. But other Atlantans have blazed their own trails and used the Olympics as an inspiration for change.

Fear of change led a noisy band of neighborhood activists to nearly scuttle plans to construct the new stadium. The $209 million arena, built without public funds, is the site of opening and closing ceremonies for the Olympics and will become the home of the Atlanta Braves major league baseball team in 1997. But plans for the new stadium contrasted sharply with the neglected, inner-city neighborhoods that ringed it. Residents complained that millions would be spent on a stadium while they would receive nothing. They worried the new stadium would lead to further decline of their neighborhoods with increased traffic and noise.

In 1993, against that backdrop of discontent, Atlanta Olympic organizers sought the approval of local governments to proceed with the stadium project. The decision ended up hingeing on the vote of one local official, Martin Luther King III, the son of the civil rights leader. King took on the cause of the stadium neighborhoods and refused to give his approval unless the neighborhoods got a piece of the deal. The brinkmanship won out: the Olympics got a new stadium, the neighborhoods won a piece of the pie.

Olympic organizers, local government, and the Atlanta Braves baseball club all agreed to contribute to a plan that might lead to long-term change for the neighborhoods. Residents became eligible for job training and employment for the construction of the sta-

dium. The baseball team promises to hire people from the community when it begins play in the new stadium. And city planners have tried to pave the way for homes and business to replace abandoned storefronts and dilapidated tenement-style housing.

But of the three stadium neighborhoods, Summerhill, Peoplestown, and Mechanicsville, Summerhill will see the most change as a result of the games. While plans are moving ahead for the other two, Summerhill's plans existed prior to the Olympics, which gave the neighborhood a head-start.

The Olympics are accelerating that change

Left, flying the flag. **Right**, Olympic mascot: the Whatizit doll.

says Douglas Dean, who leads the Summer-hill plans. Dean once opposed the new stadium, but is now convinced the Olympics will help the neighborhood attract more capital and public attention. He does not see how Summerhill can be ignored, lying in full view of the world during the summer of 1996.

"After 30 years of no-growth, we have an opportunity to make the new stadium a benefactor of our neighborhood. Atlanta needs to assure that this will be a changed neighborhood by 1996," says Dean, whose dream is for Summerhill to become a mixed-income neighborhood, complete with

schools, shops, and parks. Dean also knows generations of neglect won't be erased before the games. He's resigned to the fact that the complete makeover of the stadium neighborhoods will not happen until well after the games are over – if it happens.

Another observer is Rick McDevitt, who runs an advocacy group on childrens' issues located a few blocks from the Olympic stadium. "The Olympics won't save us. But they can be a catalyst for change. They can change Atlanta's image as a town of the Old South. But I still don't think the problems of the poor have been given enough attention."

But Olympic supporters – especially the business community – point out that the economic benefits of the games for Atlanta and the state of Georgia should top $5 billion. Beyond that, Atlanta's business leaders are counting on the games to put the city in the spotlight as it never has been before, attracting economic development that will help all Atlantans for years to come.

Those same business leaders also express frustration with the slow pace of work to make the city look good for the Olympics. While the privately-funded Atlanta Committee for the Olympic Games has been able to go about its work preparing venues and organizing the games focused on a 1996 deadline, government-sponsored projects like renovated housing for the poor, new parks, rebuilt roads, and pedestrian corridors downtown got a late start, the result of procrastination, indecision and lack of money.

It wasn't for lack of notice; Atlanta had six years to prepare. Awarded the games in 1990, the city was inspired to ask what needed to be done to get its house in order.

Fictional decision: Initially, Atlantans reacted with the same attitude of Georgia's fabled fictional heroine, Scarlett O'Hara of *Gone With The Wind* who often dealt with perplexing decisions by saying "I'll think about it tomorrow." Atlanta felt the same way until the Barcelona games of 1992.

Living in the Catalonian capital for nearly a month, Atlanta's mayor, Olympic organizers and other Atlanta visitors marveled at the twisted spires of Gaudi's architecture. They walked Barcelona's Gothic Quarter. They saw how the city had reclaimed its Mediterranean shoreline and built new roads – all as a result of the Olympics. The Atlantans returned from Barcelona with a measure of self-doubt that their 150-year-old city could compete with the millennium of history behind the Mediterranean city. But they were inspired to use the games to help change the city as Barcelona had tried to do.

City leaders were warned, however, not to look to the Olympics for the money to accomplish their goals. In a watershed speech to Atlanta's business and government leaders, Billy Payne, the president of the Atlanta Committee for the Olympic Games (ACOG), said his $1.5 billion budget would only pay for the games, not for the transformation of the city. He coined the phrases "inside the fences" and "outside the fences" to describe Atlanta's Olympic challenge.

Payne assured his audience that ACOG would take care of preparations "inside the fences" of Olympic venues. But he said parks, urban redevelopment, and other projects "outside the fences" would only result from a partnership between government and business. Payne insisted ACOG would be a cheerleader to those efforts, not the instigator.

Payne's park: But the Olympics chief ended up playing both instigator and cheerleader with one of the major "outside the fence" projects planned for 1996: Centennial Olympic Park, a signature green space for downtown Atlanta. The park, built at a cost of about $50 million, was Payne's idea. He saw a need for a gathering place for the crowds that will fill downtown Atlanta in 1996, and then convinced major private donors to finance the project. Half of the money alone comes from the Woodruff Foundation, the philanthropic arm of Coca-Cola.

In addition to providing respite for Olympic visitors, it is hoped the park will spark change in downtown Atlanta. Like many other US cities, Atlanta's Downtown has been on a downward trend as the suburbs grow. The park has been planned to help stimulate new businesses around its fringes and encourage new housing. But for now the park replaces a formerly unsightly area of decrepit warehouses, vacant lots, and shelters for homeless people.

The lofty goals of the park to foster urban redevelopment improvement will have to wait until after the games. In part, that may be due to the late start for Payne's idea: construction started with less than two years to go before the Olympics. But Payne acted only after local politicians had frittered away four years without coming up with major plans on their own.

While some projects to make Atlanta a better place to live and visit will still be works-in-progress by 1996, one change in the landscape is assured. By the time the games open on July 19, 1996, 15,000 new trees will have been planted along Atlanta's streets. The feat is the accomplishment of Trees Atlanta, a private group that began its Olympian task in 1990, shortly after Atlanta won the bid to host the games.

Although visitors often comment on how many trees seem to cover the city, the reality is that Atlanta is among the lowest-ranked US cities by this criterion. Asphalt and office towers dominate the streetscape of Atlanta's

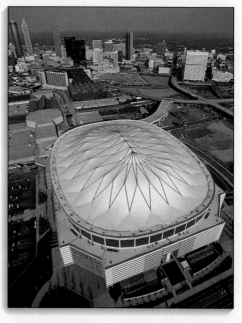

commercial districts. Trees Atlanta should be able to change that perspective by 1996 with the shade of magnolias, hollies, elms, and oaks.

The work of Trees Atlanta is taken seriously by the city, which does not have the resources to handle such an ambitious landscaping program. But while it has been a force for positive change, the group is unable to mute the forces of nature, even for the public relations good of the city. Fabled Peachtree Street winds for miles, without a peach tree in sight. Atlanta is simply too far north to grow Georgia's famous fruit.

Some years ago, two Atlantans accompanied a visitor on a tour of sparkling suburbs, busy shopping malls, and Buckhead, a hushed enclave of sprawling mansions set on manicured lots. Dinner – gravad lax and broiled salmon – was served at a post-modern Scandinavian restaurant. Back at the Marriot Marquis Hotel – a concrete monolith with a ribbed atrium seemingly designed to represent the innards of a whale – the visitor, who'd not heard a whisper of a Southern accent all day, asked his hosts where were the verandas? The cobblestone streets? The gaslit historic districts? The shotgun shacks?

Where were the peach trees? Dozens of Atlanta streets begin with the word "Peachtree." The antiquated tea rooms? Where was the fried chicken, the catfish, the okra, and collard greens?

"Right across the street," they said, pointing to a downtown restaurant, its antebellum facade gleaming like a capped tooth in the center of a grimy parking garage. "Aunt Pittypat's Porch."

Preconceived: Atlanta burned twice, once during the Civil War and again in a devastating 1917 fire. Much of what survived was uprooted by real estate speculators and urban "renewal" projects in the 1960s. What's left of the Downtown is a facade, a narrow strip of office towers, hotels, and convention centers for visitors searching for whatever preconceived "Atlanta" they imagine. No one really lives there, except the homeless.

Atlanta is no longer a Southern city. Travel 20 miles in any direction and the soy bean fields, boiled peanut stands, Baptist churches, and pick-up trucks make that exceedingly clear. As does the poster at the popular Royal Bagel shop that reads "Shalom y'all." In fact, metropolitan Atlanta, its tendrils already stretching to the foothills of the Blue Ridge Mountains, is hardly a city in any traditional

sense. Imagine, instead, a series of widely-scattered satellite communities – residential, occupational, racial, social, ethnic – revolving aimlessly, without a center.

Virginia-Highland is the intown yuppie enclave. Ansley Park equals old money; Dunwoody, new money. Middle-class blacks live in Cascade Heights, gays in Midtown, punk rockers in Little Five Points. Buford Highway has become Asia Town. The Perimeter is a second Downtown. Artists are

moving to Cabbagetown. Nightlife revolves around Buckhead.

Unbound by natural borders, its history and traditions – like its brick and mortar – swept aside by war, fire, racial liberation, mass immigration, and unbridled development, Atlanta has become, in essence, a city without walls, constantly transforming itself, endlessly proud of itself. For many, it is an Emerald City hovering above the red clay of the rural South.

It is also a mirror reflecting its ever-changing population. The elegant ladies and gentlemen attending the glittery Swan Ball

Preceding pages: underground entertainment in the heart of the city; al fresco dining in Buckhead; post-game signings. Left, Atlantans kick up their heels. Right, Sunday best.

and their debutante daughters on display at the exclusive Piedmont Driving Club are part of Atlanta's bright tapestry, as are the roller bladers and street musicians whirling outside the club windows, the gourmands eating ribs at Alex Barbecue Heaven, or Sika Venison with Spaetzle and Red Wine Pear at the Buckhead Ritz Carlton's Dining Room. The taxis ferrying black professionals to business meetings are likely to be driven by Ethiopians. The chief of police is a woman.

Like any adolescent, Atlanta is self-absorbed – from a visitor's perspective, alarmingly so. Helpful people – themselves recently arrived in most cases – will give you

natural harbor or free-flowing river. On the surface, not much character. The Big Apple and the Big Easy capture New York and New Orleans precisely. The Big Peach doesn't say much.

Yet Atlanta is a fascinating place, a city of dreamers both glorious and bizarre. A hundred years ago, newspaper editor Henry Grady predicted a "New South" rising from the ashes of the Civil War. Today, New Agers have deemed Stone Mountain, with its Confederate frieze, a focal point of the world's upcoming "harmonic convergence." Atlanta pharmacist John Pemberton gave the world Coca-Cola; Ted Turner gave it CNN. Martin

directions that are impossible to follow. Street names change without warning. Signs, particularly on MARTA, the rapid rail system, are bewildering, points of interest widely scattered. Atlanta's intown grid is bent and hopelessly incomplete. You must drive miles, for example, to cross from Piedmont Avenue to Peachtree Street, the city's main north-south thoroughfares. Traffic, particularly in the suburbs, is horrendous.

Visitors, searching for some defining core – Piccadilly Circus, Times Square, Rome's Forum come to mind – will be disappointed. Atlanta has no distinctive architecture, no

Luther King Jr. lived his dream. Peanut farmer Jimmy Carter leaped from the governor's mansion to the White House; Billy Carter, his brother, urinated on the lawn.

Epidemiologists at the Centers for Disease Control helped rid the world of smallpox. The lowly Atlanta Braves are World Series contenders; Evander Holyfield captured the heavyweight boxing championship. Former mayor Andrew Young wanted direct air travel between Atlanta and Lagos, Nigeria. He helped win the Olympics instead.

Hidden behind Atlanta's gaudy billboards, leafy parks, strip joints, pleasant suburbs, and singles complexes, a post-modern urban experiment is still underway. The catalyst: hundreds of thousands of newcomers arriving over the past 30 years, all living their own versions of Atlanta. Southerners escaping the choking grasp of small town life; Northerners fleeing the bleak realities of America's Rust Belt; blacks storming the barriers to equal opportunity; gays tasting liberation.

Atlanta is no formal "City on a Hill." Ferlinghetti's "Coney Island of the Mind" is more appropriate; an amusement park where each person is free to pursue his or her pleasure. Demographics tell the story. Between 1950 and 1960, more than 200,000

Jaguar owners line up their expensive machinery outside Abbondanza's sprawling hilltop garage. Enzo drinks espresso all day; his mechanics swig Dr Pepper.

Larry Dean grew up in a house without an indoor toilet in southwest Atlanta. Wall Street deemed his software company – Stockholder Systems Inc. – indispensible, and Dean became a wealthy man. He rewarded himself with Dean Gardens, a $40 million estate complete with amphitheater, sea shell swimming pool, "Moroccan Media Room," a 1950s soda fountain, and a bathroom complete with sarcophagus, designed like an Egyptian burial chamber. Dean, who re-

fled Georgia seeking opportunities elsewhere. Today, more than 40 percent of Atlanta's 3 million population arrived *from* somewhere else. "Sometimes I'm reminded of Aunt Pittypat in *Gone With the Wind*, says Atlanta native Susan Brooks. "Yankees in Georgia? How did they ever get in?"

And what are all these folk up to? In 1979, Enzo Abbondanza arrived from Italy with $700, a battered Volkswagen, a very pregnant wife, and some big dreams. Today,

Left, foreign affairs at Stone Mountain. **Above**, Atlanta has at least 12,000 homeless people.

cently tried to rezone his north Atlanta home as a tourist attraction, says he built Dean Gardens "for the glory of God."

Robert Blazer's dream encompassed mountains of fresh produce, meat, bread, and seafood. The reality is his astonishing Your Dekalb Farmer's Market, a cornucopia spanning the length of two football fields. Emblazoned with the world's flags and employing scores of Asian and African immigrants, the market has become one of Atlanta's most interesting attractions. Blazer, who moved south from Rhode Island, started his business with a few crates of vegetables.

Today, sales are topping a reported $55 million. "It's not about money," he insists. "I've always wanted to provide something of real value to people."

Such success, underwritten by a strong economy, has not come without a price. A city of winners is, by definition, a divided city. In 1993, Atlanta led the nation in generating new jobs, yet unemployment in the city of Atlanta, the "hole" in the metropolitan "donut," has jumped nearly fivefold since 1990, mostly because workers lack educational and job skills.

Nearly half the city's children live below the poverty line. Thirty percent of the infants

born at downtown Grady Hospital have no pre-natal care; 17 percent of their mothers are addicted to crack cocaine. Not surprisingly, the cycle of poverty, broken homes, and poor education has led to despair and violence, particularly in the southside black community. In 1994, Atlanta, per capita, was the most violent city in the United States. This is the city visitors and most residents rarely glimpse.

Ironically, Sweet Auburn, once black Atlanta's Main Street, has become a victim of integration. Given the freedom to chose, most middle-class blacks live, shop, and raise their children elsewhere – leaving the community without positive role models. Volunteer organizations such as the Coalition of One Hundred Black Men, which bonds successful black males with inner city youth, are struggling to address the problem. Recently, Auburn Avenue has slowly been revitalized. "This was the mecca," says salesman Rick Brown, a regular visitor to Auburn. "We can't forget our roots."

Such dramatic changes did not occur overnight. A hundred years after the Civil War, the South remained psychically at war with mainstream America. In the 1960s, while Birmingham, Alabama, and other Southern cities resisted the rising tide of civil rights, Atlanta's white leaders – practical burghers – opted to share political power with its black citizenry. In a telling 1961 mayoral election, Ivan Allen Jr defeated segregationist Lester Maddox. Spurned in Atlanta, Maddox went on to become a national embarrassment as Georgia's governor.

Searing television images of bombed churches, club-wielding policemen, and snarling dogs doomed Birmingham's hopes of becoming the South's pre-eminent city. Atlanta, "the city too busy to hate," stayed calm, its schools integrated peacefully. Corporate America took notice. When Martin Luther King Jr's great crusade ended, when the South's untapped markets, cheap labor, and resources became "Sunbelt dynamics," Atlanta became a magnet for entrepreneurs.

Chambodia: In the past decade, tens of thousands of Mexicans, Koreans, Vietnamese, Indians, and Ethiopians have arrived. To the outrage of its white residents, Chamblee, a somnolent working-class suburb, has become "Chambodia" – home to hundreds of Asian businesses, shops, and restaurants.

"Atlanta has become *the* place," says attorney Thomas Choi, president of the 35,000-member Korean Association. He speaks for a dozen other ethnic groups. Like Atlanta, Choi considers himself representative of the New South Henry Grady envisioned. "Discriminating against newcomers is not what America is about," he says. "The fact that your ancestors arrived earlier than I did does not necessarily make you a better citizen."

In *Southerners: A Journalist's Odyssey*,

Marshall Frady suggests such enormous change does not come without a price. "In the almost touching lust of its chambers of commerce for new chemical plants, glassy-mazed office parks and instant subdivisions, the South is becoming etherized in all those ways a people are subtly rendered pastless, memoryless, blank of identity by assimilation into chrome and asphalt and plastic."

Atlanta's past is hidden: in the Cyclorama, a Civil War museum; carved in the granite of Stone Mountain; in the aching silence of Martin Luther King Jr's grave site; whispered in the lilting accents of its senior citizens. A hundred and fifty years ago, the city

visitors. We've always been here! I don't prejudge people. But if I dare express an opinion, bang! I'm a bigoted redneck."

Cofer is struggling to accept that the old Atlanta, like the Old South, is vanishing. But the best of the South – pride, friendliness, and hospitality – are not forgotten. This new Atlanta is not so much insubstantial as inchoate – gossamer, to be shaped by all who have flocked here.

Atlanta native Patsy Bromley left for New York's School of American Ballet when she was 13 years old, determined to soar with the world's prima ballerinas. An injury ended her career before it began. Her hopes in

was a dusty railroad crossing. Today, it wants to compete with Paris, London or New York. "Actually," says Mary Lyon Jarman, a native, "we want to be better than those places."

For others, the changes have been painful. "This new Atlanta has given me a better life," admits Russell Cofer, a high school dropout who makes a good living servicing the expensive German cars favored by Atlanta's *nouveaux riches*. "But people come here and think they own this city just because they open some damn franchise. They're the

ruins, she returned home to a city that had adopted the phoenix as its symbol. Thirty years later, the dream is alive; 28 of her students are now dancing in major companies. "Being in a place where there's so much energy" she says, "gives birth to other ideas, other options."

This high octane mix of old and new, traditional and avant garde is what makes Atlanta such an exciting place. Yes, you can still get fried catfish in Atlanta. But at Tomtom, a popular restaurant in upscale Lenox Square mall, it's served with ginger, chili dip, and Chinese black beans.

<u>Left</u>, exotic blooms. <u>Above</u>, Burton's Grill.

Atlanta has been dubbed the "black mecca" for opportunity. This is in part due to its history of prosperity and civil rights activism, in part to its reputation as a gathering place for young, middle-class blacks, and in part to its sponsorship of events and historic sites that celebrate African-American culture.

This is the home of the National Black Arts Festival, the largest showcase of African-American art in the country. This 10-day biennial event is held in different venues all over town, from jazz clubs to art galleries to churches and hospitals, and attracts up to 550,000 spectators from all over America. In the two intervening years between festivals, up to 60,000 black people might relocate to Atlanta for good.

The city's black history is everywhere, from Hartsfield Airport (home of the first African-American female aviation general manager), to the many "house museums" of notable Atlantans, to streets named after civil rights leaders Martin Luther King, Ralph David Abernathy, and John Wesley Dobbs.

The city's best-known site is Auburn Avenue, on the south side of the city, the birthplace and stomping ground of the single most noted exponent of the American civil rights movement – Martin Luther King, Jr. There is no question that in Atlanta King is king, but in locations all over the city, other black families have a story to tell.

Black millionaire: Alonzo Herndon embodied all the promise that Atlanta has come to represent for black America. Born a slave in 1858 of mixed ancestry (his mother was a slave, his father a slave holder), Herndon eventually became Atlanta's first black millionaire. After learning to cut hair at an early age, he sparked his entrepreneurship by becoming the owner of a barber shop, eventually ending up with three. But the bulk of his wealth was made after he founded the Atlanta Life Insurance Company in 1905. Today Herndon's Atlanta Life Insurance Com-

pany remains one of the two largest black insurance companies in the United States.

Alonzo and his wife Adrienne were known for their philanthropy and commitment to bettering the lives of impoverished blacks, but the family's most visible local legacy is Herndon House, a 15-room mansion built primarily by black craftsmen and designed without the aid of an architect.

Overlooking the campuses of Atlanta's historically black colleges, the house is now

a museum to the city's black business community of the late 1800s and early 1900s. Historic papers about local life and society are on display, along with a fine collection of antique furniture. About 22,000 people a year visit the house to learn about the family that did much to establish Atlanta as a mecca for black business.

There is also the Wren's Nest, the Victorian-era home of white Georgia author Joe Chandler Harris, who penned the tales of a fictitious black character called Uncle Remus, known to most American children. Special guided tours, storytelling, and museum shops

Preceding pages: a pose fit for a King. **Left,** heavenly smiles. **Right,** porch patter.

with *Br'er Rabbit* memorabilia are available at the house.

Another popular destination, located in the historic African-American neighborhood of the West End, is Hammonds House. As one of the oldest homes in the area, the house's exterior is notable, while the rooms inside are filled with rarely seen works by artist Romare Bearden and other African-American and Haitian artists.

But of all the historic sites that provide evidence of an African -American past full of promise, culture, and entrepreneurship, there is one landmark that speaks most about the condition of present-day black Atlantans.

Ebenezer Baptist Church, where he preached, and the King Center. The latter was founded by the slain civil rights leader's widow, Coretta, and teaches King's philosophy of nonviolent social change. The area is also the setting for the Auburn Avenue Research Library for African American Culture and History *(see "Sweet Auburn," page 151).*

Although the legacy of a close knit and economically independent community lives on, the present has unfortunately caught up with Auburn Avenue. Most of the buildings are abandoned, and a large community of predominantly African-American men live rough on the street, part of Atlanta's home-

Money street: "The Richest Negro Street in the World," that's what they called "Sweet" Auburn Avenue in the 1930s. Home to pharmacies, grocery stores, banks, radio stations, schools, and now, the African American Panoramic Experience Museum (APEX) and powerful churches and civil rights organizations, Auburn Avenue and the people who made it thrive is why Atlanta is considered a black mecca today.

Between Jackson and Randolph streets on Auburn Avenue, the MLK Historic District, as it is called in the city, includes, not only Martin Luther King, Jr's birthplace, but

less problem. The roots of this chronic situation are also in the past, although a less-distant past than the avenue's 1930s heyday.

The racial turbulence of the 1960s had a devastating effect on Auburn Avenue and the surrounding area. With the coming of integration and a southern culture that recoiled with fear at the idea of a united black and white South, white Atlantans fled to the northern suburbs, taking jobs and opportunities with them. The shift in employment from south to north hit the black working class hardest, as nearly half of all black men made their living as factory workers. The exodus continued and, by 1985, for every one manufacturing job in the city of Atlanta, there were 2½ in the suburbs.

The isolation of Atlanta's low-income black population on the city's south side, far removed from the areas of job growth, seems to be no accident. Local government decisions in the 1950s and early '60s blocked proposals to build public housing nearby.

The situation was made worse by decisions that blocked sufficient mass transit links between the inner city and the boom-time north. As a result, the city's black neighborhoods and basic institutions began to decline, and it was only a matter of time rary counterparts of the thriving middle class of the past have fled to their own suburbs, mainly in the south.

While these people did not gain access to the economic centers of the north, they did escape the growing problems of the inner city. Those left behind in the ghettos were, and continue to be, isolated not only from whites, but from most successful blacks. This isolation from middle-class life and the professionals and institutions that center around it made black Atlanta vulnerable to the same underclass that developed in cities all across America.

Despite the holes in its profile as a mecca

before poverty began to take its toll.

Compounding the problems of the inner city was the trend by middle-class blacks to settle their own suburbs. Once described as having the best black neighborhoods in the country, during the late 19th and early 20th century, Atlantans considered it an honor to live in the West End's prestigious, segregated neighborhoods. But now, aside from those who have made the conscious decision to stay in the downtown area, the contempo-

Left, Alonzo Herndon's music room. **Above**, a christening at Big Bethel A. M. E. church.

for black business, African-Americans still look to the city as a place of opportunity. An estimated 30,000 African-Americans relocate to the city each year. Most come to get married, to raise a family, and to climb the corporate ladder at one of Atlanta's mega-companies. But a surprisingly small percentage make it to middle-class status (only 6 percent of all local black households earn above $60,000) and statistics show that the city ranks behind Baltimore, Houston, Washington, and Los Angeles in the size and income of their black middle class.

What black Atlanta does have, however, is

political clout. Influenced by the so-called "preacher and teacher" elite of the 1960s, Atlanta has long garnered national and international recognition as a city that makes leaders. As disciples of the community-service oriented philosophies of Martin Luther King, Jr, many present-day local civil rights leaders have continued to represent the concerns of the underprivileged, not only Atlanta's, but the nation's as a whole. The civil rights-era pledges of service and community instilled in the city's black politicians a creed that links power to the ability to serve – and to be seen to be serving. That philosophy is best exemplified in the case of

Andrew Young.

Young served as a pastor before working as a top aide to Martin Luther King, Jr. Later, he was elected three times to the US Senate, and in the 1980s served two successful terms as mayor. So effective was Young, both as a politician and as a symbol of a powerful, young black community, that since his terms as mayor the city has chosen two other African-American mayors.

Atlanta's current rebound from the knocks and bruises of previous decades can be attributed not only to African-Americans in key city government positions, but to social organizations like the Coalition of 100 Black Men and the Southern Christian Leadership Conference. Influential black colleges and universities like Morris Brown College, Clark Atlanta University, Spelman College, Morehouse College, and the Interdenominational Theological Center collectively educate around 12,000 African-Americans a year from around the country.

So close are the ties of power and service, in fact, that it is almost unheard of for an African-American to run for office or head a corporate division without making his or her church affiliation and social work common knowledge. Networking between business and social leaders is how Atlantans operate. In effect, it is the unified efforts of artistic, governmental, social, and educational leaders that are forging the way for a better community.

Revitalization: Much of the black population is committed to development. The historic African-American neighborhoods of the West End and Cascade Road are experiencing revitalization. Atlanta won its bid to host the Olympic Games by marketing itself as "The city too busy to hate," and many black schools and companies are reaping the financial benefits that come with playing host to the world.

A trend for black music powerhouses has made even some of the sober-minded city government officials star-struck. The former Atlanta mayor Maynard Jackson set up an entertainment commission in 1993 to look at ways of making Atlanta the next Motown. And it isn't just artists who are coming here looking for fortune. Other newcomers include nurses, entrepreneurs, doctors, and every profession in between.

Statistics in black and white may not tell the tale of a city that has lived up to its legend, but Atlanta's past record of community, entrepreneurship, and service holds it in good stead. The closer the new black vanguard can come to building on its existing foundations as practiced by its well-known leaders, the closer Atlanta will resemble the mecca that it once was, and would like to be.

Left, biology lecture, Morehouse College. **Right** *Behold* statue at the MLK Memorial.

While he was mayor of Atlanta in the 1980s, Andrew Young was once asked why people kept moving into the metropolitan area. He smiled, held up a hand, and rubbed two fingers against a thumb. The gesture, of course, is the international sign meaning "to make money."

Atlanta's unusual pro-business culture has propelled it in a relatively short time from an overblown southern backwater into a metropolis of several million people. Since the end of World War II, it has vigorously marketed itself to the world as a city of progress, while competing southeastern centers were content with the status quo. Outsiders were always welcome in Atlanta while other southern cities viewed them with suspicion. Many of the pillars of corporate Atlanta are originally from the north, first attracted to the city by its unabashed boosterism, something that other southern cities viewed as unseemly – until they saw the dividends it paid. Now many of them are playing catch up, trying to compete themselves.

Corporate giants: Atlanta is home to some of the best known companies in America. Among them are BellSouth Corp. and Coca-Cola Co., owner of the world's most famous trademark. The long-time presence of both of these homegrown companies, which date back to the late 1800s, serves as reassurance to executives of companies contemplating moving to Georgia's capital.

Other well-known Atlanta companies include Turner Broadcasting System Inc., the empire of media mogul Ted Turner; United Parcel Service Inc., the world's largest package delivery company; Delta Air Lines Inc., the nation's third largest airline; Georgia-Pacific Corp., the country's leading forest products company; as well as Home Depot, the rapidly expanding building supply retailer, and Southern Co., the country's biggest shareholder-owned electric utility. In

addition, more than 400 of the country's largest 500 companies maintain branch operations in Atlanta to service their customers throughout the Southeast. And the city is fast gaining as a center of international business, as more than 750 foreign companies have moved into the South's business capital.

Atlanta's internationalism is bound to expand due the 1996 Olympic Games, an event that is building more recognition for the city than the most expensive marketing campaign could ever have garnered.

United Parcel Service is one example of a major corporation that pulled up its northern stakes to move south and settle in Atlanta. The company's chairman and chief executive officer, Kent Z. (Oz) Nelson, explained that the shift was forced on UPS because talented managers were rejecting promotions to corporate headquarters in suburban New York; they complained about the region's having the highest cost of living among all the major US markets. UPS could have moved anywhere in the country, but in 1991 it settled in Atlanta, which has one of the country's lowest costs of living. Atlanta was not, however, picked solely for that reason.

Excellent infrastructure: The city is often praised for having an excellent infrastructure, facilities which include telecommunications, commercial air travel, three major interstate highways, and an extensive freight rail service. Another leading Atlanta corporation, Delta Air Lines, moved to the city in 1941. It was unrealized then, but this relocation would be the harbinger of Atlanta's tremendous economic and population growth after World War II.

Delta's founder, C. E. Woolman, moved the company from Monroe, Louisiana, the year the airline became a publicly traded company. Delta was pursued by Richard Courts, president of Courts & Co., the Atlanta firm that underwrote Delta's stock offering. Courts convinced Woolman that Atlanta would develop into the South's major commercial air center.

Delta's invention of the hub-and-spoke

Preceding pages: Cable Network News began in 1980. **Left**, Scarlett checks the Dow Jones industrial average.

flight pattern in the early 1960s is the key piece of infrastructure on which Atlanta has subsequently prospered. Business executives in such "spoke" cities as Nashville, Tennessee; Tallahassee, Florida; or Montgomery, Alabama who want to fly to key centers like California, Chicago or New York, first must fly by commuter airline to the South's "hub" city of Atlanta.

There they board the wide-bodied jets that whisk them to their distant destinations. This system gives Atlanta a disproportionately large number of long-haul flights because the air service accommodates not only a market of 3 million local residents but also

rent standing as a friendly home to business, it's essential to know about the city's recent past. The vision of Atlanta as a major air travel center can be traced back to William B. Hartsfield, mayor for 25 years until his retirement in 1961. Without this facility, business executives unanimously admit that Atlanta would not be what it is today. Until 1961, the city's airport terminal was little more than an oversized Quonset hut. This is because Hartsfield spent all available funds to extend runways to handle aircraft that were increasing in size and power.

When jet planes began making an appearance in 1959, the Atlanta airport was one of

one of 40 million Southerners.

Having a higher number of non-stop flights than most cities is a convenience that often lures to Atlanta those companies whose executives must travel extensively. According to former Georgia-Pacific chairman Robert Floweree, Atlanta's superior commercial air service is the major reason for the move from Portland, Oregon in 1982 by G-P, a manufacturer of lumber, paper and cardboard. For G-P the relocation was something of a homecoming; the company moved to Portland from Augusta, Georgia, in 1954.

Recent past: To understand Atlanta's cur-

the few with runways long enough to accommodate them, solidifying the city's position as its region's air travel center. Fittingly, the airport is now named Hartsfield/Atlanta International.

Hartsfield always worked hand-in-glove with the city's business elite, believing that what was good for business was good for the city. His successor, Ivan Allen Jr., followed the same path. During Allen's leadership in the 1960s, the civil rights decade, calm more or less prevailed in Atlanta, while many other Southern cities were convulsed by violent racial upheavals. This is no small point in explaining Atlanta's current position as a business leader.

The 1960s were prosperous for the country, and northern companies looked south for new markets. With its environment of racial peace and the city's other advantages, Atlanta was selected as the place to expand into by many companies seeking growth in the South. This growth provided the city with a corporate critical mass that remains a magnet for continued economic development.

Atlanta's corporate citizens, however, are not all behemoths like Coke or Delta. The area is also alluring to hundreds of entrepreneurs, particularly the owners of high-founded Hayes Microcomputer Products Inc. in Atlanta.

Call him Ted: But the best known Atlanta entrepreneur is, without doubt, Robert E. Turner III. Or Ted, as everybody calls him. And if you do not call him Ted, even on first meeting, he gets hopping mad. So he is known as Ted.

A native of Cincinnati who grew up in Savannah, Turner came to Atlanta in 1973 at the age of 24 to prop up his late father's faltering billboard company. Years later Turner would admit his business naivete led him to prohibit a television set in his home, figuring the ban would help his company by

technology firms who are attracted by the region's first-class telecommunications system. They also benefit from the presence of Georgia Institute of Technology, a local state university whose resources they may use.

These high-tech entrepreneurs hope someday to become corporate bigwigs themselves, of course. In fact, some have already succeeded. For example, Dennis Hayes, a South Carolina native who invented the modem,

Left and right, Atlanta's economic and population growth is due in large part to its excellent airline communications.

reducing television ratings.

His anti-TV stance changed shortly when he bought another business that had been hemorrhaging badly, an ultra high-frequency television station that he would quickly turn into the profitable foundation of his $1.5 billion TV empire, Turner Broadcasting System Inc. In the mid-1970s he stunned the city by purchasing the Atlanta Braves baseball team and the Atlanta Hawks basketball team. He was hailed as a civic hero because, due to poor attendance, the previous owners were threatening to move the franchises.

But civic duty was not his motive; he

simply wanted the teams as cheap staples for his TV outlet, which he developed into the country's first superstation by selling its programming to cable systems throughout the country via satellite.

When Turner announced Cable Network News in 1980, doubters far outnumbered supporters. Critics conceded the idea made sense but maintained he lacked the financial wherewithal to sustain start-up losses. They also claimed that he lacked the necessary experience in news-gathering. Turner, who often uses far-out analogies, shrugged and noted that aerodynamically a bumble bee cannot fly because its body is too heavy for

its small wings to carry. But bumble bees do fly, and so did CNN under Turner.

These days, Turner spends little time in the office, preferring to be with his wife Jane Fonda at their ranches in Montana or Arizona. Their marriage raised many eyebrows among Turner-watchers; how could the epitome of an American capitalist get involved with an actress known for her left-wing views? One answer seemed to be their abiding interests in the environment. "They both want to save the whales," quipped one person who knows Turner well. World peace is another mutual concern, and the reason for

his superstation's sponsorship of the Goodwill Games, even though the event is a money loser. The two-week games between teams from the United States and Russia are held every four years.

Shy sage: His remarkable success as an entrepreneur and his thoughtfulness on issues beyond business cause many people to view Turner as a sage with an answer for everything, an image that exasperates him. For instance, after he delivered a rare public speech, a person in the audience asked, "What do you think of the animal rights movement?" Noting that everyone had just consumed chicken, Turner responded, "I love animals. I just ate one for lunch."

Even though he is not in the office every day, Turner still makes the big decisions. During the 1990 Gulf War, he personally countermanded CNN news executives' order for the network's three reporters in Baghdad to get out. Turner's decision enabled CNN to be the only visual and voice sources of news from Iraq's capital during the conflict, winning enormous publicity for the network. After the war, the CNN staffers departed Iraq safely. Tom Johnson, president of CNN, says if the network had existed during World War II, Turner would have tried to place reporters in Berlin. He sees CNN not as an American entity but as a world network that happens to be US-based. The verdict is still out as to whether the rest of the country feels the same way.

Back to the future: Atlanta in the 1990s has not escaped the inner city problems affecting other US cities, however. The city proper is losing population, and companies have all but abandoned the central business district, which is being transformed into a government center instead.

But just north of Downtown, in Midtown and Buckhead, business is thriving. The suburbs are prosperous and they are growing dramatically, with both residents and commerce. Twenty-five years ago, metropolitan Atlanta consisted of three counties; today there are 18 counties. By the year 2000, it is projected that Atlanta will have expanded to 20 counties.

<u>Left</u>, **Ted Turner, head of a $1.5 billion empire.**

How Coca-Cola Became The Real Thing

Coca-Cola is the most ubiquitous consumer product in the world. Its waisted glass bottle is featured in books about design. Photos in nature books show ethnic tribes, colorful and seemingly untouchable, sitting around campfires with Coke bottles in their hands. A recent BBC/Discovery Channel documentary, showing a fragment of a bottle washed up on the sands of a deserted beach, claimed it as significant an artefact of the 20th century as the soapstone beads are to ancient Egypt. The words "Coke" and "Coca-Cola" have even been programed into many computer spelling checkers.

It was Robert Woodruff's ambition to put Coca-Cola "within an arm's reach of desire," and in this he has succeeded. The Coca-Cola Company sells nearly half of all soft drinks consumed around the world. It has operations in nearly 200 countries. The Coca-Cola Company claims it is the most successful product in the history of commerce.

On May 8, 1886 Dr John Styth Pemberton, an Atlanta pharmacist, produced a thick, sweet syrup and took it to Jacobs' Pharmacy. It was placed on sale for 5¢ a glass as a soda fountain drink, but was not an immediate hit; during that first year, sales averaged only around nine drinks a day. The name came from Dr Pemberton's partner and bookkeeper because he thought "the two Cs would look well in advertising," and it is the bookkeeper's flowing script that became the famous trademark. Later, Pemberton sold his interests in the drink to, among others, an Atlanta businessman named Asa G. Candler.

Candler promoted Coca-Cola aggressively, advertising in *The Atlanta Journal*, distributing coupons, and turning out clocks, calendars, and countless novelties, all with the company's trademark. So successful was the drink becoming that imitators were quick to act, and it was this battle against other cola drinks that produced the distinctively shaped bottle. A variety of straight-sided containers had been used up to 1915, but, after rival drinks hit the marketplace, Coca-Cola decided on an unusual contoured shape to distinguish itself from the competition.

Atlanta banker Ernest Woodruff bought The Coca-Cola Company from Candler in 1919 (to-

Coca-Cola has operations in nearly 200 countries.

day, the names "Candler" and "Woodruff" are widespread in Atlanta, appearing on everything from office blocks to arts centers), then passed the business to his son Robert, who presided for more than 60 years. Well-known illustrators such as Norman Rockwell and Haddon Sundblom produced striking advertising images. According to Coke, it is because of Sundblom's Yuletide image for the company that the public has come to think of Santa Claus as the tubby, ruddy-faced man now found on most contemporary Christmas cards.

At the outbreak of World War II, Coke was bottled in 44 countries, including those on both sides of the conflict. Robert Woodruff saw his chance and issued the order "to see that every man in uniform gets a bottle of Coca-Cola for 5¢,

wherever he is and whatever it costs the Company." More than 5 billion bottles were consumed by military service personnel during that war, not to mention the countless drinks consumed by local people, many tasting Coke for the first time.

Armed forces overseas were also behind the invention of soft drinks in metal cans, which, by 1960, had become available to shoppers in supermarkets. That same decade, the radio jingle "Things Go Better With Coke" was recorded by The Supremes, the Moody Blues, and The Four Seasons. Less than 30 years later, three independent worldwide surveys conducted by Landor & Associates confirmed Coca-Cola as the best-known trademark in the world. ∎

During the Civil War, newspaper advertisements in the *Atlanta Daily Intelligencer* announced theatrical spectacles at The Athenaeum, the principal theater for the city's more than 6,000 residents. Built in 1854 on Decatur Street near today's Georgia State University in downtown Atlanta, it stood next to the elegant Trout House, one of the city's premier hotels. Throughout 1863, the theater's company offered a wide variety of entertainments, from musicals to farces to vocal concerts.

On September 22, 1863, a guard was detailed during the performances "to preserve order," as the Confederates feared disruption of its nightly entertainments by Union troublemakers. The performances continued nonetheless. Admission was $1.50, with children and servants admitted at half price.

When Union General William Tecumseh Sherman, commander of the Army of Tennessee and conqueror of Atlanta, decided to abandon the city and march to Savannah, he torched the buildings that he deemed most militarily important. It's said that as the fires burned, spreading throughout the city, the general ordered his band to play the "Miserere" from *Il Trovatore*.

Music: The irony of that moment cannot be lost on anyone interested either in opera or Atlanta's cultural history, because after the city went through a frenetic year-long postwar construction period, culture became paramount once more. In 1866, the city hosted its first full-length opera, and then, as the population soared past the 20,000 mark, life started to return to normal. Other operatic events continued throughout the latter part of the 19th century, but it was in the early 20th century that opera made its firm beginnings.

The Metropolitan Opera of New York included Atlanta in its tour season in 1901 and 1905, but it was a 1909 visit by Met star Geraldine Farrar that really got Atlanta's

contemporary cultural life going. The great American soprano appeared as part of a cultural event organized by socially important Atlantans Colonel and Mrs William Lawson Peel, driving forces behind the Atlanta Music Festival Association. Attendance at the four-concert event topped 25,000 – an impressive figure for a city of about 155,000.

While being driven around the city, Farrar suggested to her hosts that Atlanta develop its own opera season. Colonel Peel gathered

200 leading citizens and shortly afterwards collected the $30,000 guarantee required by the Metropolitan Opera. The company's performance of *Lohengrin* on May 2, 1910, was a stunning success: some 1,000 disappointed fans were turned away after "Standing Room Only" was unavailable. That initial season reached an audience of 27,000.

For more than seven decades, interrupted only by war and economic depression, the Metropolitan Opera made an annual pilgrimage to Atlanta, and the city responded with glitter and galas. Although the Met's annual spring tour no longer takes place, its

Preceding pages: symphony by candlelight, Chastain Park. Left, *Carmina Burana* by the Atlanta Ballet. Right, Modern Primitive Gallery.

effect has been to seed the ground for local opera companies throughout the country. Atlanta is no exception.

Alfred Kennedy, Jr, whose father headed the Atlanta Music Festival Association and who was responsible for bringing the Metropolitan Opera tour to town, is now general manager of the Atlanta Opera.

Atlantans themselves have been included among the operatic stars who perform here. From Tucker, Georgia, a local suburb, Richard Clement starred in the 1992 production of *Albert Herring*; Delores Ziegler, a native of nearby Decatur, held center stage in the 1992 production of *Carmen*; and Jan

cording honors, including 14 Grammy Awards, and was one of two American orchestras nominated for "Best Orchestra of the Year" by the First Annual International Classical Music Awards. One of the most pleasant ways to enjoy a concert by the orchestra is to spend a summer's evening at Chastain Park, in north Atlanta , and have an al fresco meal at the same time.

This outdoor amphitheater hosts everything from classical music to pop to rock and country, but the picnics deluxe come out in spades when the symphony is playing. At least half the evening is given over to this dining exercise, in many instances complete

Grissom, who lives just north of Atlanta, took the role in *The Pearl Fishers* in the 1994 season. All are nationally recognized operatic artists.

Atlanta also has more than 60 choral organizations, remarkable for both their number and for their quality. Many are based at area churches, always good sources of information on choral performances, especially around holiday time.

The Atlanta Symphony Orchestra celebrated its first half century of performance in 1995, with a series of gala events. Launched in 1945, the orchestra has earned major re-

with silver, china, and crystal. As darkness falls, candles are lit, and the livelier fans may produce sparklers for extra effect. Musical concerts celebrating patriotic holidays or anniversaries tend to wrap up everything in fireworks displays.

Local heros: The South's devotion to classical music, will never, however, supplant its love of its own musical heritage. Georgians know and appreciate that the state was the inspiration behind Ray Charles, Lena Horne, James Brown, and Gladys Knight. In the 1970s, the Allman Brothers raised the flag; in the 1980s the baton passed to Athens,

Georgia where the B-52s, R.E. M. and other bands made music heard around the world. The '90s saw The Indigo Girls soar from local clubs to coast-to-coast TV. Some musicians born out of state, or even out of the country, have made Atlanta a base of operation: Elton John, Curtis Mayfield, and Freddy Cole (Nat King Cole's brother) currently have homes here in Atlanta.

Cajun and zydeco, the musical traditions of Louisiana, are popular favorites here, too, often played at such nightclub venues as Blind Willie's, which is also known as a major source for blues music.

Significant country music stars perform at

Dance and theater: The Atlanta Ballet, on the stage for more than six decades, is the oldest continuously performing ballet company in America. In Cobb County, the Georgia Ballet has been performing the classics for more than 30 years.

Theater, as well as dance, is a thriving part of Atlanta's performance-arts history. Headquartered at the Alliance Theatre in the Woodruff Arts Center on Peachtree Street, the company is known for its repertoire of both classical and new work. The Woodruff's sister theatre, the intimate Alliance Studio Theatre, was home for many performances of the local production of *Driving*

Lanierland (also known as "Concerts in the Country") north of Atlanta near Lake Lanier, and many rising and established country music stars appear at local clubs, like Cobb County's Miss Kitty's Saloon and Dance Hall. The best spots to listen to jazz include Dante's Down the Hatch, Cafe 290 and the La Carrousel Lounge at Pascal's Motor Lodge. A highlight of summer is the Atlanta Jazz Festival, where the sounds of the South are guaranteed.

<u>**Left**</u>, croonin' at Miss Kitty's. <u>**Above**</u>, story-tellin' at the Wren's Nest.

Miss Daisy, written by Atlantan Alfred Uhry. This award-winning play later became an Academy-award winning movie, some of which was filmed locally.

Limit yourself to the Alliance, however, and you'll miss much of what's special about local theatrical life, because theater can be enjoyed in a variety of unusual venues. Hoist a brew and nibble pub-style fare while waiting for Shakespeare or his contemporaries to perform at the Shakespeare Tavern.

In the summertime, savor Shakespeare with a picnic supper that you bring to the Georgia Shakespeare Festival, where plays are performed under a tent on the campus of north Atlanta's Oglethorpe University. Hand-held puppets of all kinds prevail at the Center for Puppetry Arts, where not all the productions are geared toward young audiences.

Visual arts: Only four short decades ago, the visual arts were in short supply in Atlanta. As if the town simply didn't have time for such matters after World War II, the terms "gallery" and "picture-frame shop" seemed interchangeable. Whereas in the early 1960s, Atlanta galleries devoted to good art were scarce, today the city has many.

What perplexes gallery owners, however, is that so much of their business seems to

tion, the High Museum evolved slowly, then suffered a severe setback in 1962, when a plane carrying 122 Atlanta art patrons crashed at Paris's Orly Field, killing all who were on board. A copy of Auguste Rodin's *L'Ombre* ("The Shade"), a gift of the French government, recalls this loss. As well as the High Museum, the Woodruff Center houses Symphony Hall, the Alliance Theatre, and the Atlanta College of Art.

Atlanta also embraces other museums of significant specialty interests. Hammonds House, lodged in the West End home of the late Dr Otis Thrash Hammonds, contains more than 250 works by artists of African

come from out-of-towners, rather than local residents. Customers who have the whole of Los Angeles' Rodeo Drive to shop, will fly in to select work from an Atlanta dealer. Still, some Georgians do collect good art, as was clearly demonstrated in a special exhibition called "Georgia Collects" held in the High Museum.

Housed at the Robert W. Woodruff Arts Center, the High Museum of Art, designed by American architect Richard Meier, results from the generosity of Mrs Joseph High on whose property the structure stands. Founded in 1905 as the Atlanta Art Associa-

heritage, including paintings, sculpture, and masks. On the city's college campuses, two museums offer unique collections. Work from the Ancient and American classical worlds is showcased at the Michael C. Carlos Museum. Carlos, a local businessman, collected Greek art and artifacts. Local real estate developer William C. Thibadeau and his wife, Carol, pursued their passion for pre-Columbian art. The results of both these patrons' efforts form the Carlos's permanent collection. Controversial and provocative American architect Michael Graves, known for his whimsical use of color and shape, designed the museum. The small museum at Oglethorpe University, located in the Philip Weltner building, is devoted to realism.

Nexus Contemporary Art Center, near downtown Atlanta at 535 Means Street NW, has 12 studios occupied by individual artists. The main space is a gallery devoted to exhibitions of modern art, which also stages live performances. The center is a classic grunge collection of warehouses near Georgia Tech that has been beautifully rehabbed into art areas. The Georgia Council for the Arts is here; so are the offices for the Shakespeare Festival. Visiting Nexus is a great way to spend an afternoon, but if you don't know

natural history, and science all hsve their own space. Trace the city's history at Atlanta Heritage Row, near Underground Atlanta, and at the Atlanta History Center, where the Tullie Smith House and the Swan House capture the spectrum of the area's residential forms, from the grand to the modest. View the rise of Atlanta's black middle class at the APEX Museum; grasp the region's natural history at the Fernbank Museum of Natural History, or explore science at SciTrek, Georgia's science and technology adventure.

Architecture: No view of a city's culture is complete without an understanding of its architecture. Atlanta is the home of several

about it, it's doubtful you'll ever find it. Signs pointing the way can be seen once you reach the general area.

Many galleries also show work by significant local artists. Try the Abstein Gallery, The Signature Shop and Gallery, the Berman Gallery, or the Modern Primitive Gallery for Southern art and crafts, many of which also make lovely souvenirs.

Museums: Atlanta's museums devote themselves to more than art, however: history,

Left, gallery and owner, Virginia-Highland. **Above**, the Fernbank and friend.

major architects, the most famous of whom is John Portman *(see box on page 128)*.

Atlanta's best known residential, as opposed to commercial, architect is Philip Trammell Shutze, designer of the beautiful Swan House at the Atlanta History Center. Driving tours through the residential areas of Buckhead pass much of his best work.

For more information on these and other buildings, the Atlanta Preservation Center and the Atlanta/Georgia Chapter of the American Institute of Architects, both located Downtown, offer tours and information about architecture in the city.

Atlanta grew up a rowdy frontier town. Coastal Savannah was already a century old, and proud of being refined, when Atlanta was first settled. Early entertainments reflected Atlanta's hellbent lifestyle. On Whitehall Street, in the southwest downtown area, diversions were not sedate. Gambling, horse racing, displays of pistol skill, and other raucous, manly sports ruled the area's leisure life.

Saloon culture: Nearly 20 years passed before the town saw its first theater, built in 1854 on Decatur Street near present-day Georgia State University. The musicals and comic entertainments it presented offered an alternative to the less civilized activities of nearby saloons.

Atlanta is known for both its refined cultural offerings as well as its taste for rowdy street celebrations, such as the unanticipated and spontaneous gathering of about 750,000 citizens in downtown streets to welcome home the Atlanta Braves baseball team when it *lost* the 1991 World Series. Or the thousands of college kids who fill the streets for Freaknik each spring. As Lucy Peel, an early 20th-century society matron, once observed: "Atlantans love a romp." They sure do.

Having witnessed both its first opera and its first baseball game in 1866, Atlanta has emerged as a cultural town and a major professional sports town. The two currents – culture and sports – define the city's leisure in both public and private terms.

But not all leisure is savored in such public venues. Entertaining at home is viewed as an accomplished art, and some private Atlanta parties are legendary for their size as well as their opulence. One local attorney has thrown an annual oyster roast at his home for the past two decades, the guest list at the last tally topping 2,000. The size and scope of the event are unusual, but it is certainly appropriate, recalling the magnitude of the county-

wide 19th-century plantation barbecues.

Fashion is also a part of the Atlanta leisure statement. Atlanta is a city whose belles like to glitter. Visitors from other parts of this country comment on the taste for serious evening attire, with long dresses, ball gowns, sequins, and stones for the women, and black tie or white tie and tails for their escorts. Formal costume of one sort or another is *de rigueur* for galas – and Atlantans love to throw galas. Any excuse will do, from fund-

raising to private purposes. One couple threw a small gala affair at home to celebrate their 10th wedding anniversary, and specified "black tie" on the invitations. In response, ladies had to wear silk and shine, long or short being their sole personal decision, and the gentlemen wore tuxedos. This is definitely *not* California.

Plantation posh: Women may not wear antebellum crinolines anymore, and you'll see everything on the streets and in offices from elegant suits to jeans to minimal minis. But Atlantans often revert to plantation posh when it comes time to party. Even on weekdays, restaurants fill with friends celebrating special occasions, and the women may wear casual but long attire, complete with thin straps and lamé finishes. At the very next table, worn jeans may prevail. For opening night at the opera, black tie dominates, but by the last performance, everything goes.

Private homes serve as much as public venues as the setting for bashes, as well as for cultural events. The "romping" Mrs Peel and her husband, Colonel William Lawson Peel, were major figures in Atlanta society earlier in this century. They presided over many stunning galas and held private musical evenings in their home. They were not alone.

The wealthy Oscar Pappenheimers between them played numerous musical instruments, including an organ which was built into their home. Recitals and even small operatic performances formed a regular part of the Pappenheimers' at-home recreation.

Callenwolde, which is now a fine arts center, was built by Coca-Cola heir Howard Candler as his home (1917–20). The built-in organ remains as a testament to this popular early 20th-century form of upper-crust entertainment.

But here's the kicker: some folks still hold such at-home soirées. The Friends of the Atlanta Opera spend the winter off-season holding musicales in private homes. Dress for such events is business suits for men and Sunday-best dresses for women.

Culinary culture: Dining out is a significant leisure activity for Atlantans, who face a broad and rich array of culinary choices in restaurants. These range from African to Italian, from Moroccan to Thai, from sophisticated to simple. The past decade, especially, has seen an explosion in the diversity of Atlanta's restaurants.

However, dining at the tables of the universe will never alter the Southerner's taste for this region's fare. A Southerner away from his barbecue – no matter which of its many versions he or she may crave – is a rudderless ship. Barbecue, which to the rest of the nation means merely grilling, takes on the aura of ritual in the South.

Not only is the meat (traditionally pork) grilled, it is then daubed with a concoction that variously uses vinegar and tomato, pepper, and other spices, to be applied only after the meat is grilled. The traditional barbecuing of a whole hog takes hours and is an experience not to be missed. In this instance, the term barbecue denotes not just the meat to be consumed, but the affair itself, which usually constitutes a grand outdoor gathering of very hungry hordes.

Barbecue, furthermore, is not at all monochromatic. In the North Carolina version of barbecue, cole slaw (a salad of shredded cabbage, onion and carrot bound with a mayonnaise-based dressing) is piled on top of the pulled pork barbecue. Heresy in Georgia. South Carolina is noted for mustard-based barbecue. Anathema in Georgia. Georgia-style barbecue sauce is generally tomato-based (abjured in North Carolina), with some vinegar, pepper, and other tangy ingredients. There are any number of places in town to sample barbecue; among the best are Fat Matt's Rib Shack, the Auburn Avenue Rib Shack and Aleck's Barbecue Heaven.

The fish fry is another down-home Georgia entertainment-cum-culinary adventure. Catfish, especially popular with local connoisseurs, is rolled in cornmeal and deep fried. With it come cole slaw and hush puppies. The latter has nothing to do with your favorite pet: hush puppies are deep-fried corn fritters. The distinctive name may derive from the fisherman's desire to hush his accompanying hound with a delectable morsel. To get a taste of hush puppies, dine (very casually) at Stringer's Fish Camp & Restaurant.

Let's not forget that stalwart dish of Southern country cooking: fried chicken. To enjoy a classic version, prepare to dine in the most humble of circumstances. You'll rub shoulders with the downtrodden and the well-heeled alike at Burton's Grill in Inman Park. Here, fried chicken is a noble experience. A new trend elsewhere is to take homestyle

professional sports events are expensive and you would do well to book in advance. Tickets to college sports games can also be difficult to acquire, as the teams of some of the schools are nationally ranked.

For instance, the Georgia Institute of Technology (the "Yellow Jackets") at North Avenue and I-85 fields a major national basketball team, and its football team recently took the national championship. Local college baseball teams, however, get less public attention despite their high quality. So taking in a baseball game on a college campus is a good – and less difficult – sports option.

One way to get a handle on Southern

Southern dishes and give them an inventive, upscale mien. South City Kitchen and the Horseradish Grill, for instance, give catfish and grits new interpretations.

Sports illustrated: Sport, of course, is a key leisure aspect of Atlanta life. What other city can boast an airline (Delta) where the pilot comes over the airwaves to announce the score of a Braves game? Atlantans love their baseball, all right. But tickets to the major

Left, patriotic sole. **Above**, around 750,000 fans turned out to cheer the team when the Braves *lost* the 1991 World Series.

sports, as well as family culture, is to attend a high school game. The South as a whole is nuts about football and basketball; the rivalries are fearsome spectacles.

But at high school games the atmosphere is special. As these are family outings, you'll find yourself sitting next to folks who cheer their offspring either on the team or in the band. Tickets are inexpensive, the hot dogs are decent, the marching bands perform well, and the kids both in the grandstand and on the field are as passionate about the game as they could be for any professional team.

High-level tennis, in the form of the Atlanta Thunder, is becoming increasingly popular in the city. Entire communities of houses are now built around the sport in suburban areas, and Martina Navratilova and Bjorn Borg served the Thunder as the team's star professionals in its first years of play.

Dress for sporting events used to be fairly formal for college games, but while the fraternity boys tend to turn out in khaki pants, shirt and tie, outsiders may wear anything they wish. Aging Bubbas (good ol' boys of fine Southern pedigree) are likely to add a blazer to the khaki pants, and the belles accompanying them often look like they're headed to Sunday dinner at the in-laws. Any-

thing goes for dress at professional games, and sometimes the costuming, aimed at reflecting partisan sentiments, can get pretty bizarre. It makes for great people watching.

Both college and professional sporting events may be preceded by lavish pre-game repasts served out of the host's vehicle, a custom known as "tailgating." Food ranges from caviar to sloppy Joes (aptly named, as these are sandwich buns filled to overflowing with drippy meat and sauce). Tailgating is almost mandatory for alumni attending college football games, and provides another splendid people-watching opportunity.

No visit to the South is complete without a trip to a car race track. Take your choice of stock car racing or road racing. What's the difference? It goes like this: stock car racing is the country boy's racing. The cars are potential junkyard treasures that have been worked on by local mechanics operating on slim budgets. Devotees of stock car racing pick personal heros and follow them as if they were rock star idols.

Stock car racing on the NASCAR (National Association of Stock Car Racing) circuit is the highlight of Atlanta Motor Speedway, south of the city, where the racing season runs in March and November. The enormous landscaped facility features a high-banked oval asphalt track.

Road racing, on the other hand, is the realm of the gentleman sportsman. At Road Atlanta, just north of the city up I-85, the outdoor course is a magnet for a chic crowd that views its 30 or so annual events. Curving its way through beautiful, rolling north Georgia countryside, Road Atlanta attracts a notable set of drivers, including film-star Paul Newman. There's an elegance and a posh quality about road racing that's absent in stock car racing.

Go fish: Fishing is another serious pastime for Atlantans. Bubba may prefer drifting lazy afternoons away in a bass fishing boat, in quest of the biggest bass a fellow can hook. The gentleman sportsman, however, is more likely to be found in his sail boat. Both these fellows take to the waters of the closest lakes in pursuit of their respective pleasures. But fly fishing in nearby streams is a very popular activity, too.

Former president Jimmy Carter and his wife Rosalyn made fly fishing their favorite sport years ago. However, it's not uncommon to see ordinary folks dangle lines from bridges into urban lakes and streams. If you join them, be sure to get a fishing license, easily obtained at sporting goods stores.

Although Atlanta lacks a coastline, water sports are popular and easy to drive to. Named for Sidney Lanier, Georgia's Poet Laureate of the Civil War era, manmade Lake Lanier covers 38,000 acres (15,400 hectares) and lies only 45 minutes north of Atlanta. Some Atlantans have second homes on the lake, while others commute to the city and live by the lake all the year round.

Perhaps the city's favorite way of welcoming spring is with a lazy float down the Chattahoochee River. The 'Hooch, as it's fondly known, was the dividing line between the Cherokee and the Creek nations prior to 1837. With its headwaters in the mountains of north Georgia, the 'Hooch winds through the city and eventually ends up in the Gulf of Mexico. The river's Atlanta portion is a federally maintained national recreational area, which is lined with jogging and hiking trails for those who eschew water entertainments. Bird-watchers and naturalists will

running down the other side. It's like nothing I've ever seen before."

Part of the Fourth of July festivities, the Peachtree Road Race inaugurates a day that includes fireworks and parades down Peachtree Street – after the runners are through. Runners who finish in the prescribed time (55 minutes) earn a T-shirt, which they proudly wear the rest of the day. Other events include a wheelchair race which precedes the foot race, and a Master's Division for runners aged 40 and over.

Festivals: Festivals and fund-raisers are highlights of the social calendar, constituting a major source of social events. St

want to check out the Chattahoochee Nature Center, a beautiful preserve on the banks of the river.

Road runners: Summer's zenith has to be the Peachtree Road Race, sponsored by the Atlanta Track Club. Begun more than 25 years ago with only 110 runners, the Peachtree recently topped 50,000 participants. As one young runner said, "You get to the top of the hill (Cardiac Hill, it's jokingly called) and all you see before you is this mass of humanity

Patrick's Day is the unofficial kick-off of Atlanta's festival season, which merits not one but two parades in this town – one in Buckhead and one in Downtown; the Downtown parade is one of the nation's longest-running Irish events. Sponsored by the Hibernian Benevolent Society of Atlanta, it dates from the early 19th century and is a solidly family affair.

The Buckhead parade was in danger of become too raucous for officials' tastes – a little too Whitehall Street, let's say. So the authorities clamped the lid on drinking beer in the streets a few years ago, forcing the

Atlantans take dining seriously. <u>Left</u>, afternoon tea at the Ritz-Carlton. <u>Above</u>, barbecue contest.

revelers indoors to the city's few Irish pubs.

Socially speaking, the spring season is launched on a farm on the outskirts of Atlanta. It's the site, at least for now, of the Atlanta Steeplechase, usually held on one of the first Saturdays in April. The multi-race event is a fund-raiser for the Atlanta Speech School, and it draws a mob. Plan to get there early, ticket in hand as none are sold at the gate, and bring an elaborate feast to serve out of the tail (trunk) of your car.

Women attending the steeplechase often wear huge, flower-bedecked hats and fancy dresses, although totally casual clothes are also perfectly acceptable. Men wear anything from casual attire to outfits that suggest the turn-of-the-century Gaslight Era or the Great Gatsby. It's as close as we ever get to Britain's Royal Ascot.

For the dogs: The dogwood is a flowering tree that is closely associated with the city. In spring, its white and pink blossoms float like clouds over the cityscape, or carpet the sidewalks with soft, pastel petals. Atlanta is at its peak in the spring – providing a late snow storm doesn't stop the trees from blossoming.

Spring is also the time when Druid Hills, where the story *Driving Miss Daisy* was set, opens some of its best homes and gardens to visitors. This coincides with the Atlanta Dogwood Festival, which is now more than 50 years old. Other events in the Dogwood Festival are a hot air balloon race and a bike race. Many events are free, although there is a fee for the home and garden tour.

Later in April, a nearby neighborhood of Victorian-era homes, Inman Park, opens its homes and gardens to visitors for the Inman Park Spring Festival. Streets are blocked off; arts and crafts are sold; food and music are terrific. It's noted for being a relaxed and casual affair.

Other excellent festivals include the National Black Arts Festival, a bi-annual which is held in the summertime in even-numbered years. A showcase for performance and visual art by blacks from all over the world, the festival is a multi-media, highly regarded, family-oriented event which is not to be missed.

The arts are never far from the festival scene, but the biggest show of all is the Arts Festival of Atlanta, which convenes every September in Piedmont Park. Beginning as a Buckhead backyard event first held in 1954, where art was hung from clotheslines, the festival has become a serious arts-focused affair lasting nine days. Crowd estimates have hit the 2-million mark recently, making this one of the largest such events in the United States.

Stone Mountain Park is the venue for a growing number of unusual festivals. Barbecue, and all its attendant virtues (and vices) is the focus of the park's annual Springfest. Visitors can sample the same barbecue that a team of judges will taste to determine the winners in several categories. See if your palate agrees with theirs.

On Memorial Day weekend (the last weekend in May), throngs come to the Taste of the South to sample not only such Southern delicacies as crayfish (pronounced "crawfish"), alligator, Vidalia onions, Brunswick stew, and catfish but also locally made Southern wines.

Apple-head dolls: Stone Mountain Park also showcases Southern craft at the Yellow Daisy Festival on Labor Day weekend (the first weekend in September). Southern foods and wines are again major parts of the event, but the focus here is on crafts, including hand-carved wooden items like canes, furniture, musical instruments (dulcimers and flutes), animals and toys, and textiles – quilts, coverlets, embroidered and woven pieces, and needlework of all kinds. Ever hear of apple-head dolls? These old-fashioned toys are made by mountain people, and you can often find them at craft fairs.

October brings one of Atlanta's most popular fairs: the Highland Games, also held at Stone Mountain. Assembling the Southern descendants of Scottish settlers, the games are a major event for both the Atlanta area and festival participants, who sell everything from tartan fabric to books, tapes, and trinkets. On the Thursday before the appointed weekend, the games open with a military tattoo, and all the excitement of a Highland pipe and drum concert.

Right, rafting on the 'Hooch.

Atlanta is a great place to live. Its excellent air connections, extensive freeways, green suburbs and proximity to both urban attractions and rural pleasures make the quality of its residents' life an enviable one.

But Atlanta is a nightmare for visitors trying to find their way around. Many of its streets were originally based on Native American trails, which means that they snake and wander in directions which once, presumably, effectively evaded the enemy, but which now cast newcomers as the enemy. Road signs are confusing or nonexistent: just because a well-meaning local explains how to get somewhere doesn't mean you'll be able to find it. And distances are great; this is a sprawling, unconfined city, a series of satellite communities with no central core. MARTA, the efficient public transit system, goes near many of the places you might want to visit, but when you exit the stations, you'll find few indications as to where to go next.

The city's citizens are sassy and streetwise and negotiate their way through life smoothly. They know where they're going, so these things aren't a problem. But where does that leave *you*?

Although Atlanta is very different city from "Slow-vannah," as the sensuous port of Savannah is nicknamed, the local custom of allowing lots of time to travel from A to B is a good one to employ in the capital, albeit for less languorous reasons. Expect to get lost. Take a good map. Build in "circling around time" because you're probably nearer to your destination than you realize.

Think about renting a car, or better yet, cultivate a relationship with a taxi driver. Most drivers don't seem to know their way around, either, but they stand a better chance than you do. (Tip: if you're being picked up from the Atlanta History Center – impossible to reach by public transportation – stress the specific building and entrance. Then prepare for a long wait.) And when you get home again, write to the Georgia Department of Industry, Trade and Tourism, or the Atlanta Chamber of Commerce, and tell them to *do* something about all this.

Preceding pages: visitors watch while CNN works; Ebenezer Baptist Church; the pause that refreshes. **Left**, number 19 to the rescue.

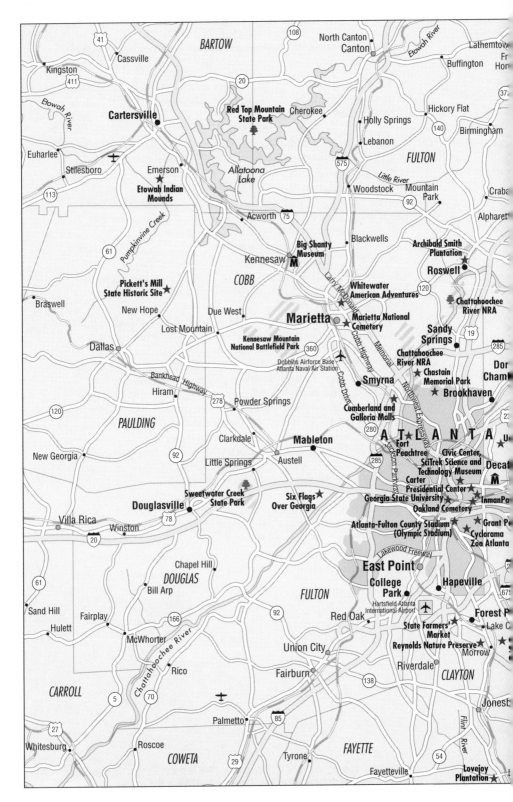

41
Kingston
411
Cassville
BARTOW
108
North Canton
Canton
Etowah River
Lathemtov
Fr
Hoi
Buffington
20
Euharlee
Cartersville
Etowah River
113
Stilesboro
Emerson
Etowah Indian
Mounds
Red Top Mountain
State Park
Cherokee
Holly Springs
Lebanon
Hickory Flat
Birmingham
FULTON
37

575
Allatoona
Lake
Little River
Woodstock
Mountain
Park
92
140
Craba
Alpharet

Acworth
75
61
Braswell
Pickett's Mill
State Historic Site
New Hope
Due West
COBB
Blackwells
Big Shanty
Museum
Kennesaw
M
Lost Mountain
Dallas
Kennesaw Mountain
National Battlefield Park
360
Marietta
Larry McDonald
Whitewater
American Adventures
Marietta National
Cemetery
120
Archibald Smith
Plantation
Roswell
Chattahoochee
River NRA
Sandy
Springs
19
285

PAULDING
120
New Georgia
Hiram
Bankhead Highway
278
Powder Springs
92
Clarkdale
Little Springs
Austell
Mableton
Cobb Highway
Memorial
Dobbins Airforce Base
Atlanta Naval Air Station
Smyrna
Chattahoochee
River NRA
Chastain
Memorial Park
Brookhaven
Cumberland and
Galleria Malls
280
ATLANTA
285
Fort
Peachtree
Jackson Parkway
Northwest Expressway
Civic Center,
SciTrek Science and
Technology Museum
Carter
Presidential Center
Georgia State University
Oakland Cemetery
Decat
M
InmanPa
Dor
Cham
23

Villa Rica
Winston
20
Douglasville
78
Sweetwater Creek
State Park
Six Flags
Over Georgia
Atlanta-Fulton County Stadium
(Olympic Stadium)
Cyclorama
Zoo Atlanta
Grant P

61
Sand Hill
Hulett
Fairplay
McWhorter
166
Chapel Hill
DOUGLAS
Bill Arp
Chattahoochee River
Rico
92
FULTON
Red Oak
Union City
Fairburn
Lakewood Freeway
East Point
College
Park
Hartsfield Atlanta
International Airport
State Farmers'
Market
Reynolds Nature Preserve
Riverdale
138
Hapeville
Forest P
Lake C
Morrow
CLAYTON
Jonesb
675

5
70
CARROLL
27
Whitesburg
Roscoe
COWETA
29
Palmetto
85
Tyrone
FAYETTE
54
Fayetteville
Flint River
Lovejoy
Plantation

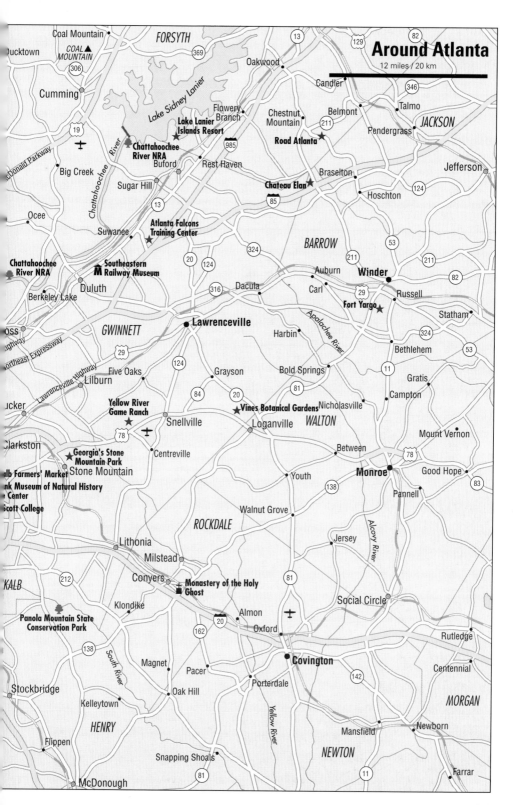

Coal Mountain

Ducktown

COAL MOUNTAIN ▲

306

FORSYTH

13

129

82

Cumming

19

Oakwood

Candler

346

Talmo

Belmont

JACKSON

Chestnut Mountain

211

Pendergrass

Lake Sidney Lanier

Flowery Branch

Lake Lanier Islands Resort

Road Atlanta

Chattahoochee NRA

985

Braselton

Jefferson

124

Chattahoochee River

Buford

Rest Haven

Chateau Elan

Hoschton

Big Creek

McDonald Parkway

Sugar Hill

Chateau Elan

85

13

Ocee

Suwanee

Atlanta Falcons Training Center

BARROW

53

Chattahoochee River NRA

20

324

211

Winder

211

Southeastern Railway Museum

124

Auburn

82

Duluth

316

Dacula

Carl

29

Russell

Berkeley Lake

Fort Yargo

Statham

GWINNETT

Lawrenceville

Harbin

Apalachee River

324

53

Ross

Northeast Expressway

29

Bethlehem

Lilburn

124

Five Oaks

Grayson

Bold Springs

11

Gratis

Lawrenceville Highway

84

20

81

Campton

Yellow River Game Ranch

Vines Botanical Gardens

Nicholasville

Tucker

Snellville

Loganville

WALTON

Mount Vernon

78

Clarkston

Georgia's Stone Mountain Park

Centreville

Between

78

Good Hope

DeKalb Farmers' Market

Stone Mountain

Youth

Monroe

83

Fernbank Museum of Natural History Science Center

Pannell

Agnes Scott College

138

ROCKDALE

Walnut Grove

Jersey

Alcovy River

Lithonia

Milstead

DEKALB

212

Conyers

Monastery of the Holy Ghost

81

Social Circle

Klondike

Almon

Panola Mountain State Conservation Park

20

162

Oxford

Rutledge

138

South River

Magnet

Pacer

Covington

Centennial

Stockbridge

Oak Hill

Porterdale

142

MORGAN

Kelleytown

Yellow River

HENRY

Mansfield

Newborn

Flippen

Snapping Shoals

NEWTON

Farrar

McDonough

81

11

DOWNTOWN

Downtown Atlanta is a maze of streets lined with soaring, modern towers punctuated by the older, more human-scale buildings that provide a link to the city's past. At Five Points, Atlanta is all business hustle and bustle, while a stone's throw away in Woodruff Park a beggar sleeps and an office worker relaxes in the sun with a take-out lunch. Down in Underground Atlanta, visitors frequent specialty cafes and bistros, while at the Capitol, state politicians strut their stuff for the folks from back home.

The architecture, the history, and the people combine to create the allure of downtown Atlanta, the part of the city the Chamber of Commerce likes to call the "sweetest part of the peach." Unfortunately, however, few people actually live here, and visitors have been known to complain about Downtown's cool, even sterile environment. City officials hope this will change with the 1996 Olympics and all its local, attendant constructions.

Underground Atlanta at Peachtree and Alabama streets is the ideal place to begin a tour of Downtown because this is where Atlanta was born. With no navigable river or seaport, Atlanta's birth was a coincidence of favorable topography and the expansion of the railroads. For many decades, the railroads would be the city's lifeblood, the cause of its destruction during the Civil War, and the reason for its dramatic rebirth after the war's devastation.

Today, the locomotives have been superceded by 747s, but the city's preeminence as a transportation center remains unchallenged. A good starting place for your explorations is **Heritage Row,** at Upper Alabama and Pryor streets, where the city's history is traced through interactive exhibits and regularly scheduled video presentations.

In 1837, surveyor Stephen H. Long was commissioned by the Western & Atlantic Railroad to lay out a line north-ward into lands recently opened for settlement following treaties with the Creek and Cherokee Indians. At the southern point, this line would intersect with the Georgia Railroad expanding westward from Augusta. Long's observations drew him to the favorable terrain of the sparsely inhabited woodlands west of the village of Decatur, and here his work gangs felled trees and laid down the thin ribbons of steel that would become the umbilical cord to the outside world for the rough settlement of Terminus.

Today, the rail lines just north of Underground follow the same route as these original beds laid down over 150 years ago. The vantage point of **Upper Alabama Street** offers a clear view of the tracks and the viaducts built over them, creating the "underground" city streets of the 1920s.

Nearby, beneath the parking garage at 90 Central Avenue, is the **Zero Mile Post**, a simple stone marker, with the inscription "W&A R.R. 00" on one face and "W&A R.R. 138" on another. When

Preceding pages: the skyline at night. Left, Westin Peachtree Plaza. Right, Emerging, by Marc Smith.

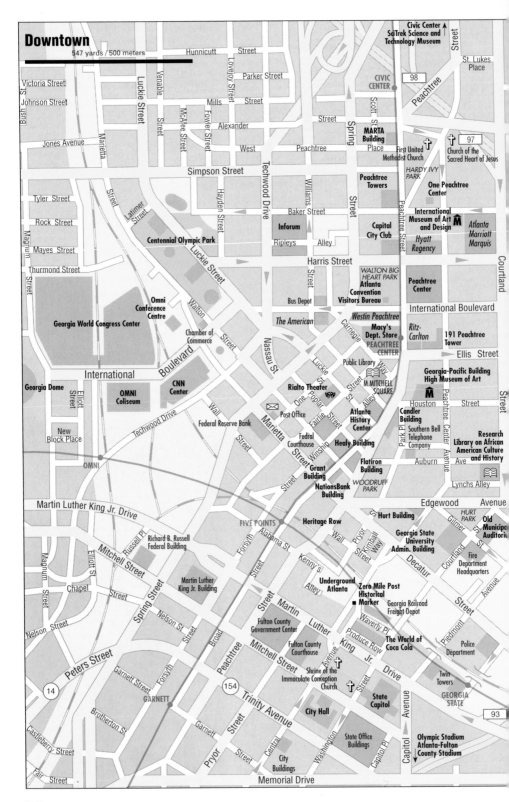

Downtown

547 yards / 500 meters

Hunnicutt Street

Victoria Street
Johnson Street
Jones Avenue
Tyler Street
Rock Street
Mayes Street
Thurmond Street

Lovejoy Street
Parker Street
Mills Street
Alexander Street
West Peachtree Street
Simpson Street

Venable Street
Luckie Street
McAfee Street
Fowler Street
Marietta Street
Latimer Street

Civic Center
SciTrek Science and
Technology Museum

St. Lukes
Place

CIVIC
CENTER 98

Peachtree Street

Scott Street
Spring Street

MARTA
Building

First United
Methodist Church

97

Church of the
Sacred Heart of Jesus

HARDY IVY
PARK

Peachtree
Towers

One Peachtree
Center

Hayden Street
Techwood Drive
Williams Street
Baker Street

Inforum

Ripleys

Alley

Capital
City Club

International
Museum of Art
and Design

Hyatt
Regency

Atlanta
Marriott
Marquis

Harris Street

Centennial Olympic Park

Luckie Street

Walton Street

Street

Bus Depot

WALTON BIG
HEART PARK

Atlanta
Convention
Visitors Bureau

Peachtree
Center

Omni
Conference
Centre

Georgia World Congress Center

Chamber of
Commerce

The American

Westin Peachtree

Macy's
Dept. Store

PEACHTREE
CENTER

International Boulevard

Ritz-
Carlton

191 Peachtree
Tower

Ellis Street

Courtland Street

International Boulevard

CNN
Center

Nassau St

Carnegie

Public Library

Luckie St

Street

M. MITCHELL
SQUARE

Georgia-Pacific Building
High Museum of Art

Georgia Dome

OMNI
Coliseum

Elliott Street

Techwood Drive

Rialto Theater

One Poplar Street

Fairlie Street

Atlanta
History
Center

Houston Street

Candler
Building

Southern Bell
Telephone
Company

Peachtree Center Avenue

Research
Library on African
American Culture
and History

New
Block Place

Post Office

Federal Reserve Bank

Wall Street

Marietta Street

Winship

Federal
Courthouse

Healy Building

Grant
Building

Flatiron
Building

WOODRUFF
PARK

Auburn Ave

Lynchs Alley

OMNI

NationsBank
Building

Hurt Building

HURT
PARK

Old
Municipal
Auditorium

Martin Luther King Jr. Drive

FIVE POINTS

Heritage Row

Alabama St

Forsyth Street

Georgia State
University
Admin. Building

Edgewood Avenue

Gilmer St

Courtland Street

Fire
Department
Headquarters

Richard B. Russell
Federal Building

Russell St

Elliott St

Mitchell Street

Magnum Street

Chapel Street

Martin Luther
King Jr. Building

Spring Street

Nelson Street

Kenny's Alley

Pryor Street

Wall Street

Kimball Way

Underground
Atlanta

Zero Mile Post
Historical
Marker

Georgia Railroad
Freight Depot

Decatur Street

Avenue

The World of
Coca Cola

Piedmont Avenue

Police
Department

Nelson Street

Peters Street

Broad Street

Forsyth Street

Fulton County
Government Center

Fulton County
Courthouse

Martin Luther King Jr. Drive

Produce Row

Waverly Pl

Twin
Towers

14

Garnett Street

GARNETT

154

Shrine of the
Immaculate Conception
Church

Trinity Avenue

Mitchell Street

City Hall

State
Capitol

Capitol Avenue

GEORGIA
STATE

93

Castleberry Street

Brotherton St

Pryor Street

Central Ave

Garnett Street

City
Buildings

Washington Street

State Office
Buildings

Capitol Pl

Olympic Stadium
Atlanta-Fulton
County Stadium

Fair Street

Memorial Drive

Long's work crews placed the marker in 1842, it marked the distance from Terminus to the end of the line in the new settlement of Chattanooga, Tennessee. For a journey back in time to the days of the steam-belching iron horse, step a few feet from the marker and buy a ticket for a ride on the **New Georgia Railroad**, an excursion train that offers several different trips, including an 18-mile (29-km) loop around the city, a trip around Stone Mountain, and a popular evening dinner train.

South of the railroad tracks and adjacent to the eastern entrance to Underground is the oldest existing building in downtown. The **Georgia Railroad Freight Depot** was completed in 1869 to replace the one destroyed by Union troops in 1864. Today, the building has been renovated by the state to serve as a conference facility. West of the depot, beneath the Central Avenue Viaduct, is **Old Alabama Street**. One of the city's original seven streets, and the first to be paved, Alabama Street was a center of commerce for nearly a century.

Today, a set of glass doors across the old brick street serve as an entrance to Underground Atlanta. Step inside and explore the old buildings that are now home to shops, bars, and cafes. On the north side was Packinghouse Row, a line of meat warehouses with their backs to the railroad tracks. Here also were the banks and businesses, Humbug Square – a haven for con-artists, traveling animal acts and patent medicine salesmen – the taverns of Kenny's Alley (a place so rough that the police put a precinct house there in 1870), and retail shops that supplied the growing city.

During the Civil War this all went up in smoke, but within a decade it was bigger and busier than ever. While no commercial buildings remain from antebellum Atlanta, an old gas lamp survived and is now located just inside the north entrance to Underground, almost on the precise spot where it originally stood. During the murderous artillery siege of the city in August 1864, this lamp was struck by a Union artillery shell and a fragment (note that a piece of the base is missing) struck, and fatally wounded, a passerby, Solomon Luckie. Ironically, Luckie was a free black man. For the 1939 world premiere of the film *Gone With The Wind*, the lamp was restored and dedicated as the **Eternal Flame of the Confederacy**.

By the 1920s, increasing automobile traffic and lengthy delays to those crossing the tracks forced the city to erect viaducts over the railroad lines, turning the commercial storefronts into neglected basements. Business owners adapted by moving their retail entrances to the second floor and the old areas were forgotten for over 40 years.

In the late 1960s, developers created Underground Atlanta, a shopping and entertainment district that was supposed to rival New Orleans' French Quarter in tourist appeal. After a meteoric rise, the area's fortunes fell when a large part of the complex was taken for construction of the MARTA Five Points Transit Sta-

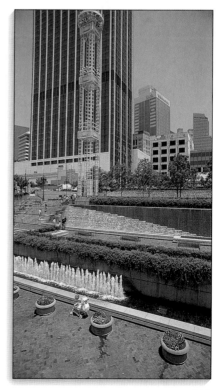

Outside Underground Atlanta.

tion and a nagging crime problem caused both tourists and locals to seek their fun elsewhere. By the early 1980s, Underground was back to where it had started – closed up and forgotten. But the idea would not die and in a joint public-private partnership, with the design expertise of the Rouse Company, the new Underground Atlanta reopened to enthusiastic crowds in 1989.

Today, Underground, encompassing six city blocks both above and below ground, blends the old and the new in a complex of shops, restaurants, street markets, and lively entertainment spots. Variety is the key here. There are shops featuring international art and rare collectibles, as well as local crafts and ethnic gifts.

For a meal, there is good dining at restaurants like Mick's and Damon's, a quick bite at the Exchange Food Court, or a rare culinary experience at Dante's Down the Hatch, Underground's most famous destination. And if you want to take a taste of Georgia back home with you, stop and sample the wares at Habersham Winery's Tasting Room and Shop on Old Alabama Street.

As it was a century ago, **Kenny's Alley** is a center for lively entertainment with bars like Fat Tuesday's, Hooters, and the Groundhog Tavern, plus live music at Fanny Moon's Beer Hall and Music Club. Throughout all of Underground, street vendors, mimes, and roving minstrels complete the festival atmosphere.

Underground's popularity with visitors and residents alike is stronger than ever. The annual illumination of a Christmas tree and the New Year's Eve celebrations a few weeks later, when a giant peach descends at midnight from the plaza tower, are two events that draw crowds in excess of 200,000. Be sure, though, to stay with groups of people if visiting after dark, and don't stray too far from the popular spots.

A recent addition to the growing Underground complex is the **World of Coca-Cola Pavilion** in the plaza lo-

Underground Atlanta is located on the site of the old city.

cated north of Martin Luther King, Jr Drive. Quickly becoming one of Atlanta's most visited attractions, the exhibits feature both rare and familiar Coke memorabilia, a theater showing the soft drink's long-running hit television commercials, an authentically reproduced soda fountain from the past, and displays of the Coke advertising art that has made so many generations reach for the "pause that refreshes."

The atmosphere is unsophisticated but fun if you're feeling in a light-hearted mood, and on a recent visit the vendor behind the soda fountain exhibited an engaging, unDisney-like frankness. Explaining the drink's origins as a cure for aches and pains, he confided that doctors could have recommended to their patients any one of a number of local syrups, but happened to choose Coca-Cola. Sales began to improve overnight.

At the end of a visit, top off your tour with free samples of more than a dozen soft drink flavors produced by Coca-Cola for countries around the world – all dispensed by a fascinating futuristic fountain of tubes and jets.

Across the street from the pavilion, at 48 Martin Luther King, Jr Drive, is the Gothic-style **Shrine of the Immaculate Conception** Roman Catholic Church, built in 1873 to replace the original sanctuary damaged in the Civil War. According to local legend, the church's pastor, Father Thomas O'Reilly, personally persuaded General Sherman (himself a Catholic) to save this and several other churches nearby from the torch. Ironically, the church was nearly destroyed in a 1982 fire but has been faithfully restored. During the rebuilding, construction workers rediscovered Father O'Reilly's tomb in the basement.

On the crest of the hill, east of the church, is the **State Capitol Building** at 206 Washington Street. It was built in 1889 on the site of Atlanta's antebellum City Hall, which surprisingly survived the Civil War. Its neo-classical design is similar to that of the United States Capi-

The World of Coca-Cola Pavilion offers free samples.

tol. An interesting feature of the building, at least by today's government standards, is that it was completed on time and under budget. What first catches your eye is the radiant golden dome. It was a gift from the citizens of the nearby town of Dahlonega, Georgia, site of America's first gold rush in the 1830s. The thin covering, made from 43 ounces (1,220g) of gold-leaf, was first applied in 1958 and refurbished in 1981.

The Capitol and the surrounding state office buildings are at their liveliest from January to mid-March, when the legislature is in session and lobbyists, school children, protesters, and constituents vie for the legislators' attention. The Capitol is open for tours and contains historical exhibits, a portrait gallery, and a small science and natural history museum. The landscaped grounds are dotted with historical markers and bronze figures of politicians, including Atlanta's only equestrian statue, that of Confederate General, and later Governor, John B. Gordon.

The Capitol anchors the eastern end of what Atlantans call **Government Walk,** probably named for the legions of lawyers and politicians who shuffle among the federal, state, county, and city buildings located in this compact area. In the distance, atop a parallel ridge, is the modern **Richard Russell Federal Building** at 75 Spring Street. Named for a long-time Georgia senator, the building occupies the site of Terminal Station, for many years Atlanta's main railway passenger depot and one of the city's lost architectural landmarks.

In the valley separating the state and federal offices are Atlanta's **City Hall** at 68 Mitchell Street and the massive **Fulton County Courthouse** at 136 Pryor Street. The Art Deco style City Hall, built in 1930, rests on the site of John Neal's antebellum residence, used by General Sherman as his headquarters during his short but inflammatory 1864 stay. A 1990 addition to the complex complements the building's original architectural design. A block west is the Fulton County Courthouse and Administrative Center.

The Beaux Arts style courthouse, with its massive Corinthian columns, was completed in 1914 and is in stark contrast to the strikingly modern county **Government Center** across the street. With today's tight budgets, the center's large glass atrium, indoor gardens, and iconoclastic design have raised the eyebrows of more than a few taxpayers.

Follow Peachtree Street northward, past Underground and the **MARTA Five Points Transit Station**. This is the hub of the city's expanding rapid rail system and home to a raucous market of sidewalk entrepreneurs offering just about anything a harried commuter might need. You arrive next at **Five Points**, the symbolic heart of Atlanta. Here, north of the railroad tracks, at the intersection of Marietta, Peachtree, and Decatur, Atlanta's bustling business district grew in the early 1840s.

On the northwest corner was Thomas Kile's grocery and tavern, where the

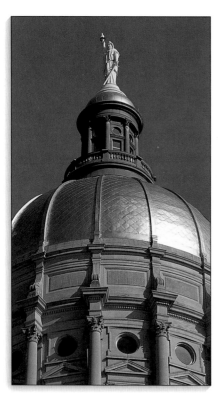

The State Capitol dome is covered in local gold.

newly incorporated city of Atlanta's first mayoral election was held in 1848. Moses Formwalt, a tinsmith noted for his manufacture of high quality whiskey stills, won the election over Jonathan Norcross, owner of a mercantile business on the southwest corner of Marietta and Peachtree. Atlanta was at that time a rough and rowdy railroad town, more Wild West than Old South, and over 60 fights between supporters of the two candidates broke out during that campaign.

In 1884, Joseph Jacobs, a former apprentice to Dr Crawford W. Long, the Georgia doctor who discovered ether-anesthesia, opened a pharmacy on the site of the old Norcross store at 2 Peachtree Street. One of the items he carried was a patent medicine produced by local druggist Dr John Pemberton. Advertised as a headache tonic, the coca leaf-based syrup was marketed under the name Coca-Cola. Sales of the product were steady but unremarkable until 1887 when, by sheer coincidence, a patron seeking relief from a headache asked the clerk, Willis Venable, to pour him a dose of the tonic mixed with tap water. Venable mistakenly added soda water, creating a refreshing carbonated drink. The rest, as they say, is history.

Following Marietta Street west, stop off to admire the main banking floor of the **NationsBank Tower** at 35 Broad Street. Built in 1901 as the Empire Building and completely redesigned in 1929 by noted architect Philip Trammell Shutze, the bank has been a long-time anchor of the city's financial district.

In the median of Marietta Street, at Forsyth, is the Alexander Doyle **sculpture** of journalist and orator **Henry Grady**. Grady's writings for the *Atlanta Constitution* and his eloquent speeches to audiences across the nation, fostered promotion of a "New South" of business, industry, and agriculture to replace the plantation-based economy destroyed by the Civil War. Through Grady's tireless efforts, Northern investors poured millions of dollars into

Hall of Flags, Georgia State Capitol.

rebuilding the devastated South and making progress toward reconciliation in the aftermath of war. Two years after Grady's untimely death in 1889, the citizens of a grateful Atlanta erected this statue in memory of his contributions to their city's renaissance.

At 72 Marietta Street are the offices of Grady's paper, now combined with the *Atlanta Journal*, where a young Margaret "Peggy" Mitchell earned her keep as a reporter while working in her spare time on the "great American novel," *Gone With The Wind*. The lobby has an exhibit of newspaper headlines concerning great local and national events and disasters. (Mitchell's home at 999 Peachtree burned down in 1994. Plans for its reconstruction are being considered.)

In the next block, at 104 Marietta Street, is the Atlanta Regional Branch of the **Federal Reserve Bank** established in 1912 by President Woodrow Wilson (who had a brief career in Atlanta as a young attorney in the 1890s). If you would like a close-up look at a $100,000 bill, with Wilson's picture on it, make an appointment to visit the **Monetary Museum** housed inside. A nearby historical marker notes that this was the site of **Thrasherville**, established by "Cousin" John Thrasher in 1839 as a rough settlement comprising tents, a general store, and a tavern for railroad laborers.

Farther west on Marietta is the shopping, dining, entertainment, and hotel complex at **CNN Center**, hub of media mogul Ted Turner's worldwide television news service. For a visit behind the scenes at Cable News Network, take what is claimed to be the world's largest free-standing escalator upstairs for the guided tour. On the tour you can see the *Headline News* newsroom in action, watch technicians pull together stories from reporters around the world, and discover the secrets of weather broadcasting (hint: don't wear blue). You can also view the extensive Turner Superstation Collection, highlighting the variety of news and entertainment pro-

Covered in weather.

gramming currently offered through the Turner cable family.

For action of a different kind, take in an Atlanta Hawks National Basketball Association game or an Atlanta Knights International Hockey League game at the **OMNI Coliseum**, located on Techwood Drive behind CNN Center. The 16,500-seat arena also hosts musical performers, tractor pulls, ice shows, circus acts, and other events. At the time of writing, the Hawks are considering relocating to a new arena to be constructed in the city's northern suburbs.

Behind the OMNI is the **Georgia Dome**, an enclosed stadium with over 70,000 seats completed in 1992. It is home to the National Football League **Atlanta Falcons**. The Dome also hosts the annual Peach Bowl football game and was the site of the 1994 Super Bowl. Both the OMNI and the Georgia Dome are event venues for the 1996 Olympics. Rounding out this extensive complex is the **Georgia World Congress Center** at 285 International Boulevard. With nearly one million square feet (9,290 sq. meters) of exhibition space, it is one of the largest conference facilities in the nation. From trade shows to scout jamborees, the center is bustling with activity nearly every day of the year.

Across Marietta Street, at 235 International Boulevard, are the offices of the **Atlanta Chamber of Commerce** and **Celebrity Walk**, a small brick plaza with markers honoring notable Georgians, including Margaret Mitchell, Lena Horne and Ray Charles, baseball home-run king Hank Aaron, long-time Coca-Cola chairman and philanthropist Robert Woodruff, civil rights leaders Dr Martin Luther King, Jr and Atlanta mayor (and UN ambassador) Andrew Young, and former president Jimmy Carter.

Adjacent to the Chamber of Commerce and bordered by Marietta Street and Techwood Drive is a 10-block area that formerly contained decaying commercial buildings and warehouses but is now the home of 21-acre (9-hectare) **Olympic Park**. This urban parkland

A night on the town.

features several tree-shaded pathways, fountains, an outdoor amphitheater, and a ceremonial plaza and fountain. At the heart of the park, to be completed after the Olympics, will be the **Olympic Centennial Museum**, erected as a permanent legacy to the first cenury of the modern Olympiad.

Inside the triangle formed by International Boulevard and Marietta Street is the compact, turn-of-the-century **Fairlie-Poplar** commercial district that earns it name from two narrow streets that intersect at its center. Captured here in masonry and brick is the city's transition from its roots as a railroad town of shops and warehouses, to its expansion as a business center of elegant skyscrapers. Wealthy Atlantans John W. Grant, William Healy, and Asa Candler constructed signature buildings here that remain as anchors of the district.

The **Healy Building** at 57 Forsyth Street, a 1913 Tudor-Gothic masterpiece with a large neo-Gothic rotunda, occupies an entire city block. Across the

street is the **Federal Courthouse**, constructed in 1911 and now home to the Eleventh Circuit Court of Appeals. A block south, at 44 Broad Street, is the Chicago-commercial style **Grant Building** designed in 1898 by Bruce and Morgan.

Probably the district's most unusual structure is the **Flatiron Building** at 84 Peachtree Street. Completed in 1897, this is Atlanta's oldest existing skyscraper. It was designed by Bradford Gilbert who, two years before, had designed the buildings for the Cotton States Exposition in nearby Piedmont Park. The building's name comes from its narrow, triangular shape, which enabled it to fit the small block on the corner of Broad and Peachtree streets.

Just south of the Flatiron Building, at **66 Peachtree Stree**t, freed-slave Alonzo Herndon opened his 25-seat barber shop in 1882. Herndon later founded the Atlanta Life Insurance Company and his businesses and investments proved so successful that he became America's first black millionaire. Atlanta Life remains an enormously successful corporation and Herndon's home, near Atlanta University, is a beautifully preserved museum.

Despite past threats of destruction for new development, Fairlie-Poplar has been preserved as a National Historic District. Today, visitors may enjoy exploring these quiet side streets and the venerable old office buildings where workers once toiled in boiled shirts and bowler hats after commuting on the trolley or in the family's Model T Ford. Soon, Fairlie-Poplar will reverberate with the sounds of music – from boomboxes to baby grand pianos – as Georgia State University renovates several buildings for use as residence halls and restores the 80-year-old **Rialto Theater** on Forsyth Street as the performance hall for its Department of Music.

Possibly the most exquisite commercial building erected in the city during the early 20th century was the **Candler Building** at 127 Peachtree Street. Coca-

The Flatiron Building was completed in 1897.

Cola Company founder Asa Candler spared no expense in erecting this marble and terracotta monument to his wealth and success. A shrewd entrepreneur and savvy investor, Candler purchased the Coca-Cola formula from Dr Pemberton in 1891 for only $2,300 and sold it to a corporation headed by Ernest Woodruff in 1919 for over $25 million. Step inside to see the ornately carved marble lobby with its highly polished bronze elevators.

In the shadow of the Candler Building, at 140 Peachtree Street, is the **Atlanta History Center – Downtown Branch**, located in the 1913 Hillyer Trust Building. Inside are changing exhibitions on Atlanta's history, and volunteers ready to assist with your explorations of the city. At the intersection of Peachtree and Forsyth streets is **Margaret Mitchell Square**, created by the city in the 1940s to honor its favorite daughter. Today, the square contains a soaring sculpture and fountain created by Kit-Yin Snyder.

Flanking the square are two other sights significant to fans of *Gone With The Wind*. At 133 Peachtree Street, the **Georgia-Pacific Building** occupies the site of the Loew's Grand Theatre, where the movie made its world premiere in December 1939 (*see photographs on page 51*). Adoring crowds lined the floodlit streets hoping to catch a glimpse of screen stars Vivien Leigh and Clark Gable with his wife Carol Lombard as they entered the theater's entrance, which was decorated for the occasion to resemble the plantation "Twelve Oaks."

The theater was lost to a fire in 1977 and the massive pink granite tower that replaced it was completed in 1982. The lobby features the **High Museum of Art at Georgia-Pacific**, with over 5,000 sq. feet (465 sq. meters) of space for frequently changing exhibits.

On the opposite corner, at Forsyth and Carnegie Way, is the Marcel Breuer-designed **Atlanta-Fulton County Public Library**, which houses an extensive collection of *Gone With The Wind* first

editions printed in foreign languages. The modern-style, precast concrete structure, built in 1980, replaced the original Carnegie Library that was on this site for nearly 80 years.

On the north side of Carnegie Way is an entrance to the **Peachtree Center MARTA Transit Station,** an attraction in its own right. Located at the crest of Peachtree on one of the highest points in the city, the station's escalators carry you nearly 100 ft (30 meters) below ground to the 770-ft (235-meter) subway tunnel, blasted from solid Stone Mountain granite. Just beyond the station, at 176 Peachtree Street, is the site of a terrible tragedy. When built in 1913 as the Winecoff Hotel, the 16-story building was considered one of the nation's most luxurious hotels. In the early hours of December 7, 1946, a raging fire gutted the building, claiming 119 lives, including that of the owner William Winecoff. It remains the worst hotel fire in America's history.

Just north of Ellis Street is the mas-

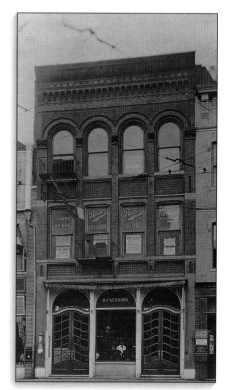

66 Peachtree is the site of Herndon's first barber shop.

JOHN PORTMAN

John Calvin Portman, Jr was born in North Carolina, but was raised in Atlanta, the place where, years later, his showpiece skyscrapers with their gleaming steel walls and soaring atriums would virtually define the skyline of the city.

So successful was Portman's concept of modern architecture that he went on to design some of America's foremost signature buildings including the Embarcadero Center in San Francisco, the Bonaventure Hotel in Los Angeles, and the Marriott Marquis hotel and theater in New York, part of that city's on-going efforts to revitalize Times Square. These modern landmarks, in turn, garnered international interest, specifically with commissions for the International Trade Mart in Brussels, and Singapore's The Regent Hotel and Marina Square.

Portman became one of the first American architects to become actively involved in China, traveling there in 1980 when that country opened its doors to the West. This visit led the Shanghai Centre project, a large, mixed-use complex of hotel, office, residential, retail and exhibition space described by the *China Daily* as "one of the five architectural stars in China mainland."

John Portman's personal style of architecture was influenced by Frank Lloyd Wright, a guest lecturer while Portman was a student at Georgia Tech. Like Wright, he focuses on the systems by which buildings are organized, and the concept of organic unity as a design ideal. Also like Wright, he believed that architecture was a comprehensive discipline that should shape and direct all aspects of life. To achieve this, Portman created the role for himself of architect/developer, a process that would enable him to have greater control over his projects.

Portman's willingness to invest money in his own ventures has roots in his first commission, the renovation of Atlanta's Fraternal Order of Eagles Building. He wanted to affix to the building the metal sculpture of a contemporary eagle. The client liked the idea, but was unwilling to finance the art, so Portman invested his own money for the sculpture. From then on, art became an integral part of his work.

Co-operation from the client was not always so forthcoming, as in the case of his first hotel. It was, Portman decided, to be the antithesis to the confining environment of traditional city hotels, constructed around a 22-story, skylit atrium with glass elevators whizzing up to a revolving restaurant on the roof. The concept was so radical for its time that the company that had initially invested in the hotel withdrew from the project.

He pitched the idea to every major hotelier in the country, but work did not begin until the Hyatt House Corporation, at that time owning only a small chain of West Coast motels, decided to fund the project. Visitors from all over America flocked to the Hyatt Regency Atlanta to take the dizzy, dazzling ride to the top. With this immediate popularity came international recognition.

Several Portman companies were established to meet the demand of design, development and financing services, swelling the organization from the two-man Atlanta team to 1,200 people world-wide. When he is not traveling for work or taking a keen interest in Atlanta's civic affairs, Portman retreats to Entelechy II, his private, showplace home on Sea Island, Georgia. ∎

John Portman redefined Atlanta's skyline.

sive brick **Macy's Department Store**, designed by Philip Shutze and opened for business in 1925 (originally called Davison's, as the parent company's name was not put on the marquee until the 1980s). The main shopping floor is an open, multi-story atrium and mezzanine, featuring large columns and marble decoration. The store is on the site of the Austin Leyden House, an antebellum mansion used by Union General George Thomas as his headquarters during the city's occupation.

Across Peachtree is the **Ritz-Carlton Hotel** and next to it the **One-Ninety-One Peachtree Tower**, a modern interpretation of a turn-of-the century skyscraper, created by architects Philip Johnson and John Burgee.

Capping the string of skyscrapers, at the summit of the ridge, is the John Portman-designed **Westin Peachtree Plaza Hotel** at 210 Peachtree Street. This soaring 70-story cylinder of glass and steel, built in 1976, was for many years the tallest hotel in the world. Atop

the building is the popular **Sundial Restaurant** which rotates to give diners an exciting aerial view of the city below. From 1870 until 1921, the Georgia Governor's Mansion occupied this site.

Atlanta's **Hard Rock Cafe** is housed in the renovated 1928 J. P. Allen clothing store at 215 Peachtree Street. If the Hard Rock is an icon of the rock generation, the nearby **Capital City Club,** at Harris and Peachtree streets, is a vestige of the men's clubs of a century ago. Founded in 1883, the club erected this building in 1911. For many years, Atlanta's main power brokers met here in the club's smoking parlors, bars, and magnificent Art Deco Mirador Room. Today, it offers a glimpse of that bygone era when life seemed simpler and the pace of life Downtown was considerably more genteel.

Surrounding the club are the buildings that make up the ever-expanding **Peachtree Center** complex, architect and developer John Portman's vision of a Southern-style Rockefeller Center,

Portman's atrium at the Marriott Marquis Hotel.

which has been a work-in-progress for more than 30 years. From the construction of the Atlanta Merchandise Mart at 240 Peachtree Street in 1961, to the completion of the **One Peachtree Center** tower at 303 Peachtree Street in 1992, Portman has redefined the downtown business district and has parlayed his design experience here into commissions around the world.

Possibly the most recognizable building in the center is the 1967 **Hyatt Regency Hotel** with its soaring 22-story atrium lobby and rotating, flying saucer-like **Polaris Room** restaurant, a bubble of deep royal blue on the roof. An evolution of this theme is the dizzying 48-story open, curving atrium lobby of the nearby **Marriott Marquis Hotel** at 265 Peachtree Center Avenue. Described by some as "Jonah's view of the belly of the whale," a glance downward from the upper floors of the hotel is not recommended for the faint of heart.

The **Merchandise Mart** is open only to wholesalers and buyers, but the

Inforum at 250 Williams Street, a center for displays of innovative technology in computing and telecommunications, and the **International Sports Plaza**, a sports retailing center with shops, restaurants, and exhibition space, are both open to the general public.

The elaborate **Peachtree Center Shopping Mall** is located beneath the corporate towers at 231 Peachtree. A feature more commonly found in northern cities than in the sunny South are the climate-controlled pedestrian walkways that connect all the Peachtree Center buildings together. These walkways also provide a respite from Downtown's more unsavory urban aspects.

At the intersection of Peachtree and West Peachtree Streets is **Hardy Ivy Park**, a small green space named in honor of Ivy, Atlanta's first permanent settler, who built his primitive cabin in the nearby woods in 1833. Ivy paid $225 in money and produce for lot No. 51, a parcel of land that now comprises much of the northern part of the downtown business district. Across from the park is the landscaped sculpture garden that Portman has created around the One Peachtree Center Tower. Dominating the grounds is *Ballet Olympia*, a whimsical adaptation of Paul Manship's 1953 sculpture of dancing maidens.

A block farther north on Peachtree are two historic churches. At 360 Peachtree Street is the **First United Methodist Church**, the oldest organized congregation in Atlanta, founded in 1847. The original wooden structure, Wesley Chapel, was located on the current site of the Candler Building. When Asa Candler acquired that property, the congregation built this Gothic Revival church from locally quarried Stone Mountain granite. Brought from the old church and included in the new building were the original pulpit, stained-glass windows, and iron fence. Also, hanging in the square tower, is the original church bell, which was rung in 1864 to warn of General Sherman's approach

Nearby, at 335 Peachtree Center Av-

Getting into her work.

enue, is the Roman Catholic **Church of the Sacred Heart of Jesus**, built in 1897. The parish was established by Marist priests in the early 1890s, and the Romanesque Revival-style red-brick church was once the centerpiece of a sprawling complex that included the Marist College and St Joseph's Infirmary. Both the school and the hospital have relocated to the suburbs, but the church remains to minister to the local community. Just south of Sacred Heart Church, in the Marquis Two Tower at 285 Peachtree Center Avenue, is the **Atlanta International Museum of Art and Design**. Located on the Garden Level, the museum displays the artwork of cultures from around the world.

Farther south, at the corner of Edgewood and Peachtree Center avenues, is **Hurt Park**, a small green space named for another Atlanta entrepreneur, Joel Hurt, who once owned the Atlanta and Edgewood Street Railroad Company. He developed Inman Park, the city's first planned suburb (at the end of his

trolley line of course), in the late 1880s. Created in 1940, this was the first public park established in the downtown area since the Civil War.

The curving lines, masonry, and fountain were designed to complement the **Municipal Auditorium** located across Courtland Street. Built in 1909, this facility was the city's main event center for several decades.

From circus shows, concerts, and grand opera; from Enrico Caruso to Jimi Hendrix, the old auditorium hosted them all during its heyday. In 1939, it was the site of an elaborate ball held prior to the premiere of *Gone With The Wind*. The facility was replaced by the new Civic Center in 1968 and in the early 1980s was purchased and extensively remodeled as an alumni center by Georgia State University. Today, only the original facade remains.

Just west of the auditorium, at 50 Hurt Plaza, is the **Hurt Building**, a beautifully restored skyscraper commissioned by Joel Hurt in 1913 and completed

SciTrek, the science museum.

over the next 15 years. The style and quality of materials used in its construction rival those of Asa Candler's nearby tower. As with that building, a tour is not complete without stepping inside to admire the ornate, domed rotunda.

The ideal spot to conclude your exploration of the central business district, to relax and people-watch, is **Robert W. Woodruff Memorial Park** at Edgewood and Peachtree Street. Woodruff, the long-time chairman of the Coca-Cola Company, purchased the land, created the park, and gave it to the city as an anonymous gift. Originally called Central City Park, it was renamed for Woodruff after his death. Today, the open meadow and plaza host an eclectic mix of lunchtime picnickers, sun worshipers, street preachers, artists, peddlers, and homeless people.

Just beyond the core of Downtown, to the four points of the compass, are other sites worth noting. To the south, is **Atlanta-Fulton County Stadium**, home of the Major League Baseball Atlanta

Braves. At Capitol and Georgia avenues is the new **Olympic Stadium**, site of the opening and closing ceremonies of the 1996 games, as well as numerous Olympic events. Following the Olympics, Atlanta-Fulton County Stadium will be demolished and the Olympic Stadium modified for the Braves.

To the west, beyond the Georgia Dome, is the campus of the **Atlanta University Center**, home of the institutions for black students: **Morris Brown**, **Morehouse**, and **Spelman Colleges**, **Clark-Atlanta University**, and the **Interdenominational Theological Center**. Founded to provide an education for freed slaves after the Civil War, the schools have grown to national prominence and claim among their alumni Dr Martin Luther King, Jr, Olympian Edwin Moses, and film maker Spike Lee.

Notable campus buildings include **Fountain Hall** (1882) and **Gaines Hall** (1869) at Morris Brown; **Graves Hall** (1889) and the **Martin Luther King, Jr International Chapel** (1980) at Morehouse, and **Sisters Chapel** (1927), **Packard Hall** (1888), and **Rockefeller Hall** (1886) at Spelman. Just north of the campus, at 587 University Place, is the 15-room, 1910 Georgian Revival mansion of **Alonzo Herndon,** now operating as a museum depicting the life of a prosperous black family during the difficult years of racial segregation. Nearby is **Paschal's Restaurant,** at 830 Martin Luther King, Jr Drive. The restaurant has been a gathering place for generations of community leaders and civil rights activists.

To the north of Downtown, at 395 Piedmont Avenue, is the **Atlanta Civic Center** and **SciTrek**, the science and technology museum of Atlanta. The Civic Center houses the city's theatrical auditorium and SciTrek, established in 1988, features more than 100 hands-on displays and exhibits. Just east of downtown is the campus of **Georgia State University**, stretching from Edgewood Avenue south to Decatur Street.

Left, Spelman College. Right, the Hilton atrium.

MIDTOWN

If Downtown is the business and historic heart of Atlanta, then Midtown, home of the Woodruff Arts Center, the High Museum, and several repertory theaters, is where the city's cultural lifeblood flows most fervently. While Midtown may be more a state of mind than a district measured by rigid boundaries, its center is without doubt the busy area around the intersection of Peachtree and 14th streets.

The boundaries in this chapter stretch to include Piedmont Park on the east; the Fox Theatre district to the south; the Georgia Institute of Technology (Georgia Tech) campus to the west; and Pershing Point Park to the north. Proximity to four **MARTA** **Transit Stations** – Civic Center, North Avenue, Midtown, and Arts Center – makes access to all points in Midtown fairly easy.

The highlight of a visit to Midtown's southern region is one of America's great movie palaces, the Moorish-style **Fox Theatre** at 660 Peachtree Street, built in 1929. Originally intended to serve as the headquarters for the Atlanta Yaarab Temple, the Order was forced to sell the building during the Great Depression. The buyer was cinema executive William Fox, who converted it to a grand movie theater with an interior reminiscent of an Arabian courtyard, filled with twinkling stars, wispy clouds, and grand balconies – like a scene from *A Thousand and One Nights*. For nearly 40 years, the Fox was the place to see a movie, listen to music on the huge Moeller organ or just to be seen during the annual performances by the Metropolitan Opera's touring company.

Nearly lost to developers in the early 1970s, the move to "Save the Fabulous Fox" is considered the foundation for citizens' efforts to study and preserve other community landmarks. Fittingly, an ideal way to see the interior of the Fox is on a guided tour offered by the Atlanta Preservation Center.

Across the street from the theater is the **Georgian Terrace**. Built in 1911, in what was still a residential suburb, it was the city's most luxurious hotel for many years before closing in the 1970s. After a decade as a vacant, derelict site, the building has been beautifully restored, expanded, and adapted for use as luxury apartments.

In 1939 the hotel played host to Clark Gable, Vivien Leigh, and other cast members from the film *Gone With The Wind* when they came to Atlanta for the movie's world premiere – at the Loew's Grand, not the Fox. Step inside to admire the ornate interior and pay a visit to the **Road To Tara Museum**, which contains a comprehensive collection of artifacts and memorabilia from the film.

Just south of the Georgian Terrace is the massive **Ponce de Leon Apartments**, a rounded, 11-story structure designed to fit the curving intersection of Peachtree Street and Ponce de Leon Avenue. Completed in 1913, this was the first luxury, high-rise apartment

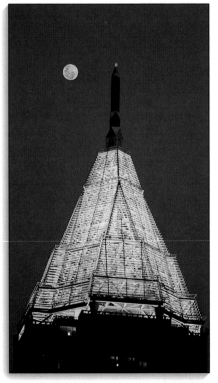

Preceding
pages and
left, the Fox
Theatre was
built to
resemble an
Arabian
courtyard.
Right,
NationsBank
Tower.

building in Atlanta. The Ponce, as it is known, and the Georgian Terrace serve as architectural complements, and their construction represented the expanding commercial growth along the spine of Peachtree Street.

A few examples of Victorian residential architecture remain nearby. One is the 1900 **Rufus Rose House** at 537 Peachtree Street, built for the founder of the Four Roses Distillery. Another is the rambling Queen Anne-style **Edward Peters Estate**, built in 1883 and located at 179 Ponce de Leon Avenue. The house is now the **Mansion Restaurant**.

Unique in Atlanta is the row of townhouses located on **Baltimore Block** off West Peachtree Street by the Civic Center Transit Station. It was completed in 1886 by architect J. S. Rosenthal of Baltimore, Maryland (a city defined by its rowhouses), but the idea never caught on in Atlanta, a city with virtually unlimited space for growth. Through the years, the buildings suffered decline and a portion of the complex was de-

molished. Recently, an ambitious project has incorporated the buildings into a sought-after residential-office complex. Other period buildings constructed to support the then-popular residential neighborhood include **All Saints Episcopal Church** (1906) at 634 West Peachtree Street, **Fire Station No. 11** (1907) at 30 North Avenue, and **North Avenue Presbyterian Church** (1901) at 607 Peachtree Street.

On Linden Avenue, "between the Peachtrees," is **Crawford Long Hospital**, built in 1910 by two local physicians, Drs E. C. Davis and L. C. Fischer. The doctors were told by skeptics that their hospital would never succeed because it was "too far from town." Donated to Emory University in 1938, the massive complex now anchors the southern edge of Midtown. The hospital lobby houses a small museum featuring medical artifacts, and furnishings from the office of **Dr Crawford Long**, who, in 1842, was the first physician to use ether as a surgical anesthetic.

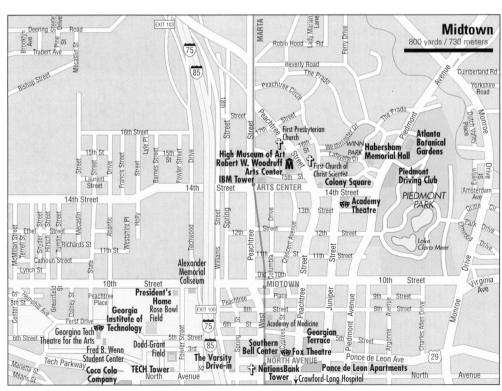

Two newer buildings dominate the area's skyline. One is the 52-story **Southern Bell Center**, at 675 West Peachtree Street, erected in 1982. It includes a small shopping center, a food court, and the **Telephone Museum**, and is built atop the North Avenue Transit Station. To the south is the **Nations-Bank Tower** at 600 West Peachtree. Currently the world's ninth-tallest building, the skyscraper is topped with an open pyramidal structure sometimes called Atlanta's Eiffel Tower.

A few blocks west, heading toward the Georgia Tech campus, is a landmark of a completely different kind. At Spring Street and North Avenue is **The Varsity**, an Atlanta culinary tradition since 1929. The current Art Moderne building, erected in 1940 and expanded numerous times, has long been a popular gathering place for Tech students and an essential stop for locals showing out-of-town guests the best – or at least the most notorious – chili-dogs, onion rings, and hamburgers in the city. The restaurant is a busy place, so be prepared with your order when the server asks, "Whatta y'all have today?"

Across Interstate 75/85 on North Avenue, new residential facilities, built as part of the Olympic village for the 1996 games, mark the entrance to the **Georgia Tech campus.** Established only two decades after Atlanta was devastated in the Civil War, Georgia Tech was a tangible outcome of journalist Henry Grady's call for a "New South" combining business, industry, and agriculture. For Grady and other visionaries, a technical college was an essential part of this plan. On the eve of the school's opening, Grady summed up his pride in the accomplishment when he said, pointing at the new administration building, "There is a light that will cast its beam over all the South. So lighted, we can move into the industrial future."

The **Tech Tower** at 225 North Avenue was completed in 1888 and is one of the original campus buildings. It anchors the Georgia Tech Historic Dis-

Midtown skyscrapers; Georgia Tech.

COLLEGE OF COMPUTING

trict, which includes the 1899 **Aaron French Building**, named for a Pittsburgh, Pennsylvania industrialist who funded the Textile Engineering program; the **Lyman Hall Building**, built for the mathematics department in 1905 and named for the school's second president; and the **Carnegie Building**, the school's first library and a 1907 gift from Andrew Carnegie. Across the driveway, and built into the side of the football stadium, is the new **William Moore Student Success Center**, a unique facility offering a variety of academic and placement services for both varsity athletes and general students. Nearby is the **Guggenheim Aeronautical and Aerospace Engineering Building**, which was built with funds from the Daniel Guggenheim Foundation in 1929.

Just west of the Tech Tower is **Dodd-Grant Field**, home to the Georgia Tech "Ramblin' Wreck" football team since 1913. The original stands were built by students and funded by Atlanta businessman John W. Grant in memory of his son, Hugh Inman Grant. The field has been the home of four national championship teams, and coaching legends John Heisman (for whom the Heisman Trophy is named), W.A. Alexander, and Bobby Dodd each served at the helm of great Tech teams. In 1988, Dodd's name was added to the storied stadium in honor of his years of success at Tech. The **Arthur B. Edge Intercollegiate Athletic Center**, at the northeast corner of the stadium, has an exhibition area featuring Tech sports memorabilia, including the 1990 National Championship Trophy.

Through the years, many great games have been played here but none is more remarkable than the 1916 contest between Tech and an outmanned team from Cumberland College. When the whistle blew to bring a merciful end to the game, Tech led 222–0. It remains the most lopsided game in American college football history.

Tech's appearance in the 1929 Rose

Park art starts here.

140

Bowl (an 8–7 victory over California in a game made famous by California player Roy Reigels' "wrong-way" run with the ball) earned the school enough money to develop **Rose Bowl Field** on Fowler and 5th streets. Today, the grounds contain the tennis complex, the football practice field, and Russ Chandler Baseball Stadium.

Across from the tennis facility is **Alexander Memorial Coliseum**, a domed gymnasium built in 1956 for the varsity basketball team. In recent years it has earned the nickname "Thriller Dome" from Tech's "pull it out at the last second" style of play. The coliseum serves as the boxing event venue for the 1996 Olympic Games. Nearby, across 10th Street, is the new Georgia Tech Natatorium, site of the swimming and water polo events during the games.

West of the athletic facilities, on 10th Street, is the **President's Home**, a Georgian-style mansion that was a gift of alumnus and textile company owner Fuller Callaway. The Callaways also provided funds for the **Fuller Callaway Manufacturing Research Center** on Ferst Drive at Hemphill Avenue.

A good place to wind up a tour of the campus is the **Fred B. Wenn Student Center** on Ferst Drive. The campus visitor center is here, along with the Ferst Place Restaurant, a cafeteria, and meeting rooms. Nearby is Houston's Bookstore, the Student Activity Center, the teepee-like Olympic Interfaith Chapel with its unusual courtyard fountain, and the **Georgia Tech Theater for the Arts** which hosts student productions by DramaTech as well as by professional artists.

At the theater's entrance are the **Richards and Westbrook Galleries**, featuring fine art and high-tech exhibits. Student creativity of the offbeat variety is the norm in the parade of "Ramblin' Wrecks," held each fall as part of the annual Homecoming festivities.

Just west of the campus, at North Avenue and Luckie Street, is the sprawling headquarters of the **Coca-Cola**

Backstage at the Center for Puppetry Arts.

Company. Legend has it that the "secret formula" for Coke could be found in only two places in the world – here, under tight security, and in the vault of the Trust Company Bank downtown, but it may have leaked out by now.

Traveling east from the campus on 5th Street and north on West Peachtree Street, look for the Philip Shutze designed, neoclassical **Academy of Medicine** at 875 West Peachtree. Constructed in 1941, it serves as headquarters for the Medical Association of Atlanta and is a popular place for meetings and wedding receptions. Step inside to admire the lobby rotunda and the magnificent chandelier which was purchased from the *Gone With The Wind* movie-set and donated to the medical society.

A few blocks further north at the intersection of West Peachtree and 14th Streets is **One Atlantic Center**, known locally as the IBM Tower. This 50-story skyscraper, designed by Philip Johnson and John Burgee and completed in 1987, was the first "post-modern" highrise in

the city and set a new standard of excellence for Atlanta's expanding skyline. Further north, at 1374 West Peachtree Street, is the **Center Stage Theatre**, venue for a mixture of performances from avant-garde drama and musical concerts, to live professional wrestling. A block west, at 1404 Spring Street, is the delightful **Center for Puppetry Arts**, which offers a variety of productions as well as classes on handling the marionettes.

Located at the intersection of West Peachtree and Peachtree streets, **Pershing Point Park** is a small green space set aside in memory of Fulton County soldiers killed in World War I. Named in honor of General John J. Pershing, the park was dedicated by French Field Marshal Ferdinand Foch in a 1920 ceremony. North of the park, at 1516 Peachtree, is **Rhodes Memorial Hall**, a 1903 Victorian Romanesque stone castle built for furniture store owner Amos G. Rhodes. Once the centerpiece of a 150-acre (60-hectare) estate, the restored

The stained-glass windows…

house on a small block of land is now headquarters for the **Georgia Trust for Historic Preservation**. If you go inside you will see a beautiful circular staircase and a unique stained-glass window commemorating the Confederacy.

Across Peachtree from Rhodes Hall is an entrance to the well-preserved, early 20th-century neighborhood of **Ansley Park**. For nearly 80 years, this land was part of the farm of pioneer George Washington Collier, a member of a large family with vast land holdings in Atlanta and adjacent DeKalb County. George's brother, Andrew Jackson Collier, owned a nearby grist mill that was the scene of terrible fighting during the 1864 Battle of Peachtree Creek. Following George Collier's death in 1904, Edwin Ansley purchased a large tract of land from the estate and began planning an upscale residential community with a new twist. Ansley's neighborhood would be tailored to the latest advance in transportation – the automobile.

Inspired by Frederick Law Olmsted's design for nearby Druid Hills, Ansley commissioned his protégé, Solon Ruff, to lay out the new development. No ramrod-straight streets suitable for trollies were part of this plan. Ansley Park would have wooded parks, large building lots, and broad, curving avenues – suitable for leisurely motoring in the family Stutz or Packard. Ruff's design was developed to such perfection that present-day drivers – in a hurry to get from place to place – curse Ansley Park's winding streets as Atlanta's equivalent of the Bermuda Triangle.

The first houses in the neighborhood were built in 1905, and residential development steadily continued for another 30 years. Unlike Grant Park, Inman Park, and other in-town communities, Ansley Park weathered the moves to the suburbs well and has maintained fierce neighborhood loyalties that bridge several generations. Today, this remains one of the most sought-after residential areas in the city.

Notable houses and buildings in

...of Rhodes Memorial Hall.

Ansley Park include: the 1905 **Michael Hoke House** at 210 Peachtree Circle, built for one of the founding physicians of Piedmont Hospital; the massive **Woodberry School Building** at 149 Peachtree Circle, built in 1915, using columns from the 1859 Austin Leyden House that once stood on the site of Macy's Department Store in Downtown; and the Italianate villa-style **Frank Ellis House** located at 1 Peachtree Circle, built in 1911.

The neighborhood also claims the elegant Beaux Arts-style **First Church of Christ, Scientist** (1914) at the intersection of Peachtree and 15th Street and the 1919 **First Presbyterian Church** at 1328 Peachtree Street, a Gothic-style, Walter T. Downing-designed sanctuary noted for its beautiful Tiffany stained-glass windows. It was also the site, in 1922, of the first religious services broadcast by radio in the South. Nearby, at 270 15th Street is **Habersham Memorial Hall**, built in 1923 as headquarters for the Joseph Habersham Chapter of the Daughters of the American Revolution. The Regency-style building was designed by Henry Hornbostel, who was the architect for the original Emory University campus.

Ansley Park's long-time popularity is attributed to its convenience to both Peachtree Street and to **Piedmont Park**, Atlanta's largest public park. Since its days as a mustering ground for Confederate veterans' reunions, Piedmont Park has been a gathering place for Atlantans from all walks of life.

In 1887, the land was acquired by the Gentlemen's Riding Club (now the Piedmont Driving Club) and a short time later a large portion of it was sold to developers of the Piedmont Exposition, a fair promoted to demonstrate the city's progress since the Civil War. Thousands, including President Grover Cleveland, traveled from across the region to attend. The event was a huge success and planning began for an even bigger event to be held a few years later. The 1895 Cotton States and Interna-

Piedmont Park is Atlanta's largest.

144

tional Exposition was the largest fair held in the South up to that time. The exposition featured over 6,000 exhibits, lasted six months, and hosted such dignitaries as Booker T. Washington, Generals John Schofield (USA) and James Longstreet (CSA), and Ohio Governor (and later President) William McKinley. President Grover Cleveland made a return visit and composer John Philip Sousa wrote a special piece, the *King Cotton March* for the exposition.

The firm of Olmsted Brothers was commissioned to landscape the fairgrounds and large portions of the present park retain distinctive elements of their original design.

Between the fairs, in 1892, the park was the site of the first football game ever played in Georgia. The game pitted teams from the University of Georgia and Alabama Polytechnic Institute (Auburn University). Just for the record, the visitors from Alabama won 10–0. For several years around the turn of the century, the park also served as an out-door home to the Atlanta Crackers professional baseball team.

In 1904, the city of Atlanta, recognizing the need for more parks, purchased the land and permanently set it aside as a public recreation area. It remains today the largest green space convenient to the central city and is an integral part of Atlanta's cultural and recreational life. Two notable events bring many thousands of visitors to the park each year. The **Peachtree Road Race**, held each Fourth of July, attracts nearly 50,000 runners who sweat their way to the finish line in the Park. And, in September, the **Arts Festival of Atlanta**, draws huge crowds to view exhibits, browse the many artisans' booths, enjoy performances by actors, musicians, mimes, and jugglers, or simply to relax and people-watch.

The northern part of Piedmont Park is now home to the **Atlanta Botanical Gardens**, an expanding complex of specialized gardens both outdoors and inside the 16,000-sq. ft (1,486-sq. meter)

Cooling down after the road race.

Dorothy Chapman Fuqua Conservatory. The conservatory provides a habitat for exotic plants from around the world and the overlook above the rotunda offers a spectacular view of the Atlanta skyline. Also part of the gardens is **Storza Woods**, a 15-acre (6-hectare) hardwood forest criss-crossed by nature trails. Entrance to the complex is through the **Garden House**, which contains the visitor center and gift shop.

The formal entrance to Piedmont Park is at 14th Street where a pair of stone columns frame a Peace Monument erected in 1911 to commemorate reconciliation between the North and South on the 50th anniversary of the Civil War. Just north of the entrance is the complex of the **Piedmont Driving Club**, the successor to the club that originally owned much of the park land. For a closer look at Ansley Park or Piedmont Park, join a volunteer from the **Atlanta Preservation Center** on a guided walking tour of each area.

South of the park is the compact **Midtown Residential District** with many restored Victorian and early 20th-century houses. One of the most notable structures is the Queen Anne-style, **William P. Nicholson House** (1892) (now the Shellmont Bed and Breakfast) at 821 Piedmont Avenue.

Traveling west on 14th Street to Peachtree returns you to the heart of Midtown. At the intersection is **Colony Square,** the first multi-use commercial/residential/hotel development in the South. Completed in 1975, the complex attracts visitors to its retail mall with a variety of shops and restaurants and a fast-food court. Across 14th Street is the **14th Street Playhouse** featuring a wide variety of theatrical events including performances by the highly regarded African-American company, Jomandi Productions.

Just north, at 1280 Peachtree Street, is the **Robert W. Woodruff Arts Center,** home to the Atlanta Symphony, the Alliance Theatre, the Children's Theater, and the Atlanta College of Art. Com-

The High's Garden in Sochi.

pleted in 1968, the center was a gift to the city in memory of over 100 local art sponsors who died in an airplane crash in France, virtually wiping out Atlanta's base of patronage for the arts.

Adjacent to the Arts Center, to the north, is the strikingly modern, Richard Meier-designed **High Museum of Art**. The name has nothing to do with the museum's exalted position but reflects the generosity of art patron Harriet High who, in 1926, donated her home for use as an art museum. The present building, constructed of white porcelain-enameled steel and completed in 1983, has been favorably compared to Frank Lloyd Wright's Guggenheim Museum in New York City.

The interior provides an excellent space for viewing the museum's exhibits. Included in its permanent collection are works of Sub-Saharan African Art, a collection of 19th-century American works, European paintings and sculpture from the Renaissance, and a diverse selection of contemporary works.

Across 15th Street to the south, amidst the skyscrapers, is **The Castle**, the unusual 1910 home of Ferdinand McMillan. In the 1980s, this odd blend of Victorian mansion and medieval fortress was called a "hunk of junk" by developers and saving it became a preservationist rallying point, as the Fox Theatre had been a decade before.

Nearly 30 years ago, Midtown was Atlanta's hippy district, an enclave of artists, musicians, poets, writers, political activists, and Vietnam War protesters in search of a community to call their own. Peachtree and the side streets were lined with coffee houses, cafes, bookstores, T-shirt shops, and places to simply gather for conversation. While the hippy movement faded long ago (those who held on now hang out and hang loose in Little Five Points) and the coffee houses have been replaced by skyscrapers and upscale restaurants, Midtown remains Atlanta's gathering place for artists and art patrons from across the city and around the globe.

The High Museum of Art.

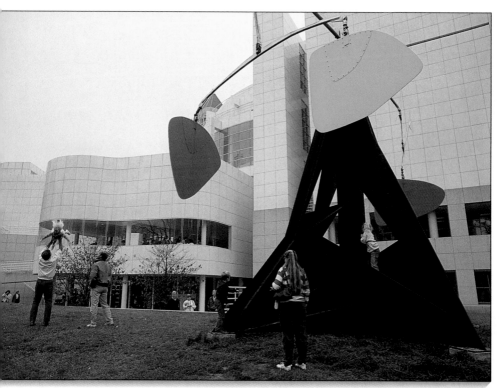

the corporation's site for day-to-day-operations, rests in some disrepair next to **Herndon Plaza,** the shiny new Atlanta Life complex. Also in that block are the **Henry A. Rucker Building** at 158-158½ Auburn, the first black-owned office building in Atlanta.

Across the street from the Rucker Building, at 145 Auburn, are the offices of the *Atlanta Daily World*, the country's oldest black-owned daily newspaper. William A. Scott II founded the paper in 1928 and parlayed it into a chain of more than 50 papers. Each covered news about the black community that the white press would not print.

Though it was one of the most successful publishing businesses of its time, the *Daily World*, which still keeps its daily schedule, is remembered most for its scathing editorials. The paper was also the training ground for such well-known black journalists as Bob Johnson, editor of *Jet* magazine; Lerone Bennett, editor of *Ebony* magazine; and Harry McAlphin, the first black journalist to join the White House Press Corps.

Across Piedmont Avenue, at 205 Auburn, is the **Mutual Federal Savings and Loan Association**. This bank was established in 1925 by 15 prominent Atlanta businessmen and professionals who each put up $100. The bank built a reputation for approving business loans to people who did not have much money. It is best known, though, for providing home loans to thousands of black people, then and now, helping

The area abounds in churches and song.

to make Atlanta a leader in the number of homes owned by blacks.

The music you hear from the moment you set foot on Auburn Avenue usually comes from the **Royal Peacock** at 186½ Auburn. In the 1950s, the Peacock was the hottest of night spots; everybody who was anybody in the black community wanted to hold their private parties and banquets here, and did.

On weekends, black people from all over town would pack the Peacock to hear the Four Tops, or B.B. King, or Gladys Knight and to dance on the polished dance floor. The Peacock hung onto its clientele through most of the '60s. In the '70s, it went disco. Although the Peacock may not burn as brightly as it used to, be sure to look for the colorful array of characters who play their drums directly outside the building and the street vendors who sell a variety of items here.

Big Bethel A.M.E. Church commands the corner of Butler and Auburn Avenue. The church grew out of one organized before the Civil War. The freedmen who founded Big Bethel established the first school for black children in Atlanta. In 1881, Rev. Wesley J. Gaines led his congregation in the founding of Morris Brown College. Construction on the imposing gray granite building that the church occupies started in 1891, but was not completed until 1921.

The building escaped the Great Atlanta Fire in 1917, but was ravaged by fire in 1922 – a day after the church's

insurance expired. The Atlanta City Council donated a substantial sum of money to the church's reconstruction fund in recognition that Big Bethel, for all its community services, was a "people's church."

Down the street from Big Bethel is the **Butler Street YMCA**. Technically it's not an Auburn Avenue attraction, but this YMCA did occupy several buildings on Auburn before moving into its present building in 1920.

The Butler Street YMCA is where NAACP (National Association for the Advancement of Colored People) leaders taught scores of Atlanta's blacks how government worked in preparation for registering them to vote in the 1930s. It is where the Atlanta Negro Voters League was formed in 1949.

Back on the main street, at 228-250 Auburn Avenue, is the **Odd Fellows Building and Annex**. This refurbished six-story complex that houses office buildings and retail stores was once the headquarters of the Odd Fellows, Georgia's largest and wealthiest black fraternal order during the early 20th century. The group operated a relief agency that paid sickness and death benefits to its members and made loans to other blacks for the purchase of businesses, homes, and land.

Across Bell Street, under the imposing I75/85 exchange, past Fort Street (and past the **Auburn Avenue Rib Shack**, home of some of the best barbecue in town), at the corner of Hillard and Auburn is the **Prince Hall Masons Building**. The building was once the center for planning and organizing much of the civil rights movement.

The man responsible for the building and the fraternal order it housed was John Wesley Dobbs, Georgia Grand Master of Prince Hall Masonic Grand Lodge. He revived the faltering organization while also leading a drive for voter registration.

Since 1960, the building has been the national headquarters of the Southern Christian Leadership Conference, the **Time out.**

organization developed by Dr Martin Luther King, Jr. In the mid 1950s, it was also the home of radio station WERD that opened its airwaves to the NAACP, the SCLC, the Atlanta Negro Voters League and, in the process, played the best black music in town.

At 407 Auburn is the most famous church on Auburn Avenue and in Atlanta, **Ebenezer Baptist Church**. It is the family church of the late Dr King, with a legacy that dates back to Dr King's maternal grandmother. Martin Luther served as co-pastor of the church with his father.

Attending one of the two Sunday services is a feat, as visitors crowd the church, which only seats about 750 people. Touring the church during one of the regular sessions is more manageable and there's the added plus of getting to hear one of Dr King's sermons that are regularly piped into the sanctuary.

Just past the church is the sight that attracts more Atlanta visitors than any other, the **Martin Luther King, Jr Center and Memorial** at 449 Auburn Avenue. Within the complex are an early learning center, a dining facility, a gift shop, and a library. There's also a mini-display of some of Dr King's personal affects including the white cap and jeans jacket he often wore on freedom marches and his Noble Peace Prize.

Of course, the center piece of the memorial is the **white marble tomb** that sits atop a circular red brick base at the foot of a long blue-watered reflecting pool.

Further down the street are the preserved homes of former Black Auburnites including a set of 1905 shotgun houses erected by the Empire Textile Company for its black workers. Other preserved homes dot the avenue all the way to **Boulevard Street**, but for many visitors Auburn's Freedom Walk ends the way it started, with a beginning – at the steps of a modest, two-story, yellow and brown house at 501 Auburn Avenue – **the birthplace of Dr Martin Luther King, Jr**.

Outside the MLK Memorial.

BUCKHEAD

Buckhead is Atlanta's best address. If Atlanta were a state, Buckhead would be its capital. If Atlanta were a super-highway, Buckhead would be the fast lane. If Atlanta were a graduating class, Buckhead would be voted Most Likely to Succeed. All the best, brightest, and most marketable projects the city has up its sleeve are in Buckhead. All Atlantans want to live here: at weekends, it seems all Atlantans, and every university student in Georgia, *do*.

Ask the concierge at any major Atlanta hotel what is the most frequent question visitors ask and the odds are it is: "How do I get to Buckhead?"

Mysterious moves: So to help tourists, a few years ago city government erected signs along Peachtree Street, Northside Drive, and other area thoroughfares letting visitors know when they had arrived in the "Buckhead Community." Then, something strange happened. Some of the signs disappeared only to reappear in new locations. Before long, the perplexed planners solved the mystery. It seems a few residents who lived just outside the boundaries were coming out after dark and moving the signs so that they were now "in" Buckhead. Silly? Not when you consider the higher property value and local prestige of a Buckhead address.

The second most-asked question about the area is: "Why is it called Buckhead?"

For centuries, this area was part of the Creek Nation and the first outsiders to locate here were soldiers sent into the wilderness during the War of 1812 to build a fort on Peachtree Creek near the Chattahoochee River, next to the village of Standing Peachtree. The original Peachtree Road was part Indian path and woodland trail connecting "Fort Peachtree" with other remote outposts. Today, a replica of the primitive wooden stockade is located on Ridgewood Road and is open to the public.

In 1821, the Creeks ceded their lands south of the Chattahoochee River to the state of Georgia and the area that would become Buckhead was finally opened for settlement. Pioneers came from across the South and some, like Hardy Pace, Thomas Moore, and Meredith Collier, acquired property that would perpetuate their family names long after they were gone.

One such settler was Henry Irby who, in 1838, paid $650 for a small tract of land at the intersection of the Peachtree road and the new wagon trail to the recently-settled village of Roswell. At this junction, Irby built a combination tavern and general store that became the place where local farmers and traders gathered to shop, gossip, and take a nip of home-made whiskey.

As the story is told, sometime in 1839 Irby went hunting in the vast woods west of his tavern, shot a buck, and mounted its head on a nearby post. Quite informally, the area became known as Buckhead, and the name stuck.

Rural retreat: For most of its early history, Buckhead remained a rural, sparsely settled community of farmers, millers, and ferry-boat men living quietly away from the hustle and bustle of Atlanta. This pastoral scene was briefly interrupted by the presence of General William T. Sherman's invading Union Army in July, 1864.

The Yankees crossed the Chattahoochee River near Buckhead and the retreating Confederates attacked them near Andrew Jackson Collier's Mill in the Battle of Peachtree Creek on July 18, 1864. The Rebels were defeated with heavy casualties and, today, the area along Collier Road between Peachtree and Howell Mill Roads is lined with historical markers providing details of the terrible fight.

The centerpiece of the battlefield is **Tanyard Creek Park**, a public greenspace with playscapes and picnic areas. It is a pleasant spot for relaxation and reflection on the history that was made here nearly a century-and-a-half ago.

For active recreation, the public **Bryan "Bitsy" Grant Tennis Center,** at 2125 Northside Drive, and the **Bobby Jones Golf Course**, at 384 Woodward Way, are nearby.

Shortly after the turn of the century, a few wealthy Atlanta businessmen purchased large tracts in Buckhead and the area became a popular place for rustic cottages, weekend retreats, and a few palatial estates. The automobile accelerated residential growth and large portions of the once-rural community were subdivided into well-to-do neighborhoods with fanciful names like Haynes Manor, Garden Hills, and Tuxedo Park.

History haven: The ideal place to begin to understand Buckhead – and Atlanta itself – is at the **Atlanta History Center** at 3101 Andrews Drive. This beautiful, tree-shaded campus occupies over 30 acres (12 hectares) and includes the **Museum of Atlanta History**. Plan to spend the best part of a day here, for the cool, flower-laden grounds and tranquil atmosphere are a perfect antidote to the urban bustle that swirls around so much of the city. Through dioramas, audio-visuals, and creative displays, the museum brings Atlanta's interesting and sometimes tragic history to life.

Across a wooded garden path from the museum is the recreated **Tullie Smith Farmstead**. The Plantation Plain-style main house was built in 1836 by cotton planter Robert Smith and was originally located on North Druid Hills Road. It was acquired by the Atlanta Historical Society and relocated to this site in 1969. The house has since become the centerpiece of a farm complex that includes a barn, blacksmith shop, kitchen, smokehouse, and an old pioneer cabin. Compact vegetable gardens, wildflowers, and farm animals add to the authenticity (and the aroma).

In contrast to the rustic simplicity of the Smith house is the 1926 **Swan House** on a hilltop above the farm. Designed by local architect Philip Shutze for businessman Edward H. Inman, it is considered one of Shutze's finest works. The **The Tullie Smith Farmstead.**

160

home blends elements of both the Italian Villa and English Manor styles and is surrounded by beautiful gardens.

The interior is noted for its grand flying staircase and delicate moldings reflecting the swan motif that gives the house its name. A large portion of the original grounds was donated to the Historical Society in the 1960s and the house and interior furnishings were purchased from the family estate in 1976. Today, a guided tour of the house reveals the lifestyle enjoyed by wealthy Atlantans during the "Roaring '20s."

Completing the complex is the **Civil War Museum**, first phase of an ambitious scheme to house one of the biggest collections in the South, and **Walter McElreath Hall**, with its Robert W. Woodruff Auditorium and an extensive library and archives of Atlanta and Georgia history.

Old money: For a walking/driving tour of the heart of Buckhead's posh residential area, start across West Paces Ferry Road from the center. Here is the **Cherokee Town Club,** a private club established in the 1950s and housed in "Craigellachie," the Walter T. Downing-designed home built in 1914 for John M. Grant, the benefactor of Dodd-Grant Field at Georgia Tech.

Continuing west, crossing Habersham Road, look for the **Southern Center for International Studies** at 320 West Paces Ferry. This privately-funded policy research center is housed in the 1929 James J. Goodrum house, designed in English Regency style. For many years, Atlantans knew this as simply the "Peacock House" for the large, colorful birds that roamed around the grounds. The center is often open to the public for symposia and workshops.

A short distance away, at 391 West Paces Ferry, is a relative newcomer to this street of stately old homes. Situated on a landscaped rise behind wrought iron gates, the **Georgia Governor's Mansion** was completed in 1968 and designed to resemble a Greek Revival plantation house. Furnished with a mix of heirloom and contemporary pieces, and filled with fine art and portraits, the house and grounds are open for tours a few days of the week.

Across the street, at 456 West Paces Ferry, is **Arden**, the large frame house built in 1914 in a style reminiscent of George Washington's Mount Vernon.

At 509 West Paces Ferry, next to the Governor's Mansion and hidden behind a huge stucco wall, is **Villa Juanita**, an Italian Romanesque villa built in 1924 for Coca-Cola heir Conkey Pate Whitehead as a wedding gift to his fiancée. Ironically, the couple lived here only a short time before getting divorced. The **James Rhodes' House** at 541 West Paces Ferry is another Italian-influenced Shutze construction.

For golfers, a must-stop is **Whitehall** at 3425 Tuxedo Road. The 1940 Shutze-designed house was the longtime home of golf legend Robert T. "Bobby" Jones. Follow the road north to 3460 Tuxedo and gaze up the tree-lined drive at **Windcrofte**, the house once owned by

One of Buckhead's many mansions.

wealthy business executive and generous philanthropist, Coca-Cola chairman, Robert W. Woodruff.

Continue along Tuxedo and then west to 281 Blackland Road. Here is **Peninsula House**, one of the most photographed homes in the city (a large mural of it once hung at Hartsfield Airport). Built in the 1930s for attorney Hugh P. Nunnally, the home gained additional notice when it was purchased by Prince Faisal of Saudi Arabia to serve as his United States residence. Financial setbacks forced the prince to sell the house in 1990. Afterwards, follow Blackland west and then left on Northside Drive back to West Paces Ferry Road. Then take West Paces Ferry east to Peachtree to enjoy the social and entertainment side of Buckhead.

Money mall: Anchoring the corner is **Buckhead Plaza**, a gable-roofed, green-glass tower that is the first phase of a planned multi-use building complex. Posh retail shops surround the street level entrances. This structure, erected

in 1988 on a 17-acre (7-hectare) site, is pink (Canadian granite) and green (reflective glass): the color of new money. With its faux-flying buttresses, it's a perfect symbol of Buckhead, whose Gothic churches have been replaced by "temples" of commerce in the former of retailers, health spas, hair stylists, galleries, and banks.

In a compact area along Roswell Road, Peachtree, and adjacent side streets such as Pharr Road, Buckhead Avenue, Irby Avenue, and East Andrews Drive, is an eclectic mix of **cafes**, **clubs**, **restaurants**, **specialty shops**, **bookstores**, and **theaters** that draws shoppers during the day, diners in the evening, and party-goers well into the night.

Many of the businesses are housed in small, one or two-story, early 20th-century mercantile buildings that have been renovated or adapted for these modern uses. The scale fosters the informal atmosphere of a cozy, small-town neighborhood ideally suited for strolling and browsing. **Buckhead Park**, a compact

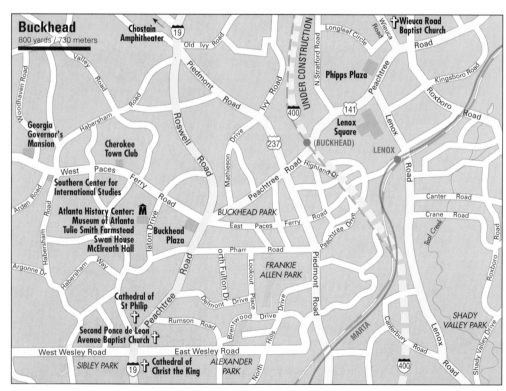

greenspace at Roswell and Peachtree, offers a pleasant spot for simply relaxing and taking in the scene.

The lineup of bars, clubs, and restaurants constantly changes with the latest yuppie whim, but some neighborhood mainstays include restaurateur George Rohrig's successful **East Village Square** (including pizza, sushi and comedy) on Pharr Road; **East Village Grille and Raccoon Lodge** on Buckhead Avenue and Bolling Way; and **Otto's Piano Bar** at 265 East Paces Ferry. While **Aunt Charley's Restaurant and Bar** at 3107 Peachtree, **Good Ol' Days Restaurant** at 3013 Peachtree, and the **Peachtree Cafe** at 268 East Paces Ferry Road have been serving crowds of faithful customers since the 1970s.

Pub crawlers nostalgic for the days of the Empire (and in search of a fast game of darts) should stop in at the **Rose and Crown** at 288 East Paces Ferry or the **Churchill Arms**, tucked away at 3223 Cains Hill Place; and sports fans will find so many big-screen TVs that they may visit a dozen bars in an evening and never miss an inning of an Atlanta Braves baseball game.

However, if you want to meet some locals, stroll down Irby Avenue and pick up a sandwich at **Henri's Bakery** or stop in for a cold beer at the **Five Paces Inn** (a place where Henry Irby would feel right at home), a neighborhood landmark since 1955.

For a formal dinner, check out one of the choices offered by Pano Karatassos' Buckhead Life Restaurant Group. From the aroma of steaks at **Chops** in Buckhead Plaza to the jazzy 1950s style of the **Buckhead Diner** at 3073 Piedmont Road, each is a Mobil four-star award winner.

Other popular destinations for the expense-account crowd include **Anthony's**, located in a restored 18th-century plantation house (moved here from Washington, Georgia) at 3109 Piedmont, and Atlanta's only Mobil five-star restaurant, the elegant dining room of the **Ritz Carlton Hotel-Buckhead** at 3434 Peachtree Road, where Atlanta's best chef (according to *Atlanta Magazine*, and everyone else), Guenter Seeger, reigns supreme. The Ritz is also the place for afternoon tea, a luxurious, completely superfluous experience that perfects suits the area.

If Buckhead is truly Atlanta's shopping mecca, then Phipps Plaza and Lenox Square are the ultimate destinations for millions of plastic-wielding "pilgrims."

Phipps Plaza, a monument in polished brass and marble, is the Taj Mahal of malls and features **Saks Fifth Avenue**, **Lord & Taylor**, **Tiffany** and over 70 other upscale shops and restaurants, including the ingenious **The Civilized Traveller**, perfect for books and travel ephemera of the highest order.

Built in 1959, **Lenox Square** was Atlanta's first mall and with continual expansion remains Georgia's largest. Anchor stores include **Rich's**, **Macy's**, **Neiman-Marcus**, **Bloomingdale's**, plus over 200 other retail shops and eateries. The malls are diagonally across

Outdoor eating is a Buckhead specialty.

from each other on Peachtree Road and both are a short stroll from the **Lenox MARTA Transit Station**. (Note: It's not well signposted. You may need to ask once you get out of the station.)

If malls are not your style, or if you are in search of rare collectibles, finely crafted furnishings, or exclusive fashions, then plan some time to visit the specialty stores and antique shops in **Buckhead Village**; the extensive galleries of **2300 Peachtree Road**; or the small shops along **Bennett Street**.

Book lovers will certainly want to visit the **Oxford Bookstore** at 360 Pharr Road. Housed in a converted Mercedes-Benz dealership that resembles a UFO, the giant store features over 135 categories of books, compact disks, and videos and is open around the clock, 24 hours a day. Browsers are welcome to relax upstairs in the Oxford Cafe or watch for the authors who frequently drop in to sign books. This is also a good place to meet people: intelligent Buckheads' answer to singles bars.

For live entertainment, there are numerous small clubs as well as stage productions and concerts at the **Buckhead Roxy** on Roswell Road across from Buckhead Park, and the **Chastain Amphitheater** in Chastain Park at 4469 Stella Drive. For avant-garde films, check out the offerings at the **Garden Hills Cinema** on Peachtree near Rumson Road.

After a weekend of sightseeing, shopping, dining, and dancing, you may want to sleep in on Sunday morning. If not, consider worshiping at one of the several large and elegant churches located in Buckhead. "Church Row" at Peachtree and West Wesley roads is home to **Christ the King Cathedral**, the largest Roman Catholic congregation in Georgia; **The Cathedral of St Philip**, the South's largest Episcopal church; and **Second Ponce de Leon Avenue Baptist Church** which, along with the **Wieuca Road Baptist Church**, located near Lenox Square, offers services for more than 6,000 people each week.

Phipps Plaza.

Etiquette School

In this fast-paced world of power lunches, presentations, networking, and negotiations, few people place etiquette training No. 1 on their list of priorities.

But if Buckhead-based Anne Oliver has her way, pleasantries won't be just a thing of the past. Armed with etiquette, Oliver has been called a feminist's worst nightmare. But according to this internationally known matron of manners, social graces are everyone's most viable commodity.

Oliver grew up knowing the rules of the social game. A former commercial print and television model, she enjoyed a stint as the Buckhead Saks Fifth Avenue's executive director of fashion, PR, and protocol. Then, during the 1970s, she escorted a group of young women on a finishing tour of Europe and "quickly realized that these girls needed to be finished before they could tour."

Increasingly aware of a generation alienated from the basics of social behavior, Oliver set out to break etiquette's bad rap and founded a group of schools based on age and development in life. She kicked off her campaign in 1976 with L' Ecole des Ingénues, a program devoted to girls' social growth, rapport, and personal confidence. Each year, college and teenage girls from around the world travel to Oliver's finishing school camp in Taos Ski Valley, New Mexico. For a $3,000 fee, the ingénues enjoy a 10-day vacation and a crash course in the ways of grace and charm.

With the program's growing popularity, it wasn't long before the executive world came knocking, wondering if they could partake of a tip or two. And *voilà*: Oliver created L' Ecole des Executifs with both the corporately sponsored executive (male and female) and the recent college graduate in mind. Touring 60 days out of the year to present lectures and workshops in world-class hotels, Oliver instructs her *executifs* in the fine arts of power dining, professional protocol, and cultural couth. "In today's world," she says, "people do business with those who are poised, polished, and comfortable to be around."

Another addition to her schools is L' Ecole des Jeunes, designed for the kindergarten and junior set, where the basics of gracious living are taught in a "couth cottage," a miniature replica of Oliver's own house in her backyard in Buckhead.

The national attention brought on by the growth of the etiquette programs spurred Oliver to take her message to the masses with the book *Finishing Touches: A Guide to Being Poised, Polished, and Beautifully Prepared for Life*. Based on the L' Ecole des Ingénues curriculum, the book prompted its author to create the popular Finishing Touches Program. Oliver hosts this one-on-one program designed to meet the needs and interests of its participants in both the Ritz-Carlton in Buckhead and in the Occidental Grand Hotel in midtown Atlanta. The charge is $100 an hour.

Why Atlanta? "Well, Atlanta truly is an international city, and, as the capital of the South, I thought it would be the perfect place for my schools," says Oliver. "Throughout its history, the South has been the center of grace and charm."

Learning the social niceties takes time, however. "Good manners come from the heart. They're not just put on like a hat and a pair of white gloves." ∎

Tea with Anne Oliver.

165

DRUID HILLS TO VIRGINIA-HIGHLAND

Located in the tree-covered hills east of downtown, the neighborhoods of Druid Hills and Virginia-Highland offer the visitor an insight into two very different styles in Atlanta's suburbanization. Druid Hills, with its large houses and winding lanes, was developed for the wealthy elite, while Virginia-Highland, defined by its narrow streets and bungalows, was considerably more middle-class. As the bank president motored into town from Druid Hills in his Packard, office clerks rode the Highland and Ponce de Leon Avenue trolleys. What the two neighborhoods have in common is their proximity to the Emory University campus, and the lasting relationship the school has had with both areas.

Architectural diamond: In the Atlanta Urban Design Commission's book *Atlanta's Lasting Landmarks*, Druid Hills is called "a diamond in Atlanta's architectural treasure chest" and is acknowledged as one of the "finest examples of … suburban residential planning in the Southeast."

These accolades attest to the creative, original design and the years of staunch, local efforts to keep intact this historically significant neighborhood.

In the early 1880s, this area was rolling hills and forest, much of it part of the estate of pioneer DeKalb County resident John G. Johnson. At that time, the Kirkwood Land Company acquired 1492 acres (604 hectares) for potential residential development. One of the company's principals was Joel Hurt, developer of Atlanta's first planned suburban community in nearby Inman Park (*see pages 184–188*). Hurt saw this new development, dubbed Druid Hills Parks and Parkways, as an even more grand residential location for the city's expanding business-class buyer.

Hurt, an engineer and landscape designer by training, was determined to preserve and emphazise the area's natural features in the new development, so he sought the expertise of the nation's premier landscape architect, Frederick Law Olmsted, for the layout of the new area. In 1893, Olmsted submitted his preliminary drawings for a development featuring a wide boulevard, curving lanes, parks, and large building lots. Unfortunately, a financial recession forced Hurt to shelve plans for the project and he was unable to turn his attention to it for several years. When he did return to it, the senior Olmsted was too ill to work, so he turned the project's design over to his sons.

Vision for visitors: Once again, though, Hurt and the Kirkwood Land Company had money problems and could not go forward with development. Then, in 1908, the land was purchased by a syndicate made up of real estate investors Forrest and George Adair, and Coca-Cola Company president, Asa Candler. The $500,000 selling price was the highest ever paid in Atlanta, up to that time, for a parcel of land. Finally, there was money to go along with the vision to make Druid Hills a reality.

Almost at once, construction work began on roadways and land subdivision and by 1911, the first large homes were completed. Notable Atlanta architects Neel Reid, Walter T. Downing, and Lloyd Preacher designed Druid Hills houses for themselves and for others. Fortunately for today's visitors, many of the finest residences remain.

A good starting point for a tour of Druid Hills is **Ponce de Leon Avenue**, a broad curving boulevard, bordered on the south by a string of linear parks with fanciful names like Virgilee, Shady Side, Springdale, and Deepdene. Overlooking the avenue and parks, and along the side streets are the marvelous period estates that help define the character of the neighborhood. Some of the most notable include the **Jacob Elsas House** at 1241 Ponce de Leon Avenue, built in 1913 by the owner of the Fulton Bag and Cotton Mill in nearby Cabbagetown.

Preceding pages: ariel view of Emory. Left, Druid Hills was a planned development.

The house has now been adapted for use as a small private school.

Farther east, at 1410 Ponce de Leon, St John's Lutheran Church has incorporated "Stonehenge" into its complex. This is the Gothic-style home of **Samuel Venable,** built in 1912 with stone from the granite quarry at Stone Mountain, which Venable owned. In 1915, Venable deeded the northern face of his mountain to the United Daughters of the Confederacy and sculptor Gutzon Borglum was commissioned to create a grand Confederate memorial carving.

Next door, at 1426 Ponce de Leon Avenue, is the former residence of Coca-Cola Company president, **Asa Candler**, who moved here from his Inman Park residence, Callan Castle, in 1916. The striking Beaux Arts-style, sandstone-brick mansion is now St John's Melkite Catholic Church.

Bordering the parks on the south side is the Neel Reid-designed **Frank Adair House** at 1341 South Ponce de Leon Avenue. One of his first Druid Hills

commissions, this residence was built in 1911 for Adair, a real estate executive and son of neighborhood developer, Forrest Adair. A block farther south, on Fairview Road, are several other houses designed by Reid. The 1913 French manor-style **Walter Rich House** at 1348 Fairview was the home of the owner of Rich's Department Store and benefactor of the School of Business at Emory University.

At 1372 Fairview is the Tudor-style **Oscar Strauss House**, completed in 1914. **Reid's personal residence** is a neo-Georgian masterpiece located at 1436 Fairview Road.

Traveling east, look for architect **Lloyd Preacher's** 1928 Italian-style villa at 1627 South Ponce de Leon Avenue and the **Cator Woolford Estate** at 1815 South Ponce de Leon. Woolford, along with his brother Guy (also a Druid Hills resident), founded the Retail Credit Company, now the huge consumer credit giant, Equifax Corporation. Today the mansion, surrounded by beautiful gardens, serves as the **Atlanta Hospitality House**, providing temporary quarters for people whose relatives are patients in local hospitals.

At the intersection of Ponce de Leon and Lullwater Road is the **Druid Hills Golf Club**, founded in 1912. The course meanders along the hillsides and creekbeds, complementing Druid Hills' parklike atmosphere. Across from the club is the **Fernbank Museum of Natural History**. Completed in 1992, Fernbank is the largest museum of its kind in the Southeast. In addition to its acclaimed permanent exhibit, "A Walk Through Time in Georgia," the facility includes an IMAX Theater, Children's Discovery Rooms, and ample space for temporary exhibitions. It also has a fine collection of dinosaurs. Two notable architectural features of the building are the soaring four-story glass lobby atrium (which is wonderful in the rain) and the fossil-embedded limestone floor.

The museum is bordered by **Fernbank Forest**, a 65-acre (26-hectare) wood-

Springtime in Atlanta.

land gem only 5 miles (8 km) from the heart of downtown Atlanta. On a visit to the forest in 1949, Charles Russell of the American Museum of Natural History called it "a unique jewel... a showpiece that no other American city can match." What makes this parcel of land different is its history. It is on record that, from the early 1800s when the area was ceded by the Creeks in a treaty, this land has never been farmed, logged, or developed. This is virgin forest – a rarity in the Piedmont region of Georgia.

There is a feisty lady to thank for preserving this botanical treasure. Emily Harrison was the daughter of Colonel Zador Harrison, who bought this land in 1881. She grew up playing in these woods and was determined to see them remain wild. As an adult she bought out her siblings' interests in the land and later sought a means to preserve the forest after her death.

Miss Daisy lived at 822 Lullwater.

With the help of Dr W. B. Baker, a biology professor at Emory, she created Fernbank, Inc. as a non-profit fund-raising body, and in 1964 gave the ground lease of the property to the DeKalb County Board of Education.

In 1967, the Board opened the **Fernbank Science Center**, with its entrance on Heaton Park Drive. The center now includes the Southeast's largest public astronomical observatory, a superb planetarium and, of course, the forest itself – safely preserved for generations to come.

Continuing the tour of Druid Hills, travel north on Lullwater Road and pause in front of the 1922 **Jacob Hirsch House** at 822 Lullwater. If the facade looks familiar, you have probably seen the 1989 film *Driving Miss Daisy* because this was the house used in the movie as the home of the Southern widow played by Jessica Tandy.

A short distance further along Lullwater is the **Lullwater Conservation Park,** a small, shady spot set aside by the Lullwater Garden Club in 1931.

Returning to Ponce de Leon along Oakdale Road, you will pass architect Walter T. Downing's Tudor Revival-

style Druid Hills home at 893 Oakdale, and the 1911 **Powers Pace House** at 858 Oakdale, one of the first homes built in Druid Hills. West of Oakdale is Springdale Road. Follow it north and look for **Boxwood** at 794 Springdale. This is the 1914 home of Charles Rainwater, designer of one of the most recognizable corporate symbols in the world – the hour-glass-shaped Coca-Cola bottle. A short distance farther on is another Neel Reid treasure, the 1917 Italian manor house designed for clothing store owner **Louis Regenstein**.

Before leaving Druid Hills, visit the **Callanwolde Fine Arts Center** at 980 Briarcliff Road. Built in 1921 for Charles H. Candler, eldest son of Asa Candler, the magnificent neo-Tudor mansion was the work of Henry Hornbostel, who crafted this estate after completing the design of the original buildings on the Emory University campus. The name is drawn from the family's Irish roots, where Candler is "Callan" and "wolde" is the old-English term for forest. In the

Haircuts $8.00
Closed on Wednesdays

early 1970s, the Candler family gave the home to DeKalb County to serve as the nucleus of an arts center. Today, Callanwolde provides studios for classes, gallery space, and music programs. One of the most popular events in Atlanta is the traditional "Christmas at Callanwolde" celebration which is held each December.

An excellent way to get a close look at many of the homes in Druid Hills is to join a walking tour organized by volunteers from the Atlanta Preservation Center. Or you could plan your visit to coincide with the Druid Hills Home and Garden Tour held each April.

Located on the northern boundary of Druid Hills, and very much a part of its history, is the 630-acre (255-hectare) campus of **Emory University**. Established by the Methodist Church in 1836 and named for Bishop John Emory, the college was originally located about 40 miles (64 km) east of Atlanta, in the community of Oxford, Georgia.

In 1888, Bishop Warren A. Candler assumed presidency of the small school and, over the next 25 years, influenced his brother Asa to provide financial support to the college. The greatest gift came in 1914 when the church leaders sought to expand the college's academic curriculum and relocate the campus to an urban center.

A Texas location was under consideration when Asa Candler came forward with a proposed gift of $1 million and 500 acres (205 hectares) of land in his new development of Druid Hills, if the college would move to Atlanta. This was an offer too good to refuse, so the Methodists quickly accepted and work on the new campus began almost immediately. In 1915 the college was rechartered as a university and Bishop Candler was installed as chancellor. New York architect Henry Hornbostel was commissioned to plan the campus and design the original buildings. Hornbostel chose an Italian villa style with red-clay tile roofs and generous use of Georgia marble for his structures.

No hair on Wednesdays.

Since the college was already functioning in Oxford, the first buildings completed on the new campus were graduate student buildings for the Law School (1916), the School of Theology (1916), and the Medical School (1917). America's entry into World War I brought construction to a halt and the college did not relocate to Atlanta until 1919. Today, all of these original buildings remain and several of them are located on the **Quadrangle** on Dowman Drive which is near the intersection with North Decatur Road.

The original building used for the Lamar School of Law (named for 1845 Emory alumnus, and US Supreme Court Justice, Lucius Quintus Cincinnatus Lamar) has been redesigned by architect Michael Graves, and greatly expanded to house the **Michael C. Carlos Museum of Art and Archaeology**. The museum contains an outstanding collection of Egyptian, Greek, and Roman antiquities as well as artifacts from other ancient cultures.

Across the Quadrangle is the complex of buildings of the Warren A. Candler School of Theology. The original building now houses the **Pitts Theological Library**, the second largest library of theological works in the United States. Adjacent to it is the strikingly modern **Bishop William R. Cannon Chapel**, completed in 1981. Also located nearby are the **Physics Building**, erected in 1919 to serve as the college's first classroom building, and the **Asa G. Candler Library**, another gift courtesy of Coca-Cola money, built in 1925.

Just south of the Quadrangle is the **Wilbur F. Glenn Memorial Methodist Church** (1931) designed by architect Philip Shutze in a style to complement Hornbostel's original work and named for Glenn, an Emory alumnus (1861) and one-time Confederate Army chaplain. East of the church is the **Robert W. Woodruff Library**. A 1969 gift to the school by the long-time chairman of the Coca-Cola Company, the building serves as the main campus library and

contains the university special collections and the **Schatten Art Gallery**.

Woodruff's name is also associated with the **Woodruff Health Sciences Center** which comprises the medical school, the Nell Hodgson Woodruff School of Nursing, Emory Hospital, the School of Public Health, and the O. Wayne Rollins Research Center. These facilities, along with the **Henrietta Egleston Hospital for Children** at 1405 Clifton Road and the US Public Health Service's **Centers for Disease Control and Prevention** located at 1600 Clifton Road, make up a scientific and medical research complex informally known as the **Clifton Corridor**. Also located on Clifton Road is the **Lullwater Estate**, built in 1925 for Walter T. Candler, another of Asa's sons. The house with its extensive grounds were acquired by Emory in 1958, and has served as the official residence of the university's president since 1963.

With the number of campus buildings bearing either the Candler or Woodruff

The Fernbank's atrium.

names, there can be little doubt that Emory has benefited greatly through the years from the world-wide popularity of Coca-Cola. It is no wonder that students at the school say: "A Coke a day keeps chalk in the tray!"

Go back through the main campus along Asbury Circle and look for the **Emory Railroad Depot**, built in 1916 and now a campus eatery and the **R. Howard Dobbs University Center**, a John Portman building, completed in 1986, that houses the post office, bookstore, cafeteria, meeting rooms, and other student gathering places. Step inside to see how Portman incorporated the neo-Renaissance exterior of the 1950 Alumni Memorial Center into the building's interior atrium lobby.

Across Asbury Circle is another building of Portman design, the **George W. Woodruff Physical Education Center**, completed in 1983. In order to blend with the landscape, the 187,000 sq. ft (17,372-sq. meter) facility is built into the hillside and decorated with foliage.

The center is the university's main intramural and intercollegiate athletic facility and is home to the varsity basketball, swimming, wrestling, soccer, and tennis teams.

Virginia-Highland: Generations of Emory students have indulged their extramural interests in the cafes, taverns, off-beat restaurants, and shops of Virginia-Highland, located about 3 miles (5 km) west of the campus at the intersection of North Highland and Virginia avenues. This compact community of craftsman-style bungalows with cozy front porches and small but comfortable interiors was developed in the 1920s as the community of North Boulevard Park. Until the late 1940s, the streetcar line ran up North Highland as far as Amsterdam Avenue, offering residents a convenient way to commute to the shops and businesses downtown.

The area suffered serious decline during the massive suburbanization of the 1950s and 1960s, but has made a dramatic comeback and is now a sought-

Dinosaurs to delight.

after residential address. Many of the bungalows have been lovingly restored or creatively adapted to suit the individual tastes of their owners. The neighborhood has become a haven for artists and artisans, members of the Emory academic community, and business people simply weary of commuting long distances from the suburbs.

Locals, students, and visitors gather in the commercial district for cold beverages, burgers, and deli-sandwiches at landmarks like **Moe's and Joe's Tavern**, or **George's Restaurant and Bar**, or for hot chicken wings and a choice of over 300 brands of beer at **Taco Mac**. An eclectic mix of antique shops, bookstores, and art galleries entice browsers and buyers alike.

Also considered part of the Virginia-Highland community is the older neighborhood of **Atkins Park**, located on North Highland near the intersection with Ponce de Leon Avenue. Its small business district includes the **Atkins Park Delicatessen** at 794 North High-

land Avenue. Opened in 1922, it is Atlanta's oldest restaurant in continuous operation. For another glimpse into the past, walk to the corner of North Highland and St Charles Place to admire the beautifully preserved, hand-painted Coca-Cola sign on the brick wall of **Fleemans Pharmacy**.

A fitting conclusion to the tour of these neighborhoods is a visit to the Art Moderne-style **Plaza Center** at Highland and Ponce de Leon avenues. Opened in 1939, the center, and especially the **Plaza Drug Store**, has long been a social melting pot. Here, Druid Hills residents, Virginia-Highland artists, Emory students, homeless people from the local shelters, and free spirits from nearby Little Five Points come together at all hours to browse, shop or just hang out. Stop in for a cold Coke and reflect on the impact this little drink, and the families who made fortunes from it, have had on these neighborhoods, on Emory University, and on the whole of Atlanta.

The Majestic diner.

VICTORIAN ATLANTA

Only two decades after Atlanta's utter destruction at the hands of Yankee invaders, *Atlanta Constitution* editor Henry Grady bragged about his city's dramatic rebirth when he told a northern audience: "We have raised a brave and beautiful city." Atlanta's rise, phoenix-like, from the ashes of war was especially visible in its expanding downtown commercial district and in the development of new upscale residential areas to meet the demands of the city's burgeoning upper and middle classes.

Victorian values: Before the Civil War, Atlanta's most prestigious residential address was Peachtree Street (after all, Scarlett and Rhett lived there) but postwar commercial expansion gradually displaced the fine estates that lined its path north of the railway tracks. So, by the 1880s, developers had their eyes on wooded lands south and east of the city and work began on the Victorian mansions of the new neighborhoods of Grant Park and Inman Park.

After a century of rapid growth followed by steady decline, these old houses have found friends in the urban pioneers who have forsaken their suburbs to renovate and restore many of the fine, rambling, old buildings to their former glory. Modern attractions that also draw visitors to these neighborhoods are the Cyclorama and Zoo Atlanta in Grant Park, and the Carter Presidential Center in Inman Park. While many visitors never get past the city's glittering skyline, it is very pleasing to slip away and spend some time away from the crowds in Victorian Atlanta.

A fitting first stop on a tour of these neighborhoods is **Oakland Cemetery** on Martin Luther King, Jr Drive. Established in 1850 and considered one of the finest Victorian cemeteries in the southeast, Oakland was for 34 years the only public cemetery in the city, leading historian Franklin Garrett to describe it as Atlanta's "most tangible link to its past."

Here citizens of all races and classes, often segregated in life, were interred together within its walls. Today, over 100,000 graves rest within the cemetery's compact 88 acres (36 hectares).

Rebel resting place: During the Civil War, Atlanta's hospitals were overwhelmed with wounded and dying soldiers and the small 6-acre (2-hectare) burial ground was hastily expanded to meet the tragic need for more space. By war's end nearly 3,000 soldiers had been laid to rest at Oakland. A handful were Union prisoners, including seven of the famed "Andrews Raiders" who, in 1862, conspired with Federal spy James J. Andrews to steal a Rebel locomotive at Marietta, Georgia and travel north, destroying railway lines as they went. On April 12, 1862, they stole the engine *General* and sped away. In hot pursuit was Captain William Fuller (also buried at Oakland) in the locomotive *Texas* (traveling in reverse). The Yankees were eventually caught near the town of Ringgold, Georgia.

This event was popularized in 1956 by the Walt Disney movie *The Great Locomotive Chase*. The seven prisoners were hanged as spies and buried in a common grave at the edge of the cemetery. After the war, the bodies were removed to northern cemeteries. Interestingly, the raiders were, posthumously, the first recipients of the newly created Congressional Medal of Honor bestowed on their families by President Abraham Lincoln. Today a small plaque on the cemetery's south wall marks the site of the one-time graves.

A fitting memorial: On April 29, 1866, the first Confederate Memorial Day observance was held at Oakland and on October 15, 1870, the day of Robert E. Lee's funeral in Lexington, Virginia, the cornerstone of a memorial to "Our Confederate Dead" was set in place. The monument, a 65-ft (20-meter) high obelisk was completed in 1874 and for many years was the tallest structure in Atlanta. Just northwest of the monument are the graves of three Confederate generals, John B. Gordon, Alfred Iverson, and Clement Evans. A fourth, General William S. Walker, is buried close to the east wall.

As a tribute to the many unknown soldiers interred at Oakland, the Ladies Memorial Association commissioned the carving, by T.M. Brady, of the **Confederate Lion**, from a single piece of marble from Tate, Georgia. The figure of a wounded and dying lion, reclining across a Confederate battle flag, was modeled after the *Lion of Lucerne,* a Swiss monument created to honor Swiss Guards killed in a 1792 massacre. Presiding over a quiet, wooded area, the memorial is a poignant reminder of the human tragedy of war.

A short distance from the Confederate section is the distinctive old Jewish section of the cemetery, notable for its closely spaced headstones and Hebrew inscriptions. Many of Atlanta's Jewish settlers came from Germany and Eastern Europe and this section reflects the burial traditions practiced in Europe.

As Oakland developed during the Victorian era, the austere tomb markers depicting frightening images of skulls and winged angels of death, common in the eighteenth century, were giving way to more artistic funerary art. Benign angels and cherubs, memorial messages of love and hope, and elaborate mausoleums, influenced by the Rural Cemetery Movement, became popular and were likened to the park-like design of Boston's Mount Auburn Cemetery. In a city without public parks, Oakland became the local rendezvous for Sunday strolls and picnics. Over a century later, Oakland remains a haven of green space amid the ever-encroaching city.

Many notable Atlantans are buried here. Among them are **Sarah Ivy** (1865), wife of Atlanta's first settler Hardy Ivy (he died in 1842 and his burial site is unknown); and **Martha Lumpkin Compton** (1917), daughter of Governor Wilson Lumpkin and namesake of the small town of Marthasville, which was renamed Atlanta in 1843. **Morris Rich** (1928), founder of Rich's Department Store in 1867, is also buried here, as is **Bishop John Wesley Gaines** (1912), African Methodist Episcopal clergyman and a founder of Morris Brown College; **Joseph E. Brown** (1894), US Senator and Civil War Governor of Georgia; and **Benjamin H. Hill** (1882), a Senator both in the United States and Confederate Congresses. Oakland is also the final resting place of the famous golfer and winner of the Grand Slam, **Robert T. "Bobby" Jones;** and *Gone With The Wind*'s author, **Margaret Mitchell.**

At the northern edge of the cemetery, amidst some of the grandest family mausoleums, is a historical marker noting the spot where, on July 22, 1864, Confederate General John B. Hood, commander of the city's defenders, watched the climactic Battle of Atlanta unfold, with devastating results.

Grant Park: Across Memorial Drive from the cemetery is the northern edge of Grant Park. Separated from the main

RIP MMM.

neighborhood in the 1960s by the construction of Interstate 20, this small area has a distinctly commercial flavor. However, once you cross the highway on Cherokee or Boulevard it is like traveling back in time as the large city park is still lined by the Victorian houses that attracted their original residents and have now drawn a new generation of "movers and shakers," handy with saws, hammers, and drills and determined to restore the fading masterpieces to their original grandeur.

The neighborhood draws its name from an early resident Colonel Lemuel P. Grant, a Maine-born Yankee who came to Atlanta in 1850 to work as a design engineer for the Georgia Railroad. In 1858 he built a large home in the wooded area that would eventually bear his name. During the Civil War, he served as a Confederate officer and, in 1863, was in charge of the design and construction of Atlanta's extensive defenses, built in preparation for the impending Union invasion. In three months, using slave labor, he built over 10 miles of trenches and breastworks along the city's northern boundaries. Considered some of the most elaborate fortifications that had ever been built, they were nonetheless no match for General Sherman's superior firepower and numbers.

Following the war, as a principal with the railroad and an active entrepreneur in the area's marketing and development, Grant was quick to capitalize on the city's rapid growth and by the early 1880s was one of Atlanta's wealthiest citizens. Seeing the need to set aside green spaces for Atlanta's growing population, Grant gave the city 88 acres (35 hectares) of land from his estate for development as a public park. A man-made pond, Lake Abana was created and curving paths were built for leisurely strolls and carriage rides. The design of the present park was completed in 1904 and is the work of J.C. Olmsted, son of the noted landscape architect Frederick Law Olmsted.

The Beath-Griggs House.

In 1890 the city bought an additional 44 acres (18 hectares) and the park was connected to the city by trolley routes. When the city annexed additional land for sale as single family plots, developers got busy building monumental Victorian houses facing the park and on the adjacent side streets. Sadly, Grant's own home, located at 327 St Paul Avenue, is in ruins after years of deterioration and failed restoration attempts.

One of the neighborhood's most notable restorations is the **James A. Burns House** at 622 Grant Street. A classic Queen Anne-style structure built by an early resident in 1868, this rambling 9,000-sq. ft (836-sq. meter) residence was reclaimed after many years as a boarding house, and carefully restored. Long-time neighborhood residents claim the house is haunted and this ghostly reputation is enhanced by the presence of several old family tombstones in the front yard.

Across the park at 620 Boulevard is the **Julius Fischer House** (1886), built

by a local contractor for his wife and 12 children. Like the Burns house, it also served as a boarding house, and was eight years in restoration to its original elegance. Each year in September, many of the restored houses and works-in-progress are opened to the public for the popular **Grant Park Tour of Homes**. The interiors of these homes offer a glimpse of the continual balancing act between preserving the past and living in the present: antique armoires mixed with video recorders, central air-conditioning, and ceiling fans. Each is a reflection of the pride and creativity of its owner, and no two are ever alike.

While the older homes give Grant Park its character, most visitors whiz right past them to visit the area's two main attractions, The Cyclorama and Zoo Atlanta, which are next to each other at 800 Cherokee Avenue and are accessible from both Cherokee and Boulevard. **The Cyclorama** contains one of the world's truly remarkable works of art, a circular painting 50 ft (15

meters) high and 400 ft (122 meters) in circumference, depicting the dramatic turning point of the Battle of Atlanta, which was fought only a short distance away on July 22, 1864.

Created by twelve European artists from Milwaukee, Wisconsin who came to Atlanta in 1885 to interview veterans and to sketch the battlefield, the work took two years to complete at a cost of $40,000. Early efforts to profit from the painting by including it in traveling exhibitions were failures and in 1893 it was nearly destroyed before Atlanta businessman Ernest Woodruff rescued it for the purchase price of $1,000. He later sold the painting to George Gress and Charles Northern, who constructed a fine building in Grant Park to house it. Gress and Northern donated the painting and the building to the city in 1898. The current Cyclorama building was erected in 1921 and renovated just over 60 years later.

The painting was restored for the first time in the 1930s under the direction of Atlanta artist Wilbur Kurtz. The three dimensional figures that give the work its realistic depth and feel were added at that time. For the world premiere of the film *Gone With The Wind*, the face of one of the figures was repainted to resemble Clark Gable. In addition to the painting, the Cyclorama houses an extensive collection of Civil War artifacts and the Western & Atlantic locomotive *Texas* that Captain Fuller used in the great locomotive chase.

Next door is **Zoo Atlanta**, now one of Atlanta's most popular destinations. The zoo's roots date from 1889 when Cyclorama promoter George Gress donated the menagerie of a defunct circus to the city. The animals were housed in a makeshift exhibit constructed adjacent to Gress's attraction. In 1935, Asa Candler, Jr tendered his private collection of exotic animals to the zoo's collection. This act of generosity was due, in part, to the ongoing complaints of Candler's Druid Hills neighbors, who were tired of the presence of predatory animals so

The Cyclorama depicts...

close to their homes and the jungle sounds emanating from his estate at all hours of the day and night.

By the 1970s, the Atlanta Zoo was a reflection of the surrounding Grant Park neighborhood: shabby, neglected, and nearly forgotten. The tragic deaths of several animals in the early 1980s prompted an investigation into the zoo's management and serious questions about its future. There was talk of relocating it to Stone Mountain but, in the end, neighborhood activists, local corporations, and people from across the whole of Atlanta came forward with the financial commitment and volunteer support to save the zoo.

Over the next several years they turned it into one of the most progressive and popular zoos in the United States. Today, few animals are kept in cages; most live in accurately recreated habitats sponsored by such corporations as the Ford Motor Company, Kroger, Eastman Kodak, and the Mars corporation. The work is far from complete and the zoo's

grounds are being continually changed.

A notable beneficiary of the zoo's improvements is its most famous occupant, the gorilla **Willie B.** (named for longtime mayor William B. Hartsfield, who grew up in Grant Park). Brought to the zoo as a youngster in the early 1960s, the gorilla lived in a solitary indoor cage for almost 30 years. Now he is at home in the African rainforest with companions on permanent loan from the Yerkes Primate Center. In 1994, in one of the city's most publicly anticipated events, he became a father for the first time. The offspring is named Kudzoo.

Before leaving Grant Park, take a stroll to the hilltop behind the zoo at the intersection of Boulevard and Atlanta Avenue. Here are the few remains of Confederate **Fort Walker**, an artillery position that rained shells on the Federals during the Battle of Atlanta. The site offers a breathtaking view of the Atlanta skyline soaring above the trees of Grant Park.

Traveling north on Boulevard from

...the Battle of Atlanta.

Grant Park, look for the massive old **Fulton Bag and Cotton Mill** and the surrounding mill village of **Cabbagetown**. Built in the early 1880s, the mill was the largest industrial settlement in a town that transported a lot of things, but manufactured relatively little – except for that certain soft drink. Although the mill ceased operations in the 1960s, the village, with its Victorian-style plain cottages lining narrow streets, remains a vibrant neighborhood filled with an eclectic mix of working-class people, artists, and retired mill workers.

Inman Park: From Boulevard, a right turn on Edgewood Avenue and a short drive leads to the second significant Victorian neighborhood, Inman Park. The formal entrance to the community is marked by a wrought iron sign at the fork of Edgewood and Euclid avenues. A fascinating historical artifact rests in **Delta Park**, a triangular expanse on the opposite side of Edgewood. Look for the small cast iron enclosure with a light on top. This is an **Iron Maiden**, an 1880s' police lock-up for a solitary prisoner, who would be placed inside until the police wagon picked him up on its rounds. Step inside and imagine being confined here on a hot August day.

Considered to be Atlanta's first planned suburb, Inman Park was laid out in 1889 and developed by Atlanta entrepreneur Joel Hurt, who named it for his friend and business associate Samuel M. Inman (who never lived there). The neighborhood's curving lanes and **Springvale Park** were designed by James Forsyth Johnson and clearly reflect the contemporary Olmsted influence. Hurt owned the Atlanta and Edgewood Street Railway Company and his new community was just a short trolley ride from the downtown business district. The 1890 **Trolley Barn** at 963 Edgewood Avenue marked the end of the railroad line. It has been carefully restored and now serves as a neighborhood community center.

Intrigued by the lure of a pastoral setting with convenient access to the

Willie B. is named for a former mayor.

city, some of Atlanta's most prominent families built homes in Inman Park and, fortunately for us, many of them survive. Some especially notable houses include the **Charles R. Winship House** (1893) at 814 Edgewood Avenue. Winship built this Eastlake-style residence for his retirement so he could be close to his daughter Emily, who was married to Ernest Woodruff. Their first Inman Park house at 882 Euclid Avenue, designed by Gottfried Norrman and built in 1890, was one of Joel Hurt's model homes. Woodruff, a financier and chairman of the Trust Company Bank, would later purchase the Coca-Cola Company from Asa Candler and place his son Robert in charge of it. In 1904, the Woodruffs moved into fancier accommodation when they commissioned Walter T. Downing to design their new 26-room, Gothic-style, brick mansion at 908 Edgewood.

Across from the Woodruff house, at 889 Edgewood, is a marvelous Eastlake-style house with a square turret, detailed lacework, and a rounded front porch. One of the first houses in Inman Park, it was built for hardware store owner **George E. King**. East of Waverly Way is Springvale Park, a green space that extends northward beneath Euclid Avenue and contains play spaces and a small pond. In Hurt's original plan, the park was supposed to be much larger but it was scaled down, as were other portions of the development, for financial reasons.

Elizabeth Street was the address of Atlanta's most prominent citizen of the day who, fittingly, lived in a castle. At 145 Elizabeth is **Callan Castle** the opulent 1903 home of Coca-Cola Company founder Asa Candler. A Greek Revival masterpiece with a distinctly Victorian flair, the building dominates the entire block. Candler lived here until he moved to Druid Hills in 1916. The castle, filled with a mix of period and contemporary furnishings, is occasionally open for tours. Across Euclid is **Joel Hurt's House** at 167 Elizabeth Street. This

large, Italianate, Victorian residence, built in 1904, was Hurt's second home in the development and projected a more elegant image than his modest cottage at 117 Elizabeth Street.

A short distance west on Euclid is the **Beath-Griggs House,** a fabulously restored rambling construction that is almost a caricature of the Queen Anne style. All the elements are here: the turret, the wrap-around porch, the massive brick chimneys, and the asymmetrical design, all surrounded by an ornate wrought-iron fence. The house is a show-stopper for the bus and walking tours. But it was not always so. When Robert Griggs ventured into Inman Park in 1969 he found the house carved up into one-room apartments. His determination to restore the structure is considered by many as the starting point of the revitalization of Inman Park and of the urban pioneering movement in Atlanta.

In the early 1980s, Inman Park was once again connected to Downtown by rail with the opening of the **Inman Park**

Inman Park mama.

THE ATLANTA PROJECT

I n a country whose citizens look to the government for answers to growing social problems, one man believes that the power to change rests with the people. In 1991, former president Jimmy Carter put a plan into action that is proving his point. Called The Atlanta Project (TAP), this community-wide effort taps the right resources to attack the social problems associated with poverty in urban areas.

Atlanta's booming economy has, over the past decade, attracted more than 1,400 new businesses and enticed scores to relocate to the area. But it is also host to 12,000–15,000 homeless people and ranks as one of the most violent cities in the nation. Some wonder if the problems are too complex and costly to solve at the local level.

But Carter and the project's 80 full-time staff members and more than 100,000 volunteers aren't taking the city's social problems lying down. "The real failure for Atlanta and cities like it would be not to try," says Carter. Praised for its comprehensive approach and overall vision, TAP, which is a private, non-profit program of the Carter Center, Inc., cuts the red tape and takes problem-solving to a grass-roots level, giving the 500,000 residents of designated "in need" neighborhoods not only a voice but also the tools to create better lives for themselves.

Residents express their needs and concerns to co-ordinators who convey the message to TAP. Steering committees define problems and create solutions to a broad range of issues, including health, children, housing, education, and jobs.

The backbone of the project is its volunteers. Under the direction of a specially appointed project co-ordinator, thousands of Atlanta executives offer their skills, contacts and community pull to the project. Companies "loan" employees full-time – salary intact – to TAP, and donate office space and equipment to help set up headquarters. They also loan out electricians and carpenters to construct homes and daycare centers. Volunteer child-care specialists and experienced parents act as mentors to teenage mothers.

Lawyers on loan represent youth offenders, doctors lecture and provide free services at health fairs, bank employees coach in the checking and savings process, and counselors work with drug abusers to help them break addictions. TAP's success is evident in the initiative of its volunteers and in the enthusiasm of the people it seeks to help.

In April 1993, TAP put on the most extensive immunization drive this country has ever seen. A complex and wide-ranging effort, the drive enlisted the help of 7,000 volunteers and succeeded in immunizing or updating the records of 17,000 pre-school children. It was proof that The Atlanta Project works. But whether TAP can maintain momentum remains to be seen. Some say the extensive involvement which helped Carter initiate TAP has led to micromanagement stumbling blocks within the organization, slowing the wheels of change.

Nevertheless, TAP continues to move forward. And with its encouragement, Atlantans who thought the voice of change came from someone else's mouth are realizing that the power to improve their neighborhoods, communities, and themselves is actually in their own hands.

Jimmy Carter founded TAP in 1991.

–Reynoldstown MARTA **Rapid Rail Station**. Across Hurt Street from the station is **Deacon Burton's Grill**, a local landmark with a distinctively southern fried flavor. Guided walking tours of the neighborhood are offered by the Atlanta Preservation Center, and restored houses are opened to the public each April during the **Inman Park Festival and Tour of Homes**.

The history of Inman Park does not begin with Joel Hurt's development nor does it end with its restoration. Twenty-five years before Hurt broke ground on his project, the land was torn asunder by the horrors of war. On July 22, 1864, this ground became hallowed in American history when the massive Rebel and Union armies clashed in the pivotal Battle of Atlanta. You can trace the movements of the battle in the text of the many historical markers that dot the neighborhood, and travel up **Degress Avenue** to the small stone East Atlanta Baptist Church building (now abandoned). Here, in 1864, stood the **Troup Hurt House,** the vortex of the heaviest fighting in the battle, and the focal point of the Cyclorama painting and diorama housed at Grant Park.

Confederate commander John B. Hood stood in Oakland Cemetery and watched the battle unfold while his adversary, Major General William Tecumseh Sherman, observed the fighting from his vantage point at the Augustus Hurt House, high on Copenhill. Today, the site marks a recent contribution to Inman Park's unfolding history, the **Carter Presidential Center** at One Copenhill Avenue (automobile access is from Cleburne Avenue). Established by former president Jimmy Carter and affiliated with nearby Emory University, the center's purpose is to foster dialogue and research in the pursuit of human rights and world peace.

The center frequently hosts conferences for political leaders, scholars, and activists to examine these issues. Not all of the projects are on a global scale: President Carter's **Atlanta Project** is

Carter Presidential Center.

also working to improve life at home. This multi-faceted effort on the part of leaders from across the community aims to address poverty, jobs, education, and civil rights concerns. Center staff are hopeful that the project may serve as a model for efforts in other cities across the United States.

Also housed within the complex is the **Jimmy Carter Library and Museum**, containing over 27 million documents, artifacts, and pictures from the Carter presidency (1977–81), as well as changing historical exhibits. Included in the museum is a replica of the White House Oval Office as it was furnished under President Carter.

The complex of low, round buildings blends with the hilltop landscape and is surrounded by open lawns, foot trails, and a beautiful Japanese garden with benches placed throughout the grounds for serious thinking or quiet reflection – or simply a chance to rest weary feet.

The location also provides a dramatic westward view towards the expanding Atlanta skyline. The center is connected to Ponce de Leon Avenue by the controversial Presidential Parkway, which was vehemently opposed by neighborhood preservation groups until the final design was modified in order to to reduce the impact on the surrounding residential areas.

After a long day exploring Victorian Atlanta, there are several nearby options for relaxation and refreshment. For a cold drink and a burger there is **Manuel's Tavern**, a fixture at the corner of Highland and North avenues since 1956. Here you can swap stories with students from Emory and Georgia Tech, or maybe spot local political figures and celebrities chatting with the tavern's proprietor, Manuel Maloof, who is the affable, retired chairman of the DeKalb County Commission.

Little Five Points: If you wish to browse in unusual shops and galleries, and people-watch from a sidewalk cafe, then head for Atlanta's so-called bohemian district at Little Five Points. This mod-

Yard sale, Little Five Points.

est collection of storefronts from the World War I era, bungalow houses, and apartments is just east of Inman Park at the intersection of Euclid, Seminole, and Moreland Avenues. Here you will find an eclectic mix of aging hippies, New Age families, punks, and weekenders trying out alternative lifestyles, all playing music in the small pedestrian park, reciting poetry, or just plain hanging around.

The neighborhood is home to three active theater companies: **Variety Playhouse** at 1097 Euclid Avenue, and **Seven Stages** next door at 1105 Euclid. These companies offer a mix of traditional, contemporary and avant garde productions. Nearby, the **Horizon Theatre** is housed in the **Little Five Points Community Center** (the old Moreland Public School) at 1083 Austin Avenue. The center is also home to the FM radio station WRFG (Radio Free Georgia), the Atlanta Jugglers Association, the Art Therapy Institute, and the Community Design Center.

For rock and roll performances visit **The Point** at 420 Moreland Avenue, where local groups, ranging from hard rock to reggae, perform nightly. Another spot for a cold drink and a sandwich is the **Euclid Avenue Yacht Club**, which has been a neighborhood gathering place since 1986. But if your tastes run toward a healthier menu, try the vegetarian fare at **Eat Your Vegetables**, just up the street from The Point at 438 Moreland. If you want to take some organically grown produce and other natural foods home with you, try shopping at **Sevananda Natural Foods**, a co-operative market at 1111 Euclid.

From poignant reminders of the Civil War in Oakland Cemetery, to the neighborhoods of carefully restored Victorian houses; from the ecologically-sound zoo to the aspirations and exhibits of the Carter Presidential Center, Victorian Atlanta has a lot to offer an adventurous visitor who is as interested in the city's roots as in its better-known contemporary attractions.

Manuel's Tavern.

STONE MOUNTAIN

To the Creek Indians it was known as *"Therrethlofkee,"* or the mountain on the side of the river (Chattahoochee) where there are no other mountains." To us it is simply "Stone Mountain," the world's largest outcrop of granite, commanding the horizon 16 miles (26 km) east of Atlanta. Large enough to swallow the city's skyline, the turtle-shell shaped mountain is truly one of the world's great natural wonders. Spend a day exploring this magnificent rock, enjoying all the activities and attractions of the park that surrounds it, and you will readily see why **Stone Mountain Park** is the most popular tourist attraction in Georgia and one of the most visited in the nation.

Geologists' gem: Known to geologists as a "monadnock," this isolated 825-ft (251-meter) high peak was born when a dome of molten rock pushed up from deep within the earth, and has evolved over the past 300 million years. Originally buried beneath 2 miles of soil, the hardened rock has slowly emerged as the land around it eroded away. Today, the nearly 600 acres (243 ha) of visible stone represent only a tiny fraction of the entire mountain. Hang around for a few hundred million years and see how big this rock really can be.

The mountain's human history is every bit as interesting as its geology. Archaeological evidence of human habitation of the area dates back nearly 5,000 years, and the high rock was, for centuries, an Indian ritual gathering place.

The first European to see the mountain is believed to have been the explorer Juan Pardo, sent into the area by the Spanish governor of Florida in 1567. When Pardo returned to St Augustine, Florida, he spoke of a marvelous "Crystal Mountain" surrounded by gems and precious stones – probably the quartz that is still seen around the mountain.

In 1790, President George Washington sent Captain Marinus Willet to Georgia as an emissary to the people of the Creek Nation, and his meetings with tribal leaders were held at a place that Willet later recorded in his diary as "Stoney Mountain."

By the 1820s, pressure for settlement had forced the Creeks to give up their lands east of the Chattahoochee to the state. DeKalb County, including Stone Mountain, was created by an act of the legislature in 1822 and land lots were put on sale. Local legend records that one early owner of land on the mountain was a man from Athens, Georgia who walked the 60 miles (100 km) from his home, took one look at the bare rock and traded the land for a mule.

Cloud's Tower: Aaron Cloud had the vision that this man lacked and was the first to see Stone Mountain's value as a tourist attraction. In 1838, he purchased a small plot of land on the mountain's summit, constructed the 165-ft (50-meter) high "Cloud's Tower," and charged visitors 50¢ for the right to climb several hundred steps to the top for the panoramic view.

Tourists first came by the stage road connecting Milledgeville and Dahlonega and, in the 1840s, by the rail line connecting Augusta with the new settlement of Atlanta. Their first stop was the growing village of New Gibraltar, a short distance from the mountain's gentle western slope. Today it is known simply as **Stone Mountain Village.** The town is filled with quaint shops located in turn-of-the-century buildings and is a popular stop for visitors. Especially notable structures are the 1857 **Stone Mountain Railroad Depot**, which survived the Civil War and today is the village's town hall; and the **Stone Mountain General Store** at Main and Manor streets, which offers a wide selection of crafts and antiques.

During the Civil War, Rebels used the heights as a lookout point but it had little strategic value. Union cavalry burned Cloud's Tower and village buildings in 1864, and General Sherman's troops followed the railway from Decatur past the mountain. But it quickly faded behind them on their March to the Sea.

In 1887, brothers Samuel and William Venable purchased the mountain for $48,000 and opened a rock quarry on the eastern side. They became wealthy by supplying high quality Stone Mountain granite for paving stones, houses and commercial buildings across the region. While the Venables exploited the mountain's commercial value, tourists continued to come out by wagon, train, and eventually automobile to see the giant rock and trek to its summit.

Stone sculpture: In 1915, the mountain's history took a new and dramatic turn when Helen Plane, a founding member of the United Daughters of the Confederacy (UDC), suggested that a statue of Confederate General Robert E. Lee be carved on the steep northern side of the mountain. Samuel Venable deeded a portion of his mountain to the UDC with the condition that the sculpture be completed within 12 years.

Sculptor Gutzon Borglum was com-

missioned for the project and he proposed a much larger and more monumental carving to include Lee, President Jefferson Davis and General Stonewall Jackson. He estimated that the project would cost $3 million and take 10 years to complete. The Stone Mountain Memorial Association was created to conduct fundraising and manage the project, but work was halted during World War I.

In 1923, Borglum announced that his design was complete and he was ready to begin blasting rock. He devised a unique projection system to cast the outline of his design on the rock-face at night so that workers could lower themselves on ropes from the cliffs above and paint the image on the mountain.

Rushmore bust up: The work on General Lee's head was completed and in 1924 was unveiled at an elaborate ceremony attended by over 20,000, on the commemoration of Lee's birthday, January 19. However, disagreements over the project flared up between Borglum and the association and, in 1925, the sculptor destroyed his models and quit. He left Georgia for South Dakota, where he would gain lasting fame for his carving of the presidents on the face of Mount Rushmore.

Augustus Lukeman was then hired to complete the project. He redesigned the carving and had the outline painstakingly drawn on the side of the mountain where he and a team of 42 men worked feverishly to make progress before the 12-year limit expired. So important was the project deemed to be that silver half-dollars were struck by the US Mint and sold for a dollar each in a hurried effort to raise more money for the continuation of the work.

An elaborate ceremony was held on May 20, 1928 to unveil the heads of Lee and Davis. Unfortunately, this was nearly a month past the deadline and the Venable brothers decided to reclaim their mountain, bringing the project to a halt. Everyone believed this was only a temporary delay, but in fact no more **Craftsman at work.**

work would be done on the carving for for more than 35 years.

Finally, in 1958, the State of Georgia realized Stone Mountain's tourist potential and re-established the Stone Mountain Memorial Association with the power to purchase the mountain and several thousand surrounding acres. Sculptor Walker Hancock was chosen to finish the carving and Roy Faulkner was hired as the foreman of a team of rock-carvers. Using thermo-jet torches capable of delicately slicing off thin layers of granite, the team worked almost daily for six years. The finished sculpture was finally unveiled to the public in a May 1970 ceremony presided over by US Vice-President Spiro Agnew. For an inside look at the carving and the men who crafted the image from the mountain, visit the **Stone Mountain Carving Museum** at 6080 Memorial Drive in Stone Mountain Village.

Despite its diminutive appearance 400 ft (122 meters) up the face of the mountain, the carving of Davis, Lee, and Jackson on horseback, measuring 90 ft (27 meters) in height and 190 feet (58 meters) in width, is, locals claim, the largest bas-relief carving in the world. It took a long time to complete but serves as an eternal tribute to the men who served the "Lost Cause" of the Confederacy.

The state was not content with simply finishing the sculpture but went on to develop Stone Mountain as the premier tourist destination in Georgia, entertaining over 3 million visitors a year. The aim was to create a complete family resort with activities to suit everyone.

A tour of the 3,200-acre (1,295-hectare) park begins at the entrance stations located on Stone Mountain Freeway (US Highway 78) or on Memorial Drive. A fee is charged for each vehicle entering the park and annual passes are also available. Visitors can also take a trip to the mountain aboard the **New Georgia Railroad** which offers weekend trips and dinner excursions from its Downtown depot near Underground Atlanta.

The best way to start your tour is with a ride on the **Stone Mountain Scenic Railroad**. From the depot on Robert E. Lee Boulevard, the vintage steam engine rocks and sways along a 5-mile (8-km) loop around the base of the mountain and provides a pleasant overview of the park's attractions and the area's unusual landscape. After the journey, it's time to explore the park more closely.

If you want to stretch your legs, try hiking to the top along the **Stone Mountain Walk-up Trail**. The well-worn path follows the route that has been used by mountain climbers since prehistoric times. The mile-long trail ascends nearly 800 ft (243 meters) and meanders through several climate zones, from the dense Appalachian mixed forest at the base, to the harsh, arid environment that prevails at the summit.

Along the way, look for the gnarled and stunted red cedar trees nestled in the cliffside rocks. Survivors of constant winds, some specimens are over more than years old. This popular trail be-

came a National Historic Trail in 1971.

If a round trip to the summit seems strenuous, then consider a ride on the **Stone Mountain Skylift**. The enclosed cars offer a breathtaking five-minute gondola ride from the base to the summit and provide the park's best close-up view of the carving. Many visitors choose to purchase one-way tickets on the skylift and complete the loop with a hike on the walk-up trail. Hikers descending the mountain may ride the railroad back to the depot which is only a short distance from the skylift.

East of the depot is **Memorial Hall** featuring displays on the geological and human history of the mountain, photographs and artifacts from the carving work, and a museum of Civil War weapons. The large lawn in front of the hall is a popular spot for picnickers and draws large nightly crowds during the summer and the Christmas holidays, when the famous Stone Mountain **Laser Show** paints a vivid palette of moving lights against the darkened mountainside.

Across Robert E. Lee Boulevard from Memorial Hall, the **Stone Mountain Inn** offers pleasant accommodations and a family restaurant in a building designed to resemble an Old South plantation. For a glimpse of the real thing, plan to spend a few hours touring the park's **Antebellum Plantation** located on John B. Gordon Drive. This complex recreates a working plantation through the use of authentic, restored buildings brought to the site from across Georgia. Each has been meticulously researched and is furnished with period antiques to give a true glimpse back in time.

The centerpiece of this exhibit is the **Charles M. Davis House**, a beautifully proportioned neoclassical structure built in 1850 as the main residence of a 1,000-acre (40-hectare) plantation near Albany, Georgia. Across the lawn is the **Kingston House,** built near Kingston, Georgia by the Bryan Allen family in 1845. Here it serves to represent a typical home of a plantation overseer.

At the western end of the complex the

Prize pork.

196

Thornton House, constructed by Thomas Thornton for his plantation near Greensboro, Georgia in 1790, is one of the few 18th-century homes still standing in Georgia. Acquired by the Atlanta Arts Alliance in 1959, it was restored and placed on the grounds of the High Museum of Art. However, expansion necessitated the removal of the house and, in 1967, it was donated to the Stone Mountain Memorial Association. It was the first of the antebellum buildings to be sited here. Surrounding the house are boxwood gardens planted in the same way as indicated by archaeological excavations at the original site.

Just south of the Thornton House are two 150-year-old **Slave Cabins** that came from the Graves Plantation near Covington, Georgia. One is a small, single-person dwelling and the other is a larger house designed for a family. The primitive structures stand in stark contrast to the elegant homes of the plantation owner and overseer.

Adjacent to the main plantation complex is a building relocated from Athens, Georgia and undergoing restoration. This is the 1830 **Thomas R. R. Cobb House** built by Cobb, a prominent Athens attorney and author of the Confederate Constitution. While in command of Cobb's Legion under General Lee, he was killed in the 1862 Battle of Fredericksburg.

Among the many outbuildings that make up the remainder of the plantation are the **Barn and Coachhouse Complex,** the **Cookhouse,** the **Plantation Office,** the **Doctor's Office**, and an 1830s country store that now serves as a gift shop.

If the visit to the plantation has whetted your appetite for the Old South, you could take a ride on an old-fashioned steamboat. Travel east on Lee Boulevard to the **Riverboat Dock** on the shores of **Stone Mountain Lake** where you can book passage on the sternwheeler *Scarlett O'Hara*. While out on the lake, listen for the soft musical tones of the **Stone Mountain Carillon** lo-

Festival of Cultures.

AROUND ATLANTA

Atlantans enjoy the close proximity of the natural world to their urban landscape. Natural attractions surround the city, and places like the Chattahoochee River National Recreation Area, Panola Mountain State Conservation Park, and Reynolds Nature Preserve annually draw thousands to swim, fish, paddle, or hike the day away.

Others are drawn to the area's human history. Whether it's a visit to antebellum communities like Marietta, Roswell, Decatur, or Jonesboro, the battlefield at Kennesaw Mountain, or a trip to the mysterious mill ruins at Sweetwater Creek, Atlanta's nearby communities offer much to explore.

American adventures: But all the appeal is not just to hikers or historians. There are places such as Chateau Elan Winery, Lake Lanier Islands, Road Atlanta, Six Flags Over Georgia, Whitewater, and American Adventures that cater to a wide range of interests. In fact, visitors may well run out of time and money – or both – before they run out of things to see and do in the areas surrounding Atlanta.

This chapter begins above the city to the north and works its way around the compass. Meandering along Atlanta's northern border, the **Chattahoochee River** has been a place for recreation since Cherokee Indians built villages along its banks and fished its waters centuries ago. Chattahoochee is a Cherokee word meaning "river of painted rocks," and paddlers negotiating its boulder-filled rapids certainly understand what the Cherokee were thinking when they named it.

Because it is not navigable above Columbus, Georgia, the parts of the river near Atlanta have never been developed for commercial use. Large sections remain wooded and undisturbed within a short drive from almost anywhere in the city. Residential development has encroached in places, but many miles of shoreline, wetland, and forest were preserved through the creation of the **Chattahoochee River National Recreation Area (CRNRA)** in 1978, during the presidency of Georgia native, Jimmy Carter.

The 13 units of the CRNRA, stretching like a "strand of pearls" from the western suburbs to Lake Lanier, collectively preserve over 4,000 acres (1, 618 hectares) of woodlands, with nearly 50 miles (80 km) of shoreline for fishing and water sports. More than 70 miles (112 km) of trails criss-cross the units, providing excellent opportunities for wildlife-watching, hiking, and exploring.

Commercial raft trips are offered during the summer months and naturalists guide walks in different units throughout the year. Detailed maps and information are available from park headquarters at the Island Ford Unit in Dunwoody, a short distance from Georgia 400. For insights into the river's ecosystem, visit the **Chattahoochee Nature Center** at 9135 Willeo Road in

Preceding pages: peanuts, peaches and onions. **Left** and **right**, life on the Chattahoochee.

Roswell. The center is a non-profit organization dedicated to the preservation of the river's wildlife habitat and providing public education about the waterway. The center has a visitor center with classroom spaces, animal rehabilitation facilities, and several woodland and marsh trails.

Marietta: To the northwest is the town of Marietta, founded in 1833 and still simmering with small-town Southern charm. The town square, where farmers used to bring their produce to market and Confederate militia once mustered, is ringed by turn-of-the-century buildings housing cafes, restaurants, and antique shops. Like Atlanta, Marietta's growth came from the railroad and the village was the destination of the first train from Atlanta (then Marthasville) – a Christmas Day round trip in 1842.

Two notable sights around the square are the **Marietta Welcome Center** and the **Kennesaw House**. The center is housed in the 1898 railroad depot at 4 Depot Street. Stop in to find out what is

going on in town and pick up a walking/driving tour map of the city. Across Depot Street, the Kennesaw House is steeped in Civil War history. It was built in 1855 as the Fletcher House Hotel, and James J. Andrews' Federal raiders met here on the night of April 11, 1862 to iron out their plan to steal a locomotive and head north toward the Union lines, destroying the railway behind them.

The next morning, they stole the *General* at Big Shanty (Kennesaw), while its crew breakfasted, and steamed north. Pursued by Confederate Captain William Fuller in the engine *Texas*, the raiders were captured near Ringgold, Georgia, ending the colorful episode we know today as the "great locomotive chase" (*see page 179*). A few miles north, in Kennesaw, the **Big Shanty Museum**, at 2829 Cherokee Street, houses the *General,* various exhibits about the chase, and other Civil War artifacts. (The *Texas* is located at the Cyclorama in Grant Park.)

In June 1864, heavy fighting came to Marietta's doorstep during the ferocious Battle of Kennesaw Mountain. Citizens huddled in their homes while the massed armies of Confederate General Joseph E. Johnston and Union General William Tecumseh Sherman slugged it out on the heavily wooded slopes of the mountain. (After days of heavy artillery shelling, soldiers called the denuded heights "Bald Mountain.")

Casualties from the battlefield streamed into makeshift hospitals and houses as the Rebel defenders tried in vain to halt the invaders. Finally, on July 2, 1864, the Confederates abandoned their mountain-top fortress when Union troops marched south toward the railway lines. The detailed story of the fighting around the mountain can be found at the **Kennesaw Mountain National Battlefield Park** on Stilesboro Road and Old US 41.

Notable sites in the park include the Visitor Center, with its small museum, the mountain summit lined with long silent artillery pieces, Pigeon Hill, **Georgia mailbox.**

Cheatham Hill, and the Peter Kolb family's 1836 farmhouse. Today, the woods are serene, filled only with the sounds of songbirds – a far cry from the hellish roar of musketry that broke the peace over a century ago.

Following the Rebel withdrawal from the mountain, Sherman's troops briefly occupied Marietta before moving on toward Atlanta. As they departed, they destroyed much of the commercial district but several antebellum buildings remain. Among them are the Kennesaw House; **Ivy Grove Plantation** (1843) at 473 Cherokee Street, built by Edward Denmead as the main house of his 1,800-acre (728 hectares) plantation; and several well-preserved residences along Kennesaw Avenue.

These include **Oakton** at 581 Kennesaw Avenue, built in 1838 by Judge David Irwin and used by General W. W. Loring during the battle; **Fair Oaks** at 505 Kennesaw, headquarters for Confederate commander General Joe Johnston; and **Tranquilla** at 435 Kennesaw,

Big Shanty Museum.

built in 1849 for Andrew Hansell. Legend has it that, during the Federal occupation, Hansell's wife stood on the front steps with a pistol threatening to shoot the first Yankee who dared to set foot on her property.

A block south, the **McClellan-Birney House** at 354 Kennesaw was the childhood home of **Alice Birney**, co-founder of the National Parent Teacher Association. Across Kennesaw Avenue is the **Archibald Howell House** built in 1848, and used by General Henry M. Judah, commander of the Federal occupying forces in 1864.

Shortly after the Civil War, Marietta resident Henry Cole, a native New Yorker, offered part of his land for a cemetery to house the dead from both armies. Local citizens refused, preferring to inter the Confederates in a section of the city cemetery on the Powder Springs Road. But the Federal government did accept Cole's offer and established the **Marietta National Cemetery** on Washington Street in 1866. The in-

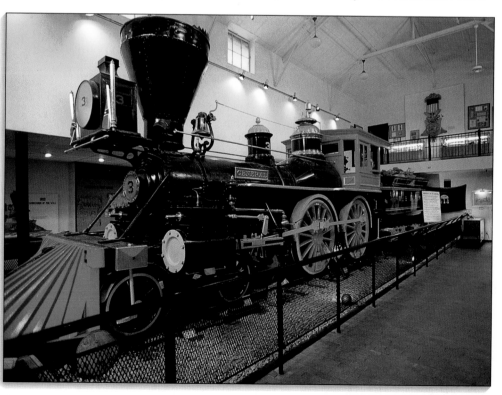

scription above the formal stone entrance dedicates the ground "To the 10,432 Men (buried here) Who Died in Defence of the Union." Today, veterans of every US war from the American Revolution to the Persian Gulf war are interred here.

On a considerably lighter note, Marietta is home to two of Atlanta's most popular family attractions. Located next to each other at 250 North Cobb Parkway, **Whitewater** and **American Adventures** offer fun and relaxation. Whitewater, open during the warmer months, is the South's largest water-park and features the Atlanta Ocean wave-pool. Next door, American Adventures is open all year round with amusement rides, mini-golf, go-kart racing, and the Imagination Station play area.

Adults may find a touch of culture at **Theater In the Square**, a popular local repertory theater to which even Atlantans travel, which is on Park Street; or do a lot of shopping at **Cumberland** and

Galleria malls, located south of town on Cobb Parkway.

Roswell: Like Marietta, the community of Roswell, located about 20 miles (32 km) north of Atlanta near Georgia 400, has a colorful history and a wealth of historic buildings to explore. The ideal place to begin your tour is the 1846 **Archibald Smith Plantation House** at 935 Alpharetta Street, one of the city's best preserved landmarks and home to the Roswell Historical Society. Society volunteers offer guided tours as well as information for those who want to explore on their own.

At the center you will learn about Roswell King, a banker from the coastal community of Darien, Georgia, who first glimpsed this land on a trip from his home to the newly opened US Mint in Dahlonega, Georgia in the early 1830s. Although this area was part of the Cherokee Nation at the time, King was so struck by the land's natural beauty and ready access to the Chattahoochee River that he decided to return if the land were opened for settlement.

With the forced removal of the Cherokee to Oklahoma on the infamous "Trail of Tears," the region was opened and in 1839, King, his son Barrington, and six other pioneer families arrived in the wilderness and established a village which they named for their leader.

The Kings built a textile mill on the northern banks of the river and soon their Roswell Manufacturing Company was also producing lumber, cornmeal, and flour for the town's expanding population. The endeavor made the Kings wealthy and Barrington's Greek Revival home, **Barrington Hall**, constructed in 1840, remains a town landmark. Look for it on Marietta Street, in the woods just south of the Square.

Another town founder was James Bulloch and his 1842 home, **Bulloch Hall**, sits on a hill at the end of Bulloch Avenue. In 1853, Bulloch's daughter Martha married Theodore Roosevelt in the dining room. Their son, Theodore, would lead the "Rough Riders" in the

Bulloch Hall was built in 1842.

Spanish-American War, and later serve as 26th President of the United States. Next door to Bulloch Hall, at 127 Bulloch Avenue, is **Mimosa Hall**, the 1847 estate of John Dunwody. In 1918, architect Neel Reid moved here from his earlier home in Atlanta's Druid Hills.

Several other antebellum structures line Mimosa Boulevard. These include **Holly Hill** at 632 Mimosa, built as a summer house for Savannah cotton merchant Robert Lewis; **Primrose Cottage**, built in 1839 for Roswell King's widowed daughter, Eliza Hand; **Roswell Presbyterian Church**, the first church in the village, constructed in 1840; and at 786 Mimosa, **Great Oaks**, the home of the Presbyterian pastor, Nathaniel Pratt, built two years later. In 1864, it served briefly as the headquarters of Union General Kenner Garrard, after his cavalry troops captured Roswell.

North of Mimosa, the Victorian-era **Canton Street Stores** today house various antique shops, restaurants, and cafes. Other shops line **Roswell Square** at the intersection of Atlanta and Marietta streets. The **Roswell Visitor Center**, at Sloan and Atlanta streets, occupies the old Mill Commissary built in 1839. It later served for many years as City Hall. Staff are available to offer information on local attractions and upcoming events. Stroll across the square and relax in the covered bandstand where, in 1908, President Roosevelt spoke to a large crowd during a visit to his mother's home.

At the eastern end of Sloan Street is the **Founders' Cemetery**, containing the remains of Roswell King, James Bulloch, John Dunwody, and other pioneer families. Across the street is the entrance to **Vickery Creek Park**. A steep path leads to the decaying ruins of the old Roswell Manufacturing Company Mill and Vickery Creek dam.

During the Civil War, the mill produced cloth for Confederate uniforms and was a target for Union cavalry raiders in July 1864. Ignoring an attempt by mill superintendent Theophil Roche to

Roswell's Visitor Center is in the former City Hall.

claim neutrality by flying the French flag over the mill, the soldiers torched it and many of the surrounding buildings. The mill was rebuilt and expanded after the War, but burned down a second and final time in 1926. The surviving structures have been creatively adapted as the **Roswell Mill Shopping and Dining Center**, which is now located on Vickery Street.

East of Roswell, near the town of Duluth, is the **Southeastern Railway Museum** at 3966 Buford Highway. Not to be missed by serious railroad buffs, the museum contains an extensive collection of antique railroad cars, locomotives, and other artifacts. The museum is maintained by volunteers from the Atlanta chapter of the National Railway Historical Society. A short distance north of the museum, in Suwanee, is the headquarters and training complex of the National Football League **Atlanta Falcons**. Regular season practices are closed to the public but visitors are welcome at summer workouts and scrimmages.

But if you prefer a summer activity more peaceful than watching very large men knocking each other down under the blazing sun, just drive a short distance north to **Lake Lanier Islands Resort** at 6950 Holiday Road in Buford. Located on the southern shores of one of the nation's largest man-made lakes, this 1,200-acre (485-hectare) resort features both rustic campsites and a luxury hotel, golf and tennis, boat rentals, walking and equestrian trails, a white-sand beach, and an enormous water park highlighted by the Kiddie Lagoon and Wild Waves, Georgia's largest wave pool.

If you like your action motorized, **Road Atlanta** on Georgia Highway 53, 10 miles (16 km) south of Gainesville, offers several annual events sanctioned by the Sports Car Club of America. One of the track's most popular races is the "Walter Mitty Challenge" held each April, featuring vintage sports cars and racing cars.

The perfect complement to a weekend of races or a visit to the nearby North Georgia Mountains is a tour of the **Chateau Elan Winery** on Georgia 211 at Interstate 85. Established in 1984, the complex has become very popular. In addition to the French chateau-style winery building with its visitor center, wine shop, cafe, restaurant, and art gallery, there is an elegant inn, a tennis center, 45 holes of golf, a European-style spa, and an equestrian center.

At the center of it all are over 200 acres (80 hectares) of vineyards producing wines that are gaining a national reputation for taste and quality.

A fitting stop after a tour of the winery would be **Vines Botanical Gardens** on Oak Grove Road near Loganville. This 90-acre (36-hectare) estate features woodlands and spectacular formal gardens surrounding a manor house that is available for weddings, conferences, and parties. Closer to Atlanta, on US 78 near Stone Mountain Park, is the **Yellow River Game Ranch** a 24-acre (9-hectare) wildlife preserve where visitors are welcome to walk among and feed **Chateau Elan Winery...**

the highly socialized animals. The ranch also serves as a wildlife rehabilitation center, assisting injured creatures to return to their natural habitat.

Decatur: If you want to explore the oldest permanent settlement in the Atlanta area, you should visit the historic town of Decatur. Established in 1823 at the intersection of two ancient Indian trails, and named for War of 1812 naval hero Stephen Decatur, the town has prospered in Atlanta's advancing shadow. To learn its story, visit the **DeKalb County Historical Society Museum** located in the Old Courthouse at 101 East Court Square. Inside you will find exhibits tracing the community's history from Native American times, through the Civil War, and on to the present day.

Nearby, at 720 West Trinity Place, the society maintains a complex of historic buildings including the **John Biffle Cabin**, a primitive structure built in 1822 by Biffle, a Revolutionary War veteran; the **Benjamin Swanton House,** the 1830s frame house of a pioneer Decatur family; and the **Thomas-Barber Cabin**, another early log house. Next door is the 1830s **Mary Gay House**. Gay lived here for nearly 90 years and recounted her experiences as a young girl in Decatur during the Civil War in a popular book, *Life in Dixie During the War.*

Decatur is also home to **Agnes Scott College**, a women's college founded in 1888 as the Decatur Female Seminary. The school received early financial support from Colonel George W. Scott who donated funds for its first permanent building, which he named Agnes Scott Hall, after his mother. In appreciation, the school changed its name in 1889. Many of the older campus buildings are designed in the ornate Collegiate Gothic style and the compact campus is a delight to explore.

If you wish to expand your culinary repertoire or learn a new language in your spare time, pay a visit to the sprawling **DeKalb Farmers' Market** at 3000

East Ponce de Leon Avenue, dubbed the "UN of Fresh Food." From modest beginnings in an old warehouse near Decatur during the late 1970s, the modern market now offers acres of shelves featuring international cheeses, spices, meats, seafood, fresh-cut flowers, baked goods, and fresh produce from the four corners of the globe. Atlanta's growth as an international city is highly evident here, and you will hear a variety of languages spoken by the shoppers.

Continuing south of the city to the rolling hills of Henry County, look for the remarkable and fragile geological treasure preserved at **Panola Mountain State Conservation Park**. Centerpiece of the 600-acre (242-hectare) park is Panola Mountain, a granite outcropping that is a smaller version of its neighbor, Stone Mountain.

But while recreation and commercialism prevail at Stone Mountain, Panola is a laboratory where nature rules. As the park brochure states, Panola is a "million-year-old mountain, in the process of evolution, unhindered by anyone." To safeguard the area's ecology, access to the mountain is limited to naturalist-led walks, but the park also has two popular nature trails and an Interpretive Center with exhibits about this unique environment.

Jonesboro: If you are one of the millions of fans of Margaret Mitchell's classic, *Gone With The Wind,* and wish to explore the land from which she drew her inspiration for the epic novel, you'll enjoy a visit to the small town of Jonesboro, about 16 miles (25 km) south of Atlanta via I-75 and Georgia Highway 54. As a child, Margaret would visit aging relatives in this area and hear their stories of the Civil War. She developed a life-long fascination with the people, their struggles, and their courage. She spent many hours in the archives of the turn-of-the-century **Clayton County Courthouse** researching local history and framing in her mind the image for what would become Tara.

Several antebellum homes remain in

Jonesboro is thought to have been...

Jonesboro and may have served as the model for her fictional plantation. One is **Stately Oaks**, in **Margaret Mitchell Park**, an 1830s Greek Revival mansion that was relocated to this site in 1972 and restored by Historical Jonesboro. Along with several outbuildings, the house is open to the public for tours and is the site of the annual "Tara Ball."

Jonesboro was established in the 1820s and grew with the construction of the Georgia railroad line that connected Atlanta with Macon, Georgia. In August 1864, Atlanta's desperate Confederate defenders looked south to this railway as their last supply link with the outside world.

As a result, when General Sherman marched troops toward the town, Confederate Commander General John B. Hood hastily ordered 24,000 men, under the command of Generals William Hardee and Patrick Cleburne, to rush to Jonesboro and hold the railway.

The decisive Battle of Jonesboro was fought in the late afternoon heat of August 31, 1864 and by day's end, the Federals had routed the weary Rebels, and Hood was forced, finally, to abandon Atlanta. On the morning of September 1, 1864, Atlanta mayor James Calhoun surrendered the city.

Several local buildings survived the battle and remain standing today. Among them are the 1859 **Warren House** at 102 West Mimosa Drive, which was the scene of fierce fighting during the battle and served briefly as the regimental headquarters of the 52nd Illinois. Nearby, at 155 North Main Street, the **Johnson-Blalock House**, built in 1840, served as a Union hospital during the same battle.

Across the railroad tracks, at 168 North McDonough Street is the **Pope Dickson and Son Funeral Home**, an antebellum structure that now houses an exhibit area containing the horse-drawn hearse used for the funeral of Confederate Vice-President, and later Georgia Governor, Alexander Stephens.

Just north of town, at the intersection

...Margaret Mitchell's inspiration.

of North McDonough and Johnson streets, is the **General Patrick Cleburne Memorial Confederate Cemetery** housing the remains of several hundred soldiers who died in the fighting around Jonesboro. For many years, the grounds have been maintained by the Jonesboro Chapter of the United Daughters of the Confederacy.

In the heart of the commercial district, the 1867 stone **Railroad Depot**, built to replace the depot destroyed during the battle, houses a *Gone With The Wind* gift shop and is the focal point of the community's annual and well-attended Fall Festival. Nearby, the attractive brick **Ashley Oaks Mansion** at 144 College Street, built in 1879, attests to Jonesboro's rebuilding in the years following the Civil War. The house has been preserved as a museum and is open to the public for tours.

A few miles south of Jonesboro on Talmadge Road is **Lovejoy Plantation**, built by Thomas H. Crawford in 1835. Here, General Hood assembled his rag-ged army after Atlanta's fall. Later, visits by a young Margaret Mitchell to her great-grandfather Philip Fitzgerald's house, now located on the grounds, served as an inspiration for "Twelve Oaks" in her book.

North of Interstate 75, on Georgia 54 in Morrow, is the 130-acre (52-hectare) **Reynolds Nature Preserve**. A gift to Clayton County by Judge William Reynolds, the preserve features nature trails, ponds, an amphitheater, and an activity center. Nearby, on Lee Street, the campus of **Clayton State College** is home to **Spivey Hall**, a modern performing arts center that hosts theatrical and musical events many evenings throughout the year.

For performances of a completely different kind, stop in and watch the hustle and bustle of the **Atlanta State Farmers' Market** on Interstate 75 in Forest Park. This 143-acre (58-hectare) complex is open 24 hours a day and features an almost endless variety of farm produce, meats, and other local wares. It is

Farmer's market.

212

the largest market of its kind in the world, so if you do not find what you are looking for here, just wait a few minutes, and a truck carrying it is bound to arrive. If the visit makes you hungry, afterwards dine in the market's cafeteria where you can sample some fresh "down-home cookin'."

West of Forest Park are the decaying brick walls of the **New Manchester Manufacturing Company Mill**, along the banks of Sweetwater Creek. Built in 1847, the textile mill once prospered, supporting a thriving village of workers and their families. Then, on July 2, 1864, Federal cavalry rode south from Kennesaw Mountain and burned the mill to the ground. The mill workers were loaded aboard trains and carried north, never to be heard from again. Unlike the mills in Roswell, the plant never reopened and the fate of the people who lived and worked here remains shrouded in mystery.

In 1976, the ruins and the surrounding forest were protected by the creation of **Sweetwater Creek State Park** and the construction of Sparks Reservoir, a popular spot with local fishermen and boaters. Stop at the park information center on Mount Vernon Road in Lithia Springs to learn about park activities, or to begin your journey into the mysterious past.

Finally, no visit to Atlanta would be complete without a day at one of the Southeast's most popular family theme parks, **Six Flags Over Georgia**. Located on Six Flags Parkway and I-20, Six Flags features over 100 rides – including wild roller coasters such as the Georgia Cyclone or the Ninja, the "black belt" of roller coasters.

If the thought of climbing into one of those rides causes you to break out in a cold sweat, you might prefer a wet ride on Thunder River or a journey down the Log Flume. For spectators, the park also offers live entertainment at the Crystal Pistol Saloon, action stunt shows, and seasonal attractions throughout the spring, summer, and fall.

**Six Flags
Over
Georgia.**

· COVRT · HOVSE ·

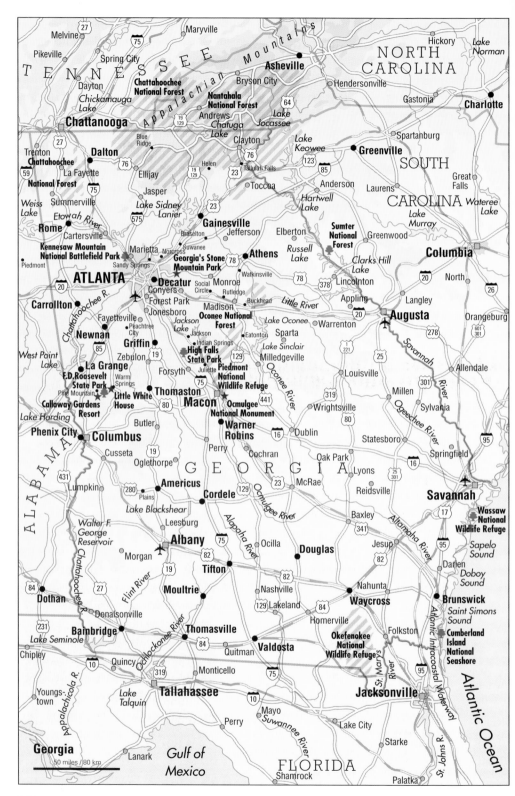

philanthropist George Foster Peabody. The building served as the university library for nearly 50 years until completion of the present facility in 1953. That year, this building was renovated to house the Alfred Holbrook Collection of American Paintings, donated to the university in 1945. Since then, the permanent collection has grown to over 7,000 works including the Kress Collection of Italian Renaissance Art; Oriental prints and drawings; and other works from cultures around the world.

Other notable structures on the North Campus include the magnificent Greek Revival-style 1832 **Chapel** where the bell was once rung to summon students to compulsory religious services and is now tolled to celebrate athletic triumphs; **Demosthenian Hall** (1824) and **Phi Kappa Hall** (1836), small buildings used by early students as literary and debating (and partying) societies; **Lustrat House** (1847), an early faculty house that is now the office of the university president; and **Waddel Hall**, a Federal-style structure erected in 1821.

Just south is the **Main Library**, which contains nearly 3 million documents including the original 1861 handwritten Confederate Constitution.

Stroll west to Lumpkin Street and visit the **Founders Memorial Garden** and the **Headquarters of the Garden Club of Georgia**. Established in 1891, this is the oldest garden club in North America and the grounds are beautifully maintained with the aid of the university's Landscape Architecture Department. The headquarters building and museum is a restored 1857 faculty house. At Lumpkin and Baldwin streets, the **Fine Arts Building** (1941) houses a 750-seat auditorium that provides performance space for the Georgia Repertory Theater, visiting artists, dancers, musicians, and student performers from the university's highly-regarded Fine Arts Department.

Behind the hall, on Sanford Drive, is the **University Bookstore** and the modern **Dean William Tate Student Center**. These are popular student gathering places and hubs of campus social activity. **Campus Visitor Parking** is located on Lumpkin Street adjacent to these buildings.

Across Sanford Drive from the Tate Center is the **Steadman V. Sanford Stadium**. Home to the Georgia Bulldog football team since 1929 (the inaugural game was a 17–0 victory over a mighty Yale University team), the facility has undergone numerous expansions and now seats over 90,000. Considered one of the finest stadiums of its kind in the nation, the grass playing field is surrounded by a distinctive boxwood hedge that has become the amphitheater's "trademark." Another notable feature of the stadium is the **set of small graves** near the western entrance. These are the final resting places for past team mascots – English Bulldogs named "UGA," for the University of Georgia at Athens.

Sanford Stadium marks the division between the old north campus and the more modern **south campus**. A natural

The tree that owns itself.

feature of this part of the campus is the steep **Ag Hill** that leads up to the complex of buildings housing the university's College of Agriculture.

Follow Soule Street east to Brooks Drive. Take a right on Carlton Drive and you will see **The Coliseum**, a 12,000-seat arena that serves as home to the university's varsity basketball teams.

The final stop on the campus tour is **Butts-Mehre Heritage Hall** on Pinecrest Drive. Named for two famed Georgia football coaches, Wallace Butts (1939–60) and Harry Mehre (1928–38), the hall was built in 1987 to house the offices of the university's wide-ranging intercollegiate athletic programs. The lobby contains a 2-story exhibit space featuring artifacts and memorabilia illustrating Georgia's athletic history.

History lesson: Laid out on land purchased from the university by Governor John Milledge, Athens began as a rough settlement with a few shops, inns, and businesses to support the fledgling college. Before long, solid commercial buildings were erected across from the campus; while faculty members and local businessmen constructed fine Federal and Greek Revival-style houses befitting their wealth and academic stature. By 1860, while enrollment at the university remained small (at the outbreak of the Civil War in 1861, the school had only 100 students), the population of Athens numbered over 4,000 with new industries established to supplement the needs of the university.

Today, university enrollment approaches 30,000, while the population of Athens and the surrounding area exceeds 250,000 (add another 100,000 on football Saturdays).

The **Athens Welcome Center** is at 280 East Dougherty Street. The center is located in the restored 1820 **Church-Waddel-Brumby House**, the oldest standing residence in Athens. The house served as home to two university presidents, Alonzo Church and Moses Waddel, before passing into the hands of the Brumby family in 1834. In 1971,

UGA's mascot with sweater.

the city and the Athens-Clarke Heritage Foundation restored the structure for use as a welcome center and house museum. Across Dougherty Street from the welcome center is the **History Village**, a small complex of historic buildings that includes the 1829 Rev. Nathan Hoyt House and the Athens Foundry, constructed in 1849.

A short distance west, off Dougherty at 293 Hoyt Street, is the **Lyndon House Art Center**, a community center featuring gallery, classroom and studio space for local artists and educators. The center is housed in a restored 1856 Greek Revival mansion once owned by Athens physician, Dr Edward Lyndon. Surrounding the house are exquisite perennial gardens maintained by the Athens Parks and Recreation Department.

Nearby, at 95 Hoyt Street, is **Hoyt Street Station**, an entertainment and dining complex located in a renovated railroad depot. The area is popular year-round but large crowds gather each spring to enjoy the annual StationFest celebration.

Atop the hill across Hancock Street is the ornate Beaux Arts Classical-style 1904 **City Hall**. On the northeast lawn is the unique **Double-Barreled Cannon** manufactured at the nearby Athens Foundry for the Confederate Army in 1863. The gun, designed by John Gilleland, was supposed to fire two balls tethered by a chain. These would "mow down Yankees like a scythe cuts wheat." However, Gilleland never figured out how to fire the barrels simultaneously. Tried only once, the piece was a failure and was never used in combat.

Stroll south on College Avenue toward Broad Street and you will find yourself where Athens' students and business people meet and mingle. Hidden behind the facades of 19th-century commercial buildings are popular eateries and clubs where the beer is cold, the music loud, and the fun fast-paced. Local landmarks to look for include **Harry Bisset's**, a New Orleans-style bar and restaurant at 279 East Broad; the fabled **40 Watt Club**, at 285 West Washington Street, where Athens-based bands like the **B-52s** and **REM** got their start in the 1970s; and the **Uptown Lounge**, at 120 East Washington, popular successor to a bar of the same name that introduced many new bands during the 1970s and '80s.

The original Uptown spawned the **Georgia Theatre** at 215 North Lumpkin Street, which now provides a stage for both alternative films as well as live performers. Just south, at 199 North Lumpkin, is the **Globe**, an English pub where you can sip an ale, find a good game of darts, or listen to poetry or Shakespeare. Around the corner, at 199 West Washington Street, is the recently restored 1910 **Morton Theatre**. Built by Monroe "Pink" Morton, the theater provided one of the few black-vaudeville stages in the state. Closed for years, today the stage is once again used for performances.

Walk north to Prince Avenue and follow it west to view some of the finest

antebellum houses in Georgia. The **Joseph H. Lumpkin House**, at 248 Prince, was built in 1841. Just south, at 279 Meigs Street, is the 1833 **Joseph Camak House**, an early Federal-style brick house with beautiful wrought-iron details. Camak, a mathematics professor, was a principal in the Georgia Railroad, which was founded in his home in 1834. At 489 Prince Street is **Fire Hall No. 2**, a triangular, single-bay Victorian brick station constructed for horse-drawn engines in 1901. Across Prince, at 698 Pope Street, the 1835 **Howell Cobb House** was home to a notable figure in Georgia history. Cobb served as Governor, Secretary of the United States Treasury under President James Buchanan (1856–60), president of Georgia's 1861 Secession Convention, and as a general in the Confederate Army.

The 1857 **John T. Grant House**, at 570 Prince, is an elegant Greek Revival mansion set behind a formal boxwood garden. It now serves as the **University President's House.**

In the next block, at 634 Prince, is the **Taylor-Grady House** an 1840 Greek Revival home built for local planter Robert Taylor. In 1863, the house was purchased by Confederate Major William S. Grady who would be killed at the Battle of Petersburg, Virginia in 1865. Grady's widow and five children occupied the home and his son Henry W. Grady lived here while attending the university in the late 1860s. Grady would go on to become editor of the *Atlanta Constitution* and a nationally renowned advocate of post-Civil War reconciliation between the North and South.

Today, the house is owned by the City of Athens and is used for parties, weddings, and other events. South of Broad Street, several 19th-century mansions have been preserved and adapted for use by college sororities. It is highly unlikely that any of the original owners of these fine homes could have imagined the independent, sometimes unreserved lifestyles enjoyed by the young women who occupy them today.

For something slightly different, take a stroll down Dearing Street to Finley Street and look for the small marker on the site of the "**Tree that owns itself**." Over a century ago, this site was shaded by a magnificent oak tree that so impressed local resident Col W.H. Jackson that he purchased the tree and the land around it and, in his will, bequeathed the property to the tree. The original old oak fell in 1946 and the existing tree was raised as a sapling from its progenitor and planted here by the Junior Ladies Garden Club of Athens.

For other botanical treasures, head north of town on US 441 (Commerce Road) about 5 miles (8 km) to **Sandy Creek Park and Nature Center**. The center features trails, a lake, and recreation areas in the woodlands along the banks of Sandy Creek. The Nature Center's **Discovery Hall** contains a variety of exhibits, and provides classroom spaces for educational programs for students of all ages and interests.

In the opposite direction about 3 miles (5 km) south of Athens, at 2450 South Milledge Avenue, is **The State Botanical Garden of Georgia**. Located above the Middle Oconee River on 313 forested acres (127 hectares), the garden complex was established by the University of Georgia as a "living laboratory" in 1968. While visitors come to enjoy the gardens, hike the miles of nature trails, and take classes in various aspects of gardening, the university faculty is behind the scenes conducting research on both individual plant species and the Piedmont regional ecosystem.

Garden features include the soaring 3-story glass conservatory, a cypress and glass framed chapel, and numerous specialty gardens highlighting roses, dahlias, herbs, and much more. Under development is the **International Garden**, a 3.3-acre (1-hectare) site featuring plants from around the world arranged by geographic region. Always changing, the State Botanical Garden is the ideal place to escape the frenetic pace of the student side of Athens.

Right, UGA was the first US state university.

224

around for feed, fertilizer, overalls, new shoes, and penny candy. Since Wiley's death in 1967, at age 89, the store has been kept open by his three retirement-age children. Townspeople drift in to buy a few necessities and swap the news around the old iron stove. If you're of a certain age, you can get a heavy dose of nostalgia looking at shelves laden with everything from sweet potatoes picked this morning to overalls that would fit a small elephant.

Sweet potatoes – and much, much more – are in the chafing dishes at **The Blue Willow Inn**, a short walk from Wiley's Store. Try to get here early, especially on weekends, because bus loads of hungry travelers queue up daily for Billie and Louis Van Dyke's feast. Spread out in the dining room of their restored 1890s' Victorian mansion, lunch ("dinner" in the South) always includes four meat dishes – fried chicken of course – and a cornucopia of okra, blackeyed peas, collard and turnip green, squash casserole, fried green tomatoes,

butter beans, stewed corn, cornbread, green and congealed salads, peach cobbler, pecan pie, and banana pudding. All this, for little more than you'd pay for a fast-food burger and fries.

Revival in Rutledge: Like the biblical Lazarus, Rutledge, 5 miles (8 km) east of Social Circle, has come miraculously back to life. Founded just after the Civil War, this town of 650 people was a busy retail hub until the 1930s, when the boll weevil devastated the area's vital cotton crop. Most of the businesses on Fairplay Street closed, and by the 1980s only a few small shops kept the lights burning.

Fortunately, a cadre of hard-working townsfolk have turned on the lights up and down the street. Several shops cater to visitors who come from Atlanta, Athens, Augusta, and other area cities and towns. The **Barn Raising Shop** has attractive gifts, handicrafts, and quilts hand-stitched by owner Pam Jones.

Next door, **The Yesterday Cafe**, in a brick-walled 1890s Masonic temple, serves a mixture of continental, upscale American and traditional Southern fare. Wine-tasting dinners are a regular event. On Memorial Day (the last weekend in May) thousands show up for the town's annual crafts fair.

At **Hard Labor Creek State Park**, a 5,800-acre (2,347 hectares) preserve on the outskirts of Rutledge, you can play a well-maintained 18-hole public golf course, swim, or enjoy fishing and boating in two small lakes. Heated and air-conditioned cottages are furnished with kitchen utensils and bed linens. Campsites have water and electrical hookups.

Magnificent Madison: Ten miles (16 km) east of Rutledge, Madison is renowned as the town so beautiful even "War Is Hell" himself, General William T. Sherman, couldn't bear to burn it. With Atlanta in ruins behind him, Sherman and his Union Army were at Madison's outskirts in November, 1864, when they were met by a delegation led by former US Senator Joshua Hill. An opponent of secession, Hill had known Sherman in Washington. The town had

The Barn Raising Shop, Rutledge.

no military significance, and Sherman yielded to Hill's plea to spare the torch.

Senator Joshua Hill's home, a palatial Greek Revival mansion built in 1830, is among dozens of homes, churches and public buildings that have survived the ravages of war, the Great Depression and progress. Founded in the early 1800s, Madison prospered as a center of the cotton-planting culture and as a major stop on the New Orleans-to-Charleston stagecoach route.

If the town of 3,500 looks familiar, it's probably because it's been the setting for numerous films and TV shows.

A first stop should be the **Madison-Morgan County Convention and Visitors Bureau's Welcome Center** on the courthouse square in the center of town. Inside the restored 1887 red-brick firehouse – look for the cupola with a weathervane on top – you can pick up free brochures that identify the town's scores of historic structures.

Just down the way, the **Morgan County Courthouse** is one of Geor-

Senator Joshua Hill's home, Madison.

gia's most beautiful. Capped by a gleaming white dome supported by four stately columns, the neo-classical style courthouse, built in 1905, is wrapped neatly around a corner facing the tree-shaded square. It's listed on the National Register of Historic Places.

Around the courthouse are many antique and gift shops and restaurants. The most unusual eatery is **Ye Old Colonial**. Housed in a 19th-century bank building, the restaurant serves good, and inexpensive, Southern cooking, cafeteria-style. The bank's vault, papered with Confederate money and valueless railroad bonds, is sometimes used as a small dining room.

On tree-shaded streets that fan out from the square, Greek Revival, Federal, Victorian and New England saltbox homes float like luxury liners on perfect green lawn seas and formal gardens. Many of these privately owned showplaces open their doors to visitors during the annual May and December home tours. Several homes also wel-

Senator Joshua Hill's home, Madison.

come guests for bed and breakfast.

One of the sites open year round is the **Madison-Morgan County Cultural Center**, on U.S. 441, the main route into town. At the red-brick Romanesque Revival **former schoolhouse**, built in 1895, you can step inside a turn-of-the-century classroom, see changing exhibitions of regional arts and crafts, and look at a reconstructed log cabin (*circa* 1805–20).

In August, the Cultural Center's auditorium is the setting for a theater festival usually featuring the works of a prominent Southern playwright.

You can go inside **Heritage Hall**. Also known as the Jones-Turnell-Manley House, the 1833 Greek Revival is home of the Morgan County Historical Society. Among the architectural curiosities are "window writings," personal inscriptions of antebellum owners' names and small messages. The mansion is also noted for its large verandah and ornate columns, period furnishings and rich ornamental details.

Watkinsville: The small town of Watkinsville (population 1,600), 15 miles (24 km) north of Madison, traces its beginnings to the late 1700s, when it was another stopover on the New Orleans-Charleston stagecoach route. Weary travelers quenched their thirst in the Eagle Tavern, then spent the night in the relative comforts of the upstairs bedrooms. A two-story plain frame structure typical of the style that preceded the more grandiose Greek Revival style of the 1800s, the tavern still sits on its original site in the center of Watkinsville.

It now serves as the **Oconee County Welcome Center**. While picking up brochures and information, visitors can admire the sturdy construction and handcrafted chests, tables, beds, and other antique furnishings.

A Walking Tour of Main Street, Watkinsville, a free guide available at the welcome center, describes 50 structures in Greek Revival, Plantation Plain, Gothic Revival, Queen Anne, Victorian and other styles. Many are private homes not open to the public. Others are churches, shops, and public buildings that welcome visitors.

With a *Guide to the Arts*, available at the welcome center, you can visit about 45 craftpeople with shops in Watkinsville, **Bogart, Bishop** and other Oconee County communities. Among the crafts are broom-making, weaving, forged iron, metal smithing and jewelry, calligraphy, print making, paper, painting and drawing, lead and blown glass.

Elder Mill Covered Bridge, off GA Hwy 15 just under 5 miles (8 km) south of Watkinsville, has been an Oconee County landmark since the late 19th century. Spanning Rose Creek, it's one of the last wooden bridges used on a Georgia public road.

Driving south from Madison on US 441 toward Eatonton and Milledgeville, you might want to spend a few minutes pondering the how-and-why of **Rock Eagle**. On the grounds of the Rock Eagle 4-H Center, the stone figure is believed to have been built as a ritual

1895 schoolhouse, near Madison.

effigy by Indians some 6,000 years ago. Made of boulders and milky quartz stones, the prone eagle measures 120 ft (37 meters) from wingtip to wingtip and 102 ft (31 meters) from head to tail. You can see it best from an adjacent observation tower.

Eatonton's famous authors: Two well-known authors were born and raised in Eatonton. Stories he heard on an antebellum plantation inspired Joel Chandler Harris (1848–1908) to write the folksy *Tales of Uncle Remus.* Contemporary novelist Alice Walker turned her early experiences into the Pulitzer Prize-winning *The Color Purple.*

Harris' tales of Br'er Rabbit, Br'er Fox, The Tar Baby and other "critters" are commemorated at the **Uncle Remus Museum.** In a log cabin made from original slave cabins, the museum displays first editions of many of Harris's stories, as well as illustrations and personal mementoes. It's located in **Turner Park**, once part of the plantation home of Joseph Sidney Turner, the "Little Boy" to whom the fictional Uncle Remus tells his tales. Picnic tables and restrooms are located in the tree-shaded little park.

Look for a small **statue of Br'er Rabbit** on the Putnam County Courthouse lawn. A walking/driving tour guide available at the Putnam County Chamber of Commerce on the courthouse square takes you past the childhood home, school, church, and other landmarks in the life of Alice Walker.

Scenic drive signs lead you past historic homes and churches on streets around the square. You're invited into several of these great houses during "Christmas in Eatonton," a holiday festival the first Saturday of December.

The Bronson House, a regal 1822 Greek Revival with fluted Doric columns on three sides, is open by appointment with the Eatonton-Putnam County Historical Society. Check at the Chamber of Commerce office.

The **Putnam County Dairy Festival**, the first Saturday of June, celebrates the county's reign as "Georgia's Dairy Capital." Two of the 59 dairy farms welcome guests, and downtown on the square the festivities include a parade (led by the Dairy Queen and her princesses) and street dance.

Milledgeville: If you're driving south on US 441, your first sight of Milledgeville, "the Antebellum Capital" (population 17,700), will be disappointing. Shopping malls and fast-food chains crowding both sides of the four-lane highway could be Anywhere USA. Only when you reach the historic downtown district does the city's antebellum heart reveal itself.

Other than Washington, DC, Milledgeville is the only American city to be planned as a capital. The idea was to attract Georgians away from the security of the coast into Indian lands in the interior. Came they did, and enriched the new town with some of the finest architecture of the day.

From 1803 – when it was laid out on a grid of broad, straight streets and public squares – until 1868, when Atlanta

Uncle Remus Museum, Eatonton.

was given the honor, Milledgeville served as the state of Georgia's capital.

Like Madison, Milledgeville escaped Sherman's wrath. Depending on which story you prefer, Sherman didn't want to disappoint a local lady friend, or he was met by a delegation of Masonic Lodge brothers who begged him to spare their town. Serious historians debunk the myths and say the town survived because it surrendered peacefully and had no military importance.

General Sherman slept in the governor's bed, and before marching on through Georgia, Union troops burned the arsenal and courthouse and stoked molasses down the organ pipes of the Episcopal church. The men in blue left behind a vast treasury of Greek Revival, neo-Gothic, neo-classical, Federal and early Victorian architecture.

Stop first at the **Milledgeville-Baldwin County Convention and Visitors' Bureau,** 200 West Hancock Street, for walking and driving tour maps and information. A couple of mornings a

week, the **Milledgeville Trolley Tour**, a motorized old-fashioned-looking bus, leaves from the tourist office for a 2-hour tour that hits the high points, with plenty of humor and anecdotes. Groups can reserve it any day. Visits are made to admire the interiors of the Old Governors' Mansion and the Stetson-Sanford House, or you can see these two sites on your own.

One of Georgia's most cherished historic landmarks, the **Old Governors' Mansion**, was built in Palladian Greek Revival style between 1835 and 1838. The elegant rose-colored house, with four towering Ionian columns, has been splendidly restored and furnished in period style with antiques, china, silver, and paintings. The central rotunda, illuminated by a skylight, is cleverly hidden from outside view. One of the prized artifacts here is a ticket to an 1825 ball commemorating the Marquis de Lafayette's farewell tour of America.

The **Stetson-Sanford House**, a two-story clapboard Milledgeville Federal-style house from around 1825, is notable for its unsupported main staircase and hand-grained woodwork.

Most of the town's beautiful homes are open to the public only on special occasions. The **Spring Tour of Homes**, held every other year in late April or early May, is one of these occasions. Another is "The 12 Days of Christmas Southern Style," featuring concerts, madrigals, and other festivities.

The **Brown's Crossing Craftsmen Fair**, the third weekend of October, is Milledgeville's biggest annual event. Thousands of people show up at the fair site, 9 miles (14 km) west of town, to watch artists and craftspeople do weaving, pottery, woodcarving, lace-making, quilting, and other old-timey tasks. The Southeastern Tourism Society ranks it among its top 10 annual events.

Although it's no longer the capital, Milledgeville still has a capitol. Originally constructed in 1807, the Gothic-style **Old State Capitol** is largely a reconstruction of the building partially

Flannery O'Connor Room, Milledgeville.

destroyed by two fires. Today, the chambers where legislators once pondered Georgia's secession from the Union and other weighty matters are occupied by students of Georgia Military College.

The well-known novelist and short-story writer **Flannery O'Connor** found Milledgeville's traditions and Old South Gothic paradoxes an ideal foil for her Irish Catholic wit. She died in 1964, but some townsfolk still wonder who among them was the inspiration for Francis Marion Tarwater, Hazel Motes, and other rascals, revivalists, freaks and patient suffers who populate her two novels (*Wise Blood* and *The Violent Bear It Away*) and anthologies.

In the library at **Georgia College** – her alma mater, across from the Old Governors' Mansion – the **Flannery O'Connor Room** contains her personal 700-book collection, editions of her works in many languages, battered typewriter, hand-written notes and manuscripts, letters, gifts, and mementoes from admirers around the world.

An aspiring novelist once came up to O'Connor and asked if she thought journalism schools discouraged creativity. "Not nearly enough!" she responded. "Heaven knows how many best-sellers could have been prevented by more diligent teachers."

If you like to explore old cemeteries, **Memory Hill** dates to the original town plan of 1803, when it was designated as one of the four 20-acre (8-hectare) public squares. Out of necessity, it became the resting place for early governors and legislators, slaves, soldiers, and Flannery O'Connor.

For a breather from history, spend a quiet time in **Lockerly Arboretum**. On US 441 on Milledgeville's southern limits, the 45-acre (18-hectare) preserve is threaded by trails that wind over wooden bridges and ponds, through stands of tall trees, flowering plants and shrubs native to middle Georgia.

Lakes Sinclair and Oconee: These two adjoining man-made lakes, running like a narrow thread from east of Madison to

Old Governors' Mansion, Milledgeville.

north of Milledgeville, cover about 36,000 acres (14,600 hectares) and offer a wide assortment of outdoor recreation. Georgia Power Company, which created the lakes in the 1950s, maintains three 85-acre (34-hectare) public parks with boating and fishing facilities, beaches, and campgrounds. Privately-owned marinas and campgrounds, motels and rental condos available to the public, can be found on US 441 between Eatonton and Milledgeville.

Fried Green Tomatoes: The popular 1991 film *Fried Green Tomatoes at the Whistle Stop Cafe* aroused a lot of curiosity. What do unripe tomatoes, dipped in batter and fried in hot oil, really taste like? Crowds of people find the answer at the **Whistle Stop Cafe** in the village of **Juliette,** off US 23 about 30 miles(48 km) west of Milledgeville, and about the same distance north of Macon.

After the movie was completed, enterprising people purchased the cafe set and all the props and opened a real-life Whistle Stop Cafe. A slice of the signa-

ture item comes on every plate of fried chicken, barbecue, meat loaf or fried fish. They're also available as a side dish. Southern breakfast, featuring grits and homemade biscuits, is also served. Many stores on the one-block main street now do a booming business in T-shirts, mugs and other souvenirs with the fried green tomatoes logo.

Indian Springs State Park: You can get a lesson in early Georgia history while you relax at Indian Springs State Park. On US 23, 5 miles (8 km) south of the small town of **Jackson,** the park (said to be America's oldest state park) is named for a **sulfur spring** which ancient Indians believed had curative powers. Many people still believe in the healthy benefits of the waters. If the bad-egg odor turns you off, advocates advise you to let any container with it in it sit uncovered for two or three days. The aroma will vanish, without diminishing the strength of the minerals.

The springhouse and other handsome stone buildings are a legacy of the Depression Era's Civilian Conservation Corps (CCC). Recreational opportunities include swimming, boating and fishing in a 105-acre (43-hectare) lake. You can walk nature trails, see the historical displays in the **Indian Museum** and stay overnight at campsites with electrical and water hookups, and furnished cottages with wood-burning fireplaces.

You can cook in your RV or cottage kitchen, but go at least once to **Fresh-Air Bar-B-Que.** On US 23 between Indian Springs and Jackson, Fresh-Air has prepared award-winning barbecued pork, served at long plank tables, since 1929. Experts says it's some of the best in the South. Fresh-Air has a branch in a Macon shopping center.

At **High Falls State Park**, on Georgia Highway 36 about 12 miles (19 km) south of Indian Springs, the **Towaliga River** forms a mini-Niagara as it gushes over mossy rocks. If you're tempted to wade in the waters below the falls, watch your step – the moss is as slippery as glass. Two hiking trails are on either **The Whistle Stop Cafe...**

side of the falls. The 955-acre (387-hectare) park has a swimming pool and 142 tent and trailer sites.

Macon: At the exact center of the state, Macon, with an area population of about 160,000, is the largest city on the Antebellum Trail. The city is busy preserving its Old South heritage while it dances to a modern tune. A bridge over the **Ocmulgee River** honors Macon-born bluesman Otis Redding. *Tutti Frutti*'s "Little Richard" Penniman flowered here, and so did the Allman Brothers Band. Duane Allman and fellow band member Berry Oakley – both killed in motorcycle accidents – are buried in historic **Rose Hill Cemetery** near Downtown. Capricorn Records, which produced gold and platinum records for the Allmans and other 1970s chartbusters, also called Macon home.

To get a handle on the city's many attractions, stop at the **Macon-Bibb County Convention and Visitors' Bureau**, in the old Terminal Station, downtown at 200 Cherry Street. (Driving south on I-75, you can also get information at the **Macon Welcome Center** and Rest Area.) At the downtown visitors' bureau, you can board an air-conditioned van for Sidney's Old South Historic Tours. Driver/guide Marty Willett, decked out like Macon's beloved 1850s poet, Sidney Lanier, will regale you with anecdotes and verses of Lanier's poetry as he takes you on a two-hour tour of his hometown. For something more romantic, board Colonel Bond's Carriage Tours for a horse-drawn ride through the past. But you can also see the city's sights on your own.

The **Georgia Music Hall of Fame** – opening in late 1995 – is next door to the convention and visitors' bureau. The modernistic $6-million complex showcases Macon's homegrown music stars and more than 50 others – including Ray Charles, Lena Horne, Jessye Norman, Brenda Lee, James Brown, Gladys Knight and Fletcher Henderson – who left their Georgia birthplace to find fame on the world stage.

The Hall of Fame includes interactive multi-media displays and films of Hall of Fame members in actual performances. It is connected by pedestrian plaza to the **Douglass Theatre**, built in 1911, and now restored as a forum for live entertainment. During segregated, pre-civil rights days, black audiences came to the Douglass for stage shows showcasing many big names such as Cab Calloway, Ma Rainey, Bessie Smith, and other black artists.

Most of the city's antebellum landmarks are located in the shady, hilly **In-Town Historic District** bordering the downtown business area.

If your time is short, the **Hay House** is the must-see house/museum. Completed in 1859 – two years before the fall of Fort Sumter sent Maconites off to fight the Civil War – the grand Italian Renaissance palazzo is visually stunning inside and out. Ahead of its time in modern conveniences, the house was built with indoor plumbing, hot and cold running water and an air circulat-

...was moved here after the movie.

ing system. Confederate soldiers alleg-edly eluded capture in secret rooms.

The **Old Cannonball House and Confederate Museum** owes its land-mark status to a cannonball that crashed into the foyer during the Union siege of 1864. You can still see the hole where the shot struck an interior wall. This Greek Revival house, built by a local judge in 1853, has replicas of rooms at the city's old Wesleyan College where the first national sororities (Phi Mu and Alpha Delta Pi) were formed in the early 1850s. The adjoining **Confeder-ate Museum** displays uniforms, weap-ons, photos, letters – and Mrs Robert E. Lee's wooden rolling pin.

Sidney Lanier, who romanticized his home state's natural beauty with such epic poems as "The Marshes of Glynn" and "Song of the Chattahoochee," was born at the **Lanier Cottage** in 1842, a white-frame Victorian bungalow on High Street. Original furnishings and copies of his poems are on display, but most visitors come away wondering how

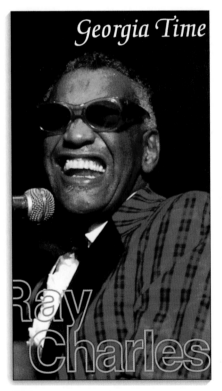

Georgia Time

Ray Charles

Lanier's wife fitted into the wedding dress with the doll-sized waist.

If you'd like to see more antebellum homes, make an appointment at the **Woodruff House**, a lordly 1830s Greek Revival commanding a high point on the Mercer University campus. Twin-spired **St Joseph's Catholic Church**, dedicated in 1903, is illuminated by Bavarian stained-glass windows. The altar and statuary were carved from Ital-ian marble. The **Harriet Tubman His-torical and Cultural Museum,** down-town at 340 Walnut Street, showcases African-American achievements with exhibits of sculpture, painting, crafts, creative writing, and other endeavors. There's also a good gift shop.

If you're fascinated by vintage theaters, take one of the regular week-day tours of the **Grand Opera House**, downtown at 651 Mulberry Street. Built in 1906, the elegant little theater, with its tiered boxes and double balconies, was a stop for such touring entertainers as Will Rogers, Sarah Bernhardt, Count Basie, and many other luminaries. Trap doors installed for a disappearance by the Great Houdini are still in the stage floor. You might be fortunate enough to be in town when local or touring artists bring the house back to life.

Antebellum homes aren't Macon's oldest landmarks. That honor goes to the **Ocmulgee Mounds National Monument**. A short drive from down-town takes you back more than 1,000 years, when these 12 ceremonial and burial mounds were built by Mississip-pian Indians. Creek Indians lived at the site until the 1830s, when the United States government forced them into exile on the tragic "Trail of Tears" to Okla-homa. Steep wooden steps take you to the top of the 45-ft (14-meter) highest mound and its surrounding smaller com-panion mounds. At the **National Park Service Visitor Center**, you can see an orientation film about the mound-build-ers, as well as artifacts and dioramas of those lost civilizations.

Macon is in all her glory during the

Macon's best-known son.

238

annual **Cherry Blossom Festival.** The 170,000 trees – more than 50 times those that adorn Washington, DC's celebrated Tidal Basin – are the living legacy of the late William Arthur Fickling, a wealthy Macon businessman who discovered that an exotic tree on his lawn was a flowering Yoshino, native to Japan. He learned to propagate the tree, and began passing seedlings to the public in 1952. His family continues the tradition by giving a pair of trees to Bibb County residents every year.

The Cherry Blossom Festival wraps conveniently around Fickling's March 23 birthday, which just happens to be the trees' traditional blooming date.

From a simple hometown party, the festival has grown to a week-long celebration of considerable stature. About 400,000 visitors come every year to events that highlight the culture and arts of two or more honored countries. The festival calendar is crowded with indoor and outdoor concerts, parades, beauty queens, arts and crafts – but the real

Christmas with Sidney.

stars are the flowering Yoshinos, whose delicate pink blooms adorn virtually every lawn and garden in town.

For a true taste of Macon, go for weekday lunch at **Len Berg's.** Downtown in the **Post Office Alley,** the maze of small dining rooms has served the city for more than 70 years. A Southern-style entree – chicken, meat loaf, pork chops, fried fish – plus two vegetables and bread is a bargain.

Warm Springs and FDR: The village of Warm Springs is forever associated with memories of President Franklin Delano Roosevelt. Then a lawyer and private citizen, the future four-time president first came to Warm Springs in 1924 to soak his polio-afflicted legs in Warm Springs' 88-degree mineral waters. The buoyant waters didn't restore his physical health, but they renewed his spirit and in 1927 he established the Georgia Warm Springs Foundation to assist others stricken by the disease.

After he was elected president for the first time in 1932, he selected a heavily

SAVANNAH

Fiction author and Savannahian Rosemary Daniell once observed: "Savannah is the kind of town where drunken, irreverent fun and thumbing one's nose at propriety are still permissible, even popular. It is said the first thing one is asked in Atlanta is, 'What do you do?'; in Charleston, 'Who were your ancestors?' and in Savannah, 'What would you like to drink?'"

Moss-draped oaks: Best known in the past for its moss-draped live oaks, steamy cobblestone streets, and pastel-colored buildings, these days an air of mystique hovers over Georgia's port city. It is not only Savannah's acclaimed beauty that is luring visitors, but curiosity that murder and misfortune has spawned. This graceful, old city is being viewed in a different light, but not one of its own choosing.

A Yankee author invaded the streets a while back. He spent eight years studying Savannah – everything from its architectural facades to its tangled web of politicians and socialites. In the end, this *grand dame* of a city, in many ways a sheltered, reclusive town, was fully exposed to tales they might have preferred to keep private.

The best-selling "non-fiction novel" *Midnight in the Garden of Good and Evil* made Savannah and author John Berendt household names in the US, with a corresponding increase in the city's tourism. Today, a visit is likely to consist of a horse-drawn carriage ride through stately squares, lunch in an outdoor market cafe, topped off by a roaring evening in a gay bar where transvestites waltz across a stage flanked by television cameras and screaming fans. Founding father James Edward Oglethorpe, who sailed up the Savannah River and charted the colony in the name of King George II of England, must be trembling in his grave.

Just a little over four hours' driving time and 252 miles (406 km) from At-

lanta, the city is reached by traveling east on I-285 and south on the long stretch of I-16 via Macon, Georgia, or by a short and inexpensive 40-minute plane ride. It is the oldest city in the state and was once, one of the wealthiest ports in the country. It is certainly one of the most beautiful.

Royal charter: In 1733, James Oglethorpe received a royal charter to establish "the colony of Georgia in America." Two of the many reasons for this were to protect the lands from Spanish Florida, and to produce wine and silk for the British Empire.

Oglethorpe designed the town on a grid of broad thoroughfares, punctuated at regular intervals with spacious public squares. Today, 21 of the 24 squares have been refurbished, forming the nucleus of Savannah's **Historic District** – one of the largest urban, national historic landmark districts in the United States. The district is bounded by the **Savannah River** to the north and **Forsyth Park** to the south, in all cover-

ing a 2½-mile (4-km) radius of downtown Savannah.

Each square has a distinctive character, defined by the structures that encompass it, whether a towering cathedral, a Confederacy statue, or an ornate fountain. **Bull Street**, running the length of the district north to south, links the most beautiful squares to each other. These squares, with names like **Monterey** and **Chippewa**, excel in Savannah's most characteristic details: fancy ironwork and Spanish moss. The ironwork, scrolled and lacy enough to rival New Orleans' finest, decorates fountains and monuments or balconies suspended from Greek Revival mansions. Sometimes the metal has been molded into the shape of animals and put to use as water spouts or foot scrapers.

Spanish moss is not really moss at all, but is an air plant, a member of the pineapple family. Its gorgeous, slender stems are not as benign as they appear, being home to insects and pests. Some visitors have tried to pack the moss in their suitcases to take home, but it is best left where it belongs, draped over the trees like ethereal canopies and contributing to Savannah's evocative, slightly spooky image.

The squares are dotted with daily activity – with vendors of art, hot dog stands and freelance musicians. Summer brings free jazz concerts to **Johnson Square**, near the river, while impromptu weddings are performed in the gazebo at **Wright Square**. A spring visit is the most opportune time to savor the myriad of colors as this is when the landscape is in full bloom. At night, fountains and monuments are lit by street lanterns, and although the squares may seem tempting, they also provide the perfect breeding ground for purse snatchers and pan-handlers: it's best to enjoy their attractions before the sun goes down.

People are drawn to Savannah because it has expanded at a leisurely pace, rather than making any attempt to keep up with cosmopolitan Atlanta. Many outsiders call the city "Slow- **Forsyth Park, Slow-vannah.**

vannah" for that same reason. Perhaps it's the high humidity that makes locals move in a slow manner. They speak slowly, drive slowly, and eat slowly. So whether you're dashing into a newsstand for the daily newspaper or picking up a cup of coffee and croissant from Barnard Street's Express Cafe, take your time: there's no reason to hurry here.

Horse-drawn carriages: A walking tour allows visitors to set their own pace, but it is difficult to cover the entire Historic District in one afternoon, especially when the heat is at its most oppressive. If time is short, the Hyatt Regency Hotel, or the Savannah Visitors' Center are best bets for catching a tour bus. Choose from a wide selection of transportation, ranging from open-air cablecar-like vehicles to modern mini-buses to horse-drawn carriages.

The **Savannah Visitors' Center** is located 14 blocks south of the river and just to the west of the Historic District, on Martin Luther King, Jr, Boulevard. A 20–30 minute walk from River Street

(a very hot stroll in the summer), the center is housed in the former passenger station of the Central of Georgia Railway. It shares its premises with the **Savannah History Museum**, where you can view films and look at a multimedia presentation of the city's past.

The visitors' center is also the place to check if you're interested in elegant accommodation. A handful of the Historic District houses have been turned into bed and breakfast inns, luxurious but quite expensive. The main location for modest rooms is the motel strip near the visitors' center, a fair walk from the town's restaurants and shops.

The Historic District is home to wealthy townspeople living in elegant 19th-century homes, side-by-side with lower-income tenants in dilapidated housing who strive to pay the rent. The contrast offers an unusual blend of cultures and it is not uncommon to see an old Savannah resident dressed in tailored clothing walking a diamond-studded miniature poodle past a fountain

Gastonian B & B.

full of black children splashing in the cool spray to escape the summer heat.

As it is the home of the **Savannah College of Art and Design**, Savannahians are joined on the downtown streets by groups of students from all over the world. From green and purple dyed hair to wild clothing, SCAD students paint the town with their talents and taste for the unusual.

Savannah's restoration efforts began in the 1950s when a mansion in the district was threatened with demolition. A small group banded together to form the Historic Savannah Foundation and raised the funds to save and restore the **Davenport House** on East State Street, the home of builder Isaiah Davenport. Today, the foundation has preserved many of the city's treasures and works with architects and residents blending old and new in the district.

Anyone interested in history or architecture should see the **Owens-Thomas House** (124 Abercorn Street), the **Hamilton-Turner Mansion**, Abercorn Street at Lafayette Square, and the **Cathedral of St John the Baptist**, also by Lafayette Square. Another notable home is **Juliette Gordon Low's birthplace** at 142 Bull Street. Juliette Gordon Low was the founder of the first US Girl Scouts troop, and scouts from all over the country can be seen scampering through the rooms and grounds of this handsome house, their trip to Savannah funded in part by the scouts' famous "cookie drives."

Horticulturists should seek out **Trustees' Garden** on East Broad Street, planted in the 1700s as Georgia's first experimental garden. It is now filled with exotic plants from around the world. "King Cotton" and Georgia peaches were cultivated here, the two crops which were to be so decisive in the state's economy. A delightful spot, the grounds also contain several gift shops, restaurants (The Pirates' House and 45 South), and apartments.

The **Pirates' House** is a former location for seafaring captains who were

Juliette Gordon Low's home.

seeking additional crew. Sailors were given mugs of high-powered alcoholic Chatham Artillery Punch and, upon passing out, were carted off to the ships via an underground tunnel. Today, visitors who dine at this popular eatery can peer at the figure of a drunken pirate lying at the bottom of the stone stairway, awaiting his fate.

After dinner at the Pirates' House, join a jovial crowd upstairs at **Hannah's East**, where Emma Kelly, a true-life character from the *Midnight* novel, plays her soul out every evening. Called the "Lady of 6,000 Songs," her repertoire ranges from blues to swing. The setting is uniquely Savannah.

Several historic buildings open to the public in the next several blocks were designed in Regency style by English architect William Jay upon his arrival in 1817. The most notable examples are now owned by the Telfair Academy of Arts and Sciences – the **Alexander Telfair home** (121 Barnard Street), once the official residence of visiting state governors, and now housing traveling art exhibits from around the world – and the **William Scarbrough house** (41 West Broad Street), which at one time hosted President James Monroe during a visit to the city.

The most talked about residence in recent memory is **Mercer House**, located on Monterey Square and built by composer Johnny Mercer's grandfather. The residence was the home of the late antique dealer Jim Williams, the subject of John Berendt's book. Williams, an eccentric but debonair millionaire, shot his 22-year-old male companion in 1981. The victim had a reputation for wildness and Williams claimed self-defense. Convicted twice of murder, jailed and released and tried a third time to a hung jury, the fourth time he was tried and successfully acquitted.

Williams died of a heart attack the same year he was freed. Today, his sister occupies the house, a magnificent structure filled with antiques, which, it is said, the late Jacqueline Onassis once

Midnight book cover; Mercer House.

tried to buy. The shutters are nearly always drawn tight, and the house is not open to the public.

How about a down-home Southern lunch? Stop by **Mrs Wilkes' Boarding House**, located on **Jones Street**. Tucked away between stately homes, her Southern-style restaurant serves up fried chicken, bowls overflowing with fresh vegetables, and lots of cups of sweet tea. Instead of waiting in the long lines, locals know to head to the lane (Savannah's term for alley), and the kitchen's back door to pick up their orders. Otherwise, plan on arriving by 11.30am latest to get a place. If you're into private dining, don't eat here: Mrs Wilkes's tables are round and comfortably seat ten to 12 diners at one time, so you might wind up sitting next to someone from California.

The Historic District's procession of squares ends at beautiful **Forsyth Park**, a 31-acre (13-hectare) setting for constant outdoor activity: jogging, frisbee tournaments, walking, football, and an annual picnic for thousands, called the Symphony in the Park. The Savannah Symphony Orchestra performs a free concert in October, where symphony lovers arrive for the performance with elaborate picnics baskets and candelabra to light at nightfall. At the centerpiece of the park stands an elaborate fountain similar to the one in the Place de la Concorde, Paris.

River city: Around the beginning of the 1800s, Savannah's commerce thrived. The creation of the steamship *SS Savannah*, the first vessel to cross the Atlantic Ocean to Liverpool, England, opened up new shipping routes and with the development of Eli Whitney's cotton gin, shipping escalated to new heights: by 1795, US exports were 40 times greater than in previous years. Savannah, positioned neatly on the Atlantic Ocean looking out towards Europe, quickly became the largest port in the Southeast.

The five-story brick warehouses and former shipping offices have now be-

Emma Kelly, lady of 6,000 songs.

come a meeting point for tourists, reached by a series of steep steps from the main part of Downtown. The buildings provide a nostalgic setting for thriving businesses, lavish inns, rustic restaurants, and novelty gift shops the length of the riverfront, called appropriately enough, **River Street**. River Street's ramps and walkways are covered with attractive stones imported from Europe; as a result, traveling by foot can be treacherous: it's best to leave the high heels in the hotel.

Sit on a bench, sip on a frozen concoction from Wet Willie's or chug a cold, draft beer from one of many riverside outlets and watch the contemporary shipping industry in motion.

Slowly moving ships carrying everything from melons, bananas, pineapples, kaolin clay, and even dogfood pass by at a snail's pace only a few hundred yards away. Escorted by tugboats that guide the huge vessels into port, crews from all over the world extend warm Southern greetings as they enter the second-largest port in the United States.

The riverfront air is always filled with music, from South American natives playing soothing pan pipes to a threesome picking guitars and banjos. There's even a roving photographer who, armed with a Polaroid, will capture you and the moment for just a few dollars.

The *Savannah River Queen*, a replica of the steamboats that plied the waters during the city's heyday, has sightseeing cruises during the day and in the evening. One of the sights pointed out is a statue of *The Waving Girl*, erected in 1971 in remembrance to Florence Martus. Every day for 44 years, Ms Martus waved a welcome to each incoming ship and a good-bye to each outgoing ship as it passed Savannah.

The riverfront skyline is dominated by the 185-ft (56-meter) tall great **Savannah Bridge**, which locals refer to as "the bridge with no name." Replacing the old two-lane Eugene Talmadge Bridge, the recently built structure hails as a landmark and its image appears on

Mrs Wilkes' Boarding House.

company logos and restaurant menus. It spans across the marshes into the state of South Carolina and, as the sun's rays illuminate its shape, camera buffs come out in hordes.

If the port evokes a yearning for food, River Street merchants offer an eclectic range of cuisine. Dining high points include mostly casual fare, from fresh seafood, steaks and hamburgers cooked every way imaginable at Fisherman's Wharf and The Chart House, to a Spanky's chicken finger (a tender strip of fried chicken dipped in honey) or a fried onion ring and barbecue sandwich oozing with flavor from Big Al's.

If your sweet tooth is longing for a fix, follow the scent of sugar-coated pralines to Savannah Sweets. The folks at the River Street shop will gladly sell praline samples straight from the oven, or ship packages of them home to friends.

Although River Street cuisine can be a bit pricey, the atmosphere is like few others in the coastal United States.

Where else can you munch on hors d'oeuvres like Crabmeat Imperial (crab and cheese stuffed in fresh mushrooms, served at The Grapevine), while sipping your favorite wine an arm's length away from huge freighters? You'd better count on the elevator at the Hyatt Regency Hotel to get you back to street level; the steep, stone steps are difficult to climb if you have indulged too heavily.

If daily River Street activities aren't colorful enough, monthly festivals are a must, and First Saturday events liven the downtown area with arts and crafts booths, outdoor food stalls and free, family-oriented entertainment. Other crowd-pleasers are the riverfront Fourth of July fireworks display, Savannah Symphony outdoor concerts and the Savannah Maritime Festival, a nine-day event celebrating the maritime history of Savannah.

Keep in mind that on March 17 the city hosts the second largest St Patrick's Day Parade in the nation, and more than 300,000 celebrants – mostly out-of-towners – drink green beer, dance in the **River Street.**

streets and commit sometimes offensive behavior in honor of the Irish.

The **City Market** is another local entertainment area, four blocks of restored buildings near **Franklin Square**. John & Linda's restaurant beckons hungry visitors with tempting dishes like Southern Pecan Grouper and a wide assortment of pasta dishes. Linda Davis and John Nichols are hospitable hosts and will fill you in on the latest gossip (who's in town and who's not, who's divorcing and who's getting married, etc). Stop over at The Bottom Line for a little jazz; get rowdy at Malone's Sports Bar where you can disco with Atlanta Braves fans; or end the evening with a game of pool at Crossroads, where local R & B bands play the blues.

Ready for dessert? Try the 606 Cafe, which specializes in cow motifs. Cows illustrate the different entrées on the menu and there are cow salt and pepper shakers. Hanging from the ceiling are a collection of tacky items, from cow udders to women's undergarments.

By the sea: Leaving downtown and heading east on Victory Drive – known for its palm trees, handsome houses and flowering azaleas – in the direction of the islands, it's possible to catch a glimpse of old wealth in **Ardsley Park**. The stately, columned homes grace middle-to-upper class neighborhoods shaded by giant trees, and driving around at random provides a visual treat.

Nearby is **Bonaventure Cemetery**, a luxurious final resting place for Savannah's most distinguished citizens. A former plantation, Bonaventure is wistfully beautiful, dripping with moss and overflowing with azaleas, jasmine, magnolias, and live oak trees. (*Midnight's* cover illustration is a tombstone from Bonaventure.)

Thunderbolt, 6 miles (10 km) from downtown, is a pretty shrimping and fishing village on the banks of the **Intracoastal Waterway**. It's easy to pass over the arched bridge and fail to see the mass of towering masts from private yachts, which are owned by some

The bridge with no name.

of the world's wealthiest individuals. This boatyard, called **Palmer Johnson**, is the only one of its kind on the east coast of the United States: vessels can be housed in an indoor facility when undergoing maintenance.

Docking portside for repairs recently have been yachts owned by King Juan Carlos of Spain and vessels from other well-known celebrities kept under wraps. Don't try to get into the boatyard and, if you do, don't ask about the owners. All work is confidential and the facilities are closed to the public.

Farther on toward the Atlantic Ocean are the neighboring islands of **Whitemarsh**, **Talahi**, **Oatland** and **Wilmington**. Great seafood is to be found, not only at Thunderbolt's The River's End, but in Williams Seafood on Talahi Island, and Snapper's Restaurant and Palmer's Seafood on Wilmington Island. **Sail Harbour** on Wilmington achieved a new status when it was announced that the boats for the 1996 Olympic Yachting Events would be berthed here. Needless to say, sailboat- and dolphin-spotting cruises are two of the activities offered here, although Olympic standards cannot always be guaranteed. The Olympic events themselves are to be held at **Williamson Island**, just opposite Wilmington, and just south of **Little Tybee Island**.

Opinions vary about **Tybee Island**, 18 miles (29 km) east of downtown and known as "Savannah's beach." To some, it's the end of the earth and the perfect refuge from the city. To others, it's a redneck riviera. A tiny beach town with colorful characters and a few choice eateries, nightlife consists of bingo at the American Legion Hall or an outing to the outdoor deck at Spanky's, where, yes, you can dine on honey-flavored chicken fingers. Bring your bathing suit if the sun is shining. Of course, with the eyes of the world on the Olympic events held right on its doorstep, the atmosphere of Tybee is ripe for change.

Left, sunset in Savannah.

FOR THOSE
WITH MORE THAN
A PASSING INTEREST
IN TIME...

Before you put your name down for a Patek Philippe watch *fig. 1*, there are a few basic things you might like to know, without knowing exactly whom to ask. In addressing such issues as accuracy, reliability and value for money, we would like to demonstrate why the watch we will make for you will be quite unlike any other watch currently produced.

"Punctuality", Louis XVIII was fond of saying, "is the politeness of kings."

We believe that in the matter of punctuality, we can rise to the occasion by making you a mechanical timepiece that will keep its rendezvous with the Gregorian calendar at the end of every century, omitting the leap-years in 2100, 2200 and 2300 and recording them in 2000 and 2400 *fig. 2*. Nevertheless, such a watch does need the occasional adjustment. Every 3333 years and 122 days you should remember to set it forward one day to the true time of the celestial clock. We suspect, however, that you are simply content to observe the politeness of kings. Be assured, therefore, that when you order your watch, we will be exploring for you the physical—if not the metaphysical— limits of precision.

Does everything have to depend on how much?

Consider, if you will, the motives of collectors who set record prices at auction to acquire a Patek Philippe. They may be paying for rarity, for looks or for micromechanical ingenuity. But we believe that behind each $500,000-plus

bid is the conviction that a Patek Philippe, even if 50 years old or older, can be expected to work perfectly for future generations.

In case your ambitions to own a Patek Philippe are somewhat discouraged by the scale of the sacrifice involved, may we hasten to point out that the watch we will make for you today will certainly be a technical improvement on the Pateks bought at auction? In keeping with our tradition of inventing new mechanical solutions for greater reliability and better time-keeping, we will bring to your watch innovations *fig. 3* inconceivable to our watchmakers who created the supreme wristwatches of 50 years ago *fig. 4*. At the same time, we will of course do our utmost to avoid placing undue strain on your financial resources.

Can it really be mine?

May we turn your thoughts to the day you take delivery of your watch? Sealed within its case is your watchmaker's tribute to the mysterious process of time. He has decorated each wheel with a chamfer carved into its hub and polished into a shining circle. Delicate ribbing flows over the plates and bridges of gold and rare alloys. Millimetric surfaces are bevelled and burnished to exactitudes measured in microns. Rubies are transformed into jewels that triumph over friction. And after many months—or even years—of work, your watchmaker stamps a small badge into the mainbridge of your watch. The Geneva Seal—the highest possible attestation of fine watchmaking *fig. 5*.

Looks that speak of inner grace *fig. 6*.

When you order your watch, you will no doubt like its outward appearance to reflect the harmony and elegance of the movement within. You may therefore find it helpful to know that we are uniquely able to cater for any special decorative needs you might like to express. For example, our engravers will delight in conjuring a subtle play of light and shadow on the gold case-back of one of our rare pocket-watches *fig. 7*. If you bring us your favourite picture, our enamellers will reproduce it in a brilliant miniature of hair-breadth detail *fig. 8*. The perfect execution of a double hob-nail pattern on the bezel of a wristwatch is the pride of our casemakers and the satisfaction of our designers, while our chainsmiths will weave for you a rich brocade in gold *figs. 9 & 10*. May we also recommend the artistry of our goldsmiths and the experience of our lapidaries in the selection and setting of the finest gemstones? *figs. 11 & 12*.

How to enjoy your watch before you own it.

As you will appreciate, the very nature of our watches imposes a limit on the number we can make available. (The four Calibre 89 time-pieces we are now making will take up to nine years to complete). We cannot therefore promise instant gratification, but while you look forward to the day on which you take delivery of your Patek Philippe *fig. 13*, you will have the pleasure of reflecting that time is a universal and everlasting commodity, freely available to be enjoyed by all.

Should you require information on any particular Patek Philippe watch, or even on watchmaking in general, we would be delighted to reply to your letter of enquiry. And if you send us

fig. 1: The classic face of Patek Philippe.

fig. 4: Complicated wristwatches circa 1930 (left) and 1990. The golden age of watchmaking will always be with us.

fig. 6: Your pleasure in owning a Patek Philippe is the purpose of those who made it for you.

fig. 9: Harmony of design is executed in a work of simplicity and perfection in a lady's Calatrava wristwatch.

fig. 10: The chainsmith's hands impart strength and delicacy to a tracery of gold.

fig. 5: The Geneva Seal is awarded only to watches which achieve the standards of horological purity laid down in the laws of Geneva. These rules define the supreme quality of watchmaking.

fig. 7: Arabesques come to life on a gold case-back.

fig. 11: Circles in gold: symbols of perfection in the making.

fig. 2: One of the 33 complications of the Calibre 89 astronomical clock-watch is a satellite wheel that completes one revolution every 400 years.

fig. 8: An artist working six hours a day takes about four months to complete a miniature in enamel on the case of a pocket-watch.

fig. 12: The test of a master lapidary is his ability to express the splendour of precious gemstones.

fig. 3: Recognized as the most advanced mechanical regulating device to date, Patek Philippe's Gyromax balance wheel demonstrates the equivalence of simplicity and precision.

PATEK PHILIPPE
GENEVE

fig. 13: The discreet sign of those who value their time.

your card marked "book catalogue" we shall post you a catalogue of our publications. Patek Philippe, 41 rue du Rhône, 1204 Geneva, Switzerland, Tel. +41 22/310 03 66.

A Wise Man Never Thinks How Far He's Come. He Thinks How Far He Can Still Travel.

REMY **XO BECAUSE LIFE IS WHAT YOU MAKE IT**

Getting Acquainted

All phone numbers in Travel Tips use area code (404), unless otherwise indicated. Numbers beginning with (800) are toll-free if dialed in the US and often Canada.

The Place

The largest state east of the Mississippi River, Georgia covers 58,876 sq. miles (152,490 sq. km) and ranks as the country's 21st largest state in size. From the southernmost peaks of the great Blue Ridge mountains in Georgia's north, to the Golden Isles on the Atlantic coast, the state is strikingly diverse in terms of topography, flora and fauna.

Hikers know the Georgia mountains as the end, or beginning, of the Appalachian Trail. Rock climbers also frequent north Georgia, where from Brasstown Bald, the highest point in the state (4,784 ft/1,458 meters), four states are visible from the summit on a clear day. Eight major recreational lakes, 12 state parks and 30 golf courses make north Georgia a magnet for campers and outdoor sports enthusiasts. Trout fishermen, whitewater rafters and naturalists in search of the state flower, the Cherokee Rose, will want to head north from the state capital, Atlanta.

Near Georgia's border with Tennessee, a valley-and-ridge terrain predominates, gradually flattening towards Atlanta, where the naked granite batholith of Stone Mountain projects 825 ft (251 meters) above the surrounding plain. The state's great rivers – the Chattahoochee; the Ocmulgee and Oconee, which become the Altamaha; and the Savannah – are all navigable below the fall line. Sandy hills form a narrow belt below which the Coastal Plain, covering more than half the state, stretches to the 100-mile-long (160 km) Atlantic coast. In the southeastern corner of the state, and shared with neighboring Florida, is the 435,000-acre (176,000-hectares) Okefenokee Swamp, source of the Suwannee and St Mary's rivers, and home to many threatened species of wildlife.

Off the coast of Savannah (along with Brunswick, one of Georgia's two deep-water ports and foreign trade zones) lies Tybee Island, beginning the chain of Georgia's 13 barrier islands. St Simons Island – with its King and Prince Beach Resort, Sea Palms, the golf and tennis resort, and Sea Island, with its five-star, four-diamond Cloister resort – is perhaps the chain's most dazzling link. Brunswick may well be the shrimp capital of the world, but the barrier isles are also renowned for their catfish and crawfish.

Time Zones

Located within the Eastern Standard Time zone, Georgia sets its clocks to the same time as New York and Miami. Atlanta is one hour ahead of Chicago, three hours ahead of Los Angeles, five hours ahead of Honolulu. When it's noon in Atlanta, it's:

    1pm in Caracas
    5pm in London
    6pm in Paris
    7pm in Athens
    8pm in Moscow and Riyadh
    11pm in New Delhi
    1am in Singapore
    3am in Sydney
    3am in Tokyo
    6am in Honolulu
    9am in Los Angeles
    10am in Mexico City
    11am in Chicago.

Daylight Savings Time begins the first Sunday in April and ends on the last Sunday in October, the clock moving ahead one hour in spring, back one hour in autumn. ("Spring forward; fall back.")

Climate

Atlanta: Atlanta enjoys a heavenly, temperate spring season from April–mid-June. Summer can be hot and humid, scorching at times. Monsoon-like rains are unpredictable in summer, however, and visitors should take note when dark cumulus clouds start piling up; a rain slicker and umbrella might come in use on a stormy-looking day. The Atlantic coast suffers through a longer, hotter, more humid summer season, but spring comes earlier. Autumn, once again, is perfect, late September–October or November.

Extremes of temperature (0°F/18°C and 100°F/40°C) have been recorded in recent years, but bitter cold rarely holds for more than a day or two in January and February. Atlanta's altitude – 1,050 ft (320 meters) above sea level – accounts for the fact that daily highs and lows may vary by 15 to 20 degrees. Annual rainfall is around 48 inches (122 cm); December–April and July are the city's wettest months.

Weather in the north Georgia mountains is cooler, and there are road closings in winter due to snow and ice. Winter snows are rare, but freak blizzards and ice storms occasionally sugarcoat the magnolias and chaos reigns for a week or so, as the state is ill-prepared. Tornado alerts are not uncommon in Georgia, though funnels rarely touch down in the metropolitan area.

Savannah: Savannahians have been known to wear short-sleeved shirts on a Monday in December and thick, winter woolens on Wednesday of that same week. The winter weather is pleasant, but unpredictable. With only occasional bouts of extreme cold (i.e. below freezing), the most delightful temperatures are from October–April, with the sticky season and highest humidity levels from June–August.

Just when the temperature seems to be perfect, the city becomes plagued by "no-see-ums," a breed of pesky sand gnats, that are virtually invisible. With their penetrating sting, these tiny insects either cause minor discomfort or severe welts, depending on their victims' resistance to allergies. The best defense against these trip-spoilers is a product by Avon called "Skin So Soft." The so-called "gnat-season" lasts from about the first of April until the first of May.

Should you need more information, call the following services:
Time and Temperature: Tel: 936-8550.
Weather: Tel: 762-6151.

Swatch. The others just watch.

seahorse/fall winter 94-95

shockproof
splashproof
priceproof
boreproof
swiss made

swatch✚
SCUBA 200

INSIGHT GUIDES

COLORSET NUMBERS

INSIGHT *pocket* GUIDES

• •

United States: **Houghton Mifflin Company, Boston MA 02108**
Tel: (800) 2253362 Fax: (800) 4589501

Canada: **Thomas Allen & Son, 390 Steelcase Road East**
Markham, Ontario L3R 1G2
Tel: (416) 4759126 Fax: (416) 4756747

Great Britain: **GeoCenter UK, Hampshire RG22 4BJ**
Tel: (256) 817987 Fax: (256) 817988

Worldwide: **Höfer Communications Singapore 2262**
Tel: (65) 8612755 Fax: (65) 8616438

66 I was first drawn to the Insight Guides by the excellent "Nepal" volume. I can think of no book which so effectively captures the essence of a country. Out of these pages leaped the Nepal I know – the captivating charm of a people and their culture. I've since discovered and enjoyed the entire Insight Guide Series. Each volume deals with a country or city in the same sensitive depth, which is nowhere more evident than in the superb photography. 99

Sir Edmund Hillary

American Express offers Travelers Cheques built for two.

Cheques *for Two*℠ from American Express are the Travelers Cheques that allow either of you to use them because both of you have signed them. And only one of you needs to be present to purchase them.

Cheques *for Two* are accepted anywhere regular American Express Travelers Cheques are, which is just about everywhere. So stop by your bank, AAA* or any American Express Travel Service Office and ask for Cheques *for Two*.

Travelers Cheques

Average Atlanta Temperatures

	Low/High
January	36/54°F (2/12°C)
February	37/57°F (3/14°C)
March	41/63°F (5/17°C)
April	50/72°F (10/22°C)
May	59/81°F (15/27°C)
June	66/87°F (19/30°C)
July	69/88°F (21/31°C)
August	68/88°F (20/31°C)
September	63/83°F (17/28°C)
October	52/74°F (11/23°C)
November	40/62°F (4/17°C)
December	35/53°F (2/12°C)

Best Times to Visit

Whether summer and the Atlanta Braves baseball season, or fall and winter's football or basketball, or late spring through early autumn for the opera, Atlanta always offers more than one could ever hope to pack into a visit. Given just one choice, come in April for the Atlanta Dogwood Festival, celebrating the snowy trees that are symbols of the city. Festival dates and a program of events may be obtained from the Atlanta Convention and Visitors Bureau, 233 Peachtree Street NE, Atlanta, GA 30303, tel: 222-6688, or the Atlanta Chamber of Commerce, 235 International Boulevard NW, Atlanta, GA 30303, tel: 880-9000.

The People

In 1990, Atlanta entered the ranks of the nation's top 10 metro regions in population. The Atlanta Metropolitan Statistical Area comprises 18 counties and 5,147 sq. miles (13,330 sq. km), and is one of America's five fastest-growing areas in population. Out of the metro area's population of 2.8 million, only around 395,000 live within Atlanta's city limits.

According to 1990 census figures, out of a total of 2,833,500 inhabitants in the greater metropolitan area, 2,020,000 are white, 736,000 are African-American, 57,000 are Hispanic, 51,500 are Asian and 5,500 are Native American. Almost half of Atlanta's population migrated from other states and countries, contributing to the city's cultural diversity. Hispanics and Asians are the state's fastest-growing minorities.

Look under the heading "Churches" in Atlanta's Yellow Pages, and you will find everything from African Methodist Episcopal to Bahai, Eastern Orthodox, Gospel Harvester, Mennonite, Moravian and Swedenborgian. Baptists comprise 54 percent of Georgians, with Methodists ranking second at 23 percent. In the metro Atlanta area, urban Fulton County reports 20–39 percent Baptist, 20–39 percent Methodist, 10–19 percent Catholic, and 6–9 percent Presbyterian. Suburban Cobb County, on the other hand, exceeds the state's percentage of Baptists, with 60–79 percent.

The Economy

Both Atlanta and Georgia consistently place at or near the top of independent studies regarding business climate and employment. Atlanta is home to such giants as Coca-Cola, Delta Air Lines, Lockheed Aeronautical Systems, Scientific Atlanta, United Parcel Service, Holiday Inn Worldwide, Georgia-Pacific and Turner Broadcasting (including CNN). Between 1980 and 1990, metro Atlanta attracted more than 1,000 US companies or business units. Over 75 percent of the *Fortune 1000* companies are represented in the city, and a recent *Fortune* survey stated that "Atlanta ranks as the single most likely US city for new company facilities and manufacturing plants."

The city's major industries are construction, distribution, high technology, manufacturing, retail and wholesale trade, and business services. More than 1,400 internationally-based business from 40 countries have operations here, with over 300 choosing Atlanta for their US headquarters.

Atlanta is the key financial center for the Southeast. Many of the nation's top 100 banks are located here, and it's the headquarters for the Federal Reserve Bank's Sixth District

Government

Atlanta is Georgia's state capital, whose governor is elected for a four-year term and may be re-elected for one consecutive term. The 56-member state senate and 180-member house of representitives comprise the general assembly, which meets each January for a 40-day session. House and senate districts are apportioned by population; members are elected every two years.

Some 100 municipalities in the Atlanta Metropolitan Statistical Area operate under a variety of government structures, predominantly mayor and council, or council and city manager. Atlanta itself is governed by a mayor and council, the mayor serving as chief executive officer, with policy making and legislation the domain of the 18-member city council, in part elected city-wide and others elected from single-member districts.

Planning The Trip

What to Bring

Clothing & Essentials

Atlantans and Savannahians dress quite smartly for dinner, but tend to be very relaxed at play. In the upscale malls, you will see the entire range of American sartorial schizophrenia: affluent housewives in tennis skirts and tennis bracelets; high-school students dressed in hip-hop eccentricity; businessmen in lightweight suits and power ties; those who should know better clad in sweats. Designer labels abound.

Natural fabrics mixed with a dollop of synthetic fibers fare best in Georgia during the humid summer season and often rainy winter. Plan to dress in layers during spring and autumn, when temperatures fluctuate wildly from morning to night. A raincoat with a warm liner is useful in winter; umbrellas are *de rigueur* most of the year, and a rain slicker takes up little room. For upscale dining or hotels, dressy evening clothes will come in handy. Almost all reputable Atlanta hotels offer valet laundry services, so leave the heavy travel iron at home.

For fair-skinned visitors, hats and dark glasses are recommended to combat the fierce Georgia sunshine.

Electricity

110–115 volts AC, 60 cycles. Plugs are standard North American, with two flat parallel prongs. A good source for converters, transformers and plug adaptors is The Civilized Traveller, in Phipps Plaza mall.

Maps

For travel and tour guides, write or phone:

Georgia Department of Industry, Trade and Tourism, PO Box 1776, Atlanta, GA 30301, tel: 656-3590. The state guide contains a fine map of the state.

The Automobile Association of America also issues superlative maps. Write or phone for their Georgia/North Carolina/South Carolina TourBook:

AAA, 1000 AAA Drive, Heathrow, FL 32746-5063, tel: (800) AAA-HELP.

For a visitors guide and map write the Savannah Area Convention & Visitors Bureau, PO Box 1628, Savannah, GA 31402–1628.

In Atlanta, The Civilized Traveller in the Phipps Plaza mall carries local and international maps.

Entry Regulations

Travelers from outside North America should check with local American embassy or consulate, according to current law, citizens of Great Britain and Japan only require passports for entry into the US. Canadians must show proof of their residence in Canada.

Recommended Inoculations

Unless your country of origin is experiencing an epidemic, no vaccinations are currently required. As is prudent when traveling anywhere international, carry prescription drugs and refill prescriptions with you, not packed in checked luggage.

Visitors planning whitewater rafting, hiking or canoeing might want to immunize themselves against tetanus before setting out, and learn about the poisonous flora and fauna of the area. Foreign visitors should be aware that rabies exists in some North American small mammal populations. Avoid encounters with animals in the wild; seek medical care immediately if bitten.

Customs

Bring no plant or animal products into the US. Check with your local US embassy or consulate concerning furs, ivory or reptile-skin clothing; customs regulations and enforcement regarding endangered species are strict and unequivocal.

Visitors wishing to bring pets along with them should check with the United States Department of Agriculture, tel: (301) 436-4394/8170, regarding regulations and restrictions. Visitors who acquire pets in Georgia and wish to export them should contact the Federal Veterinarian in Atlanta, tel: 922-7860.

You may import or export up to $10,000 in currency. Larger amounts must be declared. Allowable duty free imports for foreign visitors staying three or more days: 1 litre of wine or spirits; 200 cigarettes, 100 of any but Cuban cigars or 3 lbs (1.4 kg) of tobacco; $100 worth of gifts.

Currency

Credit Cards and Traveler's Checks

Americans primarily use credit cards when traveling, and Atlanta is no exception. Major cards are accepted by most businesses, as are traveler's checks, though the city is still provincial enough to raise an eyebrow at traveler's checks drawn on foreign banks or in foreign currencies.

Visitors from abroad should purchase traveler's checks denominated in US dollars. America is not cash-oriented for purchases in large amounts, nor for foreign currency exchange in places other than banks and hotels. It is a good thing to have at least two different credit cards on hand. Personal checks drawn on out-of-state banks, let alone banks abroad, are rarely accepted.

In the event of loss or theft call the following:

American Express: Tel: (800) 528-4800.

AT&T: Tel: (800) 222-0300.

Diners Club: Tel: (800) 525-9135.

Discover: Tel: (800) 347-2683.

MasterCard: Tel: (800) 826-2181.

Visa: Tel: (800) 336-8472.

For traveler's checks:

American Express: Tel: (800) 221-7282.

Visa: Tel: (800) 227-6811.

Outside of banks and hotels, the following provide currency exchange services:

Ruesch International, 191 Peachtree Street, lobby level, tel: 222-9300.

Thomas Cook Foreign Exchange, 245 Peachtree Center Avenue, Marquis One Tower, gallery level, (also in Buckhead), tel: 681-9700, or toll free (800) 582-4496.

Public Holidays

For a listing of festivities and celebrations, refer to *Festivals*.

New Year's Day   1 January
Martin Luther King's Birthday
   third Monday in January
Washington's Birthday
   third Monday in February
Confederate Memorial Day 26 April
Memorial Day
   last Monday in May
Independence Day   4 July
Labor Day
   first Monday in September
Columbus Day
   second Monday in October
Veterans' Day   11 November
Thanksgiving
   fourth Thursday in November
Christmas   25 December

Getting There

By Air

Atlanta is a major airline hub, both domestically and internationally. Visitors from abroad whose primary destination is Atlanta can take advantage of direct flights from major European capitals, as well as from Tokyo. As in any travel, fares vary and it goes without saying (nonetheless, we'll say it) to check around and book well in advance. An informed, energetic travel agent can put together a package including reduced rates on accommodation, car rental, and air, rail or coach travel onwards in the United States.

British Airways, JAL, KLM, Lufthansa, Sabena and Swissair all offer direct flights from their countries of origin to Atlanta. Delta, whose hub is Atlanta, offers direct service to and from Frankfurt, Hamburg, London, Madrid, Munich and Paris; USAir connects with Frankfurt, London and Paris. Carriers using New York, Miami, Los Angeles and other US gateway cities and connecting with Atlanta include American, America West, Continental, Kiwi, Northwest, TWA, USAir, and United.

Hartsfield International Airport, some 10 miles (16 km) south of downtown Atlanta, vies with Chicago's O'Hare for the title of busiest US airport, and though a beautiful structure, its international arrivals and customs areas can become congested. At peak times and season, foreign visitors may require an hour and a half to get out of the airport.

Useful Telephone Numbers
Airlines
American, tel: (800) 433-7300.
America West, tel: (800) 247-5692.
Continental, tel: (800) 525-0280.
Delta, tel: (800) 221-1212.
Kiwi Airline, tel: (800) JET-KIWI.
Northwest, tel: (800) 225-2525.
TWA, tel: (800) 221-2000.
United, tel: (800) 241-6522.
USAir, tel: (800) 428-4322.
Airport Bus Service
AAA Airport Shuttle, tel: 934-8003
Atlanta Airport Shuttle, tel: 524-3400
Visitor Assistance
Atlanta Convention & Visitors Bureau, tel: 222-6688.
Georgia Dept. of Industry, Trade & Tourism, tel: 656-3545.
Multilingual Visitor Assistance, tel: 873-6170
Travelers' Aid, tel: 766-4511 or 530-6746. With one location near the arrivals area at Hartsfield airport, this volunteer counter assists travelers.

By Road

The interstate highway system (individual interstate highways are designated by "I-number") connects Atlanta

with Chattanooga, Tennesee (I-75) to the northwest; Charlotte, North Carolina (I-85) to the northeast; Charleston, South Carolina (I-20, I-26) and Savannah, Georgia (I-75 and I-16) to the southeast; Miami (I-75 and the Florida Turnpike) to the south; New Orleans (I-85, I-65, I-12 and I-59) to the southwest; and Birmingham, Alabama, via I-20, to the west.

Travelers in a hurry travel the interstates; those who want to experience the South of James Dickey, Eudora Welty and Alice Walker take secondary roads. If planning a lot of secondary-road explorations, consider membership with the AAA – Automobile Association of America, tel: 843-4500 – for six months. In addition to emergency road service, one of their services is mapping out automobile trips with handy maps, helpful for foreign visitors adrift in rural America, especially between, say, Possum Kingdom, South Carolina, and Nankipooh, Georgia.

Rush-hour traffic in Atlanta extends from 6.30–9am and again from 3.30–7pm. It's especially congested anywhere within 'the Perimeter,' or ring highway of I-285. The speed limit on city streets is 25–35mph; 40mph minimum, 55mph maximum on interstates and highways. Seat belts are required for drivers and front-seat passengers, child restraints required for children under four, and helmets required for motorcyclists and their passengers.

By Bus

Bus travel in the south, especially in the summer, will drop you into a certain stratum of Americana. It may not be the most elegant of ways to travel, nor the most comfortable, but it does reveal parts of America that only road travel can do. If nothing else, it is considerably cheaper than air or rail travel. Call Greyhound Lines, 81 International Boulevard NW, Atlanta, tel: 522-6300.

By Rail

Amtrak, via the trusty *Crescent*, connects Atlanta with points north and south along the eastern seaboard. Amtrak, Peachtree Station, 1688 Peachtree Street NW, Atlanta, tel: 881-3060, or (800) 872-7245.

Information about Georgia:
Georgia Dept of Industry, Trade and Tourism, Tourist/Communications Division, 285 Peachtree Center Avenue NE, Suite 1000 (or PO Box 1776) Atlanta, GA 30301, tel: 231-1790; fax: 656-3567.
Information about the South:
Travel South USA, 3400 Peachtree Road NE, Suite 1517, Atlanta, GA 30326, tel: 231-1790; fax: 231-2364.
Southeast Tourism Society, PO Box 420308, Atlanta, GA 30342, tel: 255-9472; fax: 847-9518.

Practical Tips

Emergencies

Dial 911 for a medical, fire or police emergency. (Not for information.) Tell the dispatcher the nature of the emergency, location and your name. Medical emergencies will be evaluated by paramedics specializing in emergency medicine, then transported to city hospitals for treatment.

Other useful numbers in Atlanta:
Dental referrals: Northern District Dental Society, tel: 270-1635. Monday–Friday, 8.30am–5pm.
Medical referrals: Medical Association of Atlanta, tel: 881-1714. Monday–Thursday 9am–4pm, Friday 9am–3pm.
AIDS Infoline: Tel: 876-9944
Alcoholics Anonymous: Tel: 525-3178
Multilingual Visitor Assistance: Tel: 873-6170
Poison Control Center: Tel: 589-4400

Road Conditions: Tel: 656-5882, 656-5267
State Highway Patrol: Tel: 624-6077
Travelers Aid: Tel: 527-7400
24-hr pharmacy: Tel: 876-0381
Weather forecast & temperatures: Tel: 762-6151

Hospitals

ATLANTA
Crawford Long Hospital (Emory University), tel: 686-4411. Emergency, tel: 892-4411
Piedmont Hospital, Buckhead, tel: 605-5000. Emergency, tel: 350-2222
Georgia Baptist Medical Center Hospital, tel: 653-4000. Emergency, tel: 653-4136
SAVANNAH
Candler Family Health Center, tel: 748-8366
Candler Hospital, tel: 354-9211
Immediate Med, tel: 927-6832
Memorial Medical Center, tel: 350-8000
St Joseph's Hospital, tel: 925-4100

Weights & Measures

Americans are slowly (very slowly) learning the metric system. In daily use, however, the English system of weights and measurements (pounds, miles) is most common.

1 ounce (oz) = 28.50 g
1 pound (lb) = 16 ozs = 453.6 g
1 ounce (oz) = 28.400 ml
1 pint = 0.57 liter
1 quart = 2 pints = 1.14 liter
1 gallon = 2 quarts = 4.55 liter
1 inch = 2.54 cm
1 foot = 12 inches = 0.31 meter
1 yard = 3 feet = 0.91 meter
1 mile = 1,760 yards
= 1.61 km

Business Hours

Store and general business hours: Monday–Friday 9am–5pm, most shops open Saturday.

Most banks: Monday–Friday 9am–4pm, Saturday 9am–1pm.

Mall or shopping centers (which usually include pharmacies or drug stores) have later openings and clos-ings. Lenox Square, for example: Monday–Saturday 10am–9.30pm, Sunday 12.30–5.30pm.

Tipping & Taxes

Taxis: 15 percent of meter reading.
Airport skycaps: 50 cents–$1 per bag for curb service; more if bags are carried further.
Hotel bellpersons: $1 per bag.
Hair stylists, barbers: 20 percent.
Restaurants: 15 percent is standard, 20 percent for exceptional service.

Georgia's statewide sales tax is 4 percent.

Religious Services

The best source of information is the *Atlanta Journal and Constitution*, the combined weekend edition of the two daily papers. Another place to check is the telephone book yellow pages. Check the listings under *Churches and Synagogues*.

Media

Print Media

Atlanta's print media include the morning *Atlanta Constitution* and evening *Atlanta Journal* ("Covers Dixie Like The Dew") daily newspapers, and a free paper, *Creative Loafing*, plus glossy, *Atlanta Magazine* and classy *Georgia Trend: The Magazine of Georgia Business*. Easily obtained at Oxford Books in Atlanta are myriad small newspapers and journals serving smaller populations in and around the city.

Radio Stations

Big band, classic rock, news: WQXI 790 AM
Country and western: WKHX 101.5 FM
Soft rock: WPCH 94.9 FM
National Public Radio (news, classical music): WABE 90.1 FM
Soft rock: WSB 98.5 FM
All news: WGST 640 AM
All news: WCNN 680 AM
Alternative rock (university): WRAS 88.5 FM
Contemporary rock: WKLS 96.1 FM
Jazz and gospel: WCLK 91.9 FM
Talk radio: WSB 750 AM

Television Stations

Check the *Atlanta Journal* and *Constitution*, *Creative Loafing* or *TV Guide* for schedules. Cable stations, both free and pay, may be available in your hotel room.
Channel 2: WSB, ABC
Channel 5: WAGA, CBS
Channel 11: WXIA, NBC
Cable channel: includes CNN

Postal Services

There are myriad post offices throughout the Atlanta area. Consult the blue pages of the Atlanta phone book for locations and phone numbers. Useful numbers in the Atlanta area:
General postal information: Tel: 765-7266.
Passport information: Tel: 765-7266.
Philately: Tel: 765-7337.
Rate information: Tel: 765-7266.

Telecoms

There are three telephone area codes in Georgia: Atlanta, 404; Athens, 706; Savannah, 912. As elsewhere in the United States and Canada, all numbers with the 800 area code are toll-free.

Pay telephones are easily found in shopping areas, on street corners, outside 24-hour convenience stores and gas stations. Local calls cost $.25 in coin. Prepaid telephone cards are not common in the United States. Note: Some hotels mark up the price of calls, both domestic and international.

Tourist Offices

Atlanta Convention and Visitors Bureau Centers, tel: 521-6600. Locations include:

Peachtree Center Mall (downtown), Monday–Friday 10am–5pm; Lenox Square Shopping Center, Wednesday–Saturday 11am–6pm, Sunday 12.30–5.30pm; Underground Atlanta, Monday–Saturday 10am–9pm, Sunday noon–6pm.

Multilingual Visitor Assistance, tel: 873-6170, Georgia Council for Interna-

INSIGHT GUIDES

COLORSET NUMBERS

tional Visitors Language Bank, 999 Peachtree Street, Suite 770, Atlanta, GA 30309-3918. Monday–Friday, 9am–5pm.

Embassies & Consulates

Austria (trade commission): 240 Peachtree Street NW, tel: 524-4022.
Barbados: 3935 Flowerland Drive NE, tel: 454-0355.
Belgium: 229 Peachtree Street NE, tel: 659-2150
Canada, 1 CNN Center, tel: 577-1512.
Colombia: 3379 Peachtree Road NE, tel: 237-1045.
Costa Rica: 315 West Ponce De Leon Avenue, Decatur, tel: 370-0555.
Denmark: 225 Peachtree Street NE, Suite 201, tel: 614-5207.
France: 285 Peachtree Center Avenue, NE, tel: 522-4226.
Germany: 229 Peachtree Street NE, tel: 659-4760.
Great Britain: 245 Peachtree Center Avenue NE, Suite 2700, tel: 524-5856.
Greece: 3340 Peachtree Road NE, tel: 261-3313.
Iceland: 1677 Tullie Circle NE, tel: 321-0777.
Israel: 1100 Circle 75 Parkway NW, Suite 440, tel: 875-7851.
Italy: 1106 West Peachtree Street NW, tel: 875-6177.
Jamaica (tourist board): 300 West Wieuca Road NE, tel: 250-9971.
Japan: 400 Colony Square, tel: 892-2700.
Mexico: 410 South Omni International, tel: 688-3258.
Netherlands: 133 Peachtree Street NE, tel: 525-4513.
Panama: 260 Peachtree Street NW, tel: 525-2772.
Republic of China: 233 Peachtree Street NE, tel: 522-0481.
South Korea: 229 Peachtree Street NE, tel: 522-1611.
Switzerland: 1275 Peachtree Street NE, tel: 872-7874.
Turkey (honorary consulate): 1100 Piedmont Avenue NE, tel: 872-9610.

Getting Around

On Arrival

For a stressless stay in Atlanta, book your hotel accommodation well in advance, guaranteeing the reservation with a credit card (Visa, MasterCard or American Express).

Many hotels offer courtesy buses from Hartsfield International Airport. Cars may be rented at the airport or downtown; it may be more convenient to rent a car downtown at a hotel. Public transportation in the metropolitan area includes buses and MARTA trains, sublimely safe, swift, reliable and clean. Atlanta – sprawling, suburban and subject to extremes of weather – is not ideally suited for extensive walking tours. And like any city, not all areas are safe for those unfamiliar with street life. As anywhere, play it safe in unfamiliar areas, and at night, don't travel alone. Be sure to lock all car doors while traveling; keep valuables out of sight, even for short stops. Uniformed police abound in Atlanta's congested areas, and are readily available for assistance.

Public Transportation

Taxis

Taxi, limousine and even horse-drawn carriage companies are numerous. Ask at a hotel for assistance; hotels are always good places to find a taxi, or call, tel: 658-7600 for information regarding taxi companies and fares.

These fares are approximate: flag falling, $1.50; each additional 1/6 mile 20 cents; waiting, $12 an hour. Typical fares: airport to Buckhead, $25. Airport to downtown, $15. Fares are subject to 6 percent tax.

Rapid Rail/Bus

MARTA (Metropolitan Rapid Transit Authority) is a rapid-rail system compris-

ing north–south and east–west lines intersecting at the main Five Points Station in downtown Atlanta. Stations are designated N, S, E, W or P, denoting their compass relationship to Five Points. (P represents the current single-station Proctor Creek Line.) The Hartsfield International Airport Station is designated Airport S7; at present, the station closest to Buckhead is Lenox N7. Timetables/schedules are available at all stations. Atlanta's MARTA buses coordinate with the rapid-rail service. The rail system operates from around 5am to around 1am daily, trains running 8–15 minutes apart. Nearly all stations have free parking, especially after 6pm and all day on weekends and holidays.

Fares: Individual MARTA tokens are available, and transfers are free. Weekly and weekend passes available. Bus and subway fares payable in tokens, prepaid Transcards or exact change.

Useful telephone numbers for services within the city are:
Subway and bus schedule information: Tel: 848-4711.
Airport service: Tel: 848-3454.
General information: Tel: 848-5000.
Handicapped information: Tel: 848-3340/5440.

Private Transportation

Rental Cars

It's best to reserve cars in advance, especially if making specific requirements during peak seasons. Check when booking airline tickets about packages or discounts. Unless carrying huge amounts of cash, a credit card is essential. Rental companies require a credit card imprint in advance (which may also tie up some of your credit card's spending limit) as a deposit, or else a substantial cash deposit.
Avis: Tel: (800) 331-1212.
Budget: Tel: 530-3000.
Hertz: Tel: (800) 654-3131.
McFrugal Auto Rental: Tel: 431-2000.
Thrifty: Tel: (800) 367-2277.

If planning extensive car travel in North America, consider joining the AAA (Automobile Association of America), an organization offering an attractive package of services and benefits, including free emergency towing and repairs, tel: 843-4500.

On Departure

By air, confirm flights well in advance. Airport security at Hartsfield International is fairly rigorous, leading to delays. Between checkpoint and gate are numerous bars, snack shops, news and souvenir stands.

Where To Stay
Hotels & Motels

Visitors generally stay in downtown Atlanta, in Buckhead (a hotel and shopping area), or near the airport. Less-expensive hotels and motels are sited near exits of the interstate highways. It's worth contacting the Atlanta Convention and Visitors Bureau in advance, as they often have booklets giv-

ing discounts on accommodation and attractions. In addition, Georgia Travel Coupons are available, free, at the state Visitor Welcome Centers as you enter Georgia on the major interstates.

Room rates vary, depending on location and swankiness. Non-discounted rack rates downtown range from $150–$250 for "Very Expensive" to $50–$120 for "Moderate."

Atlanta

Downtown

Very Expensive
Ritz-Carlton Atlanta, 181 Peachtree Street NE, Atlanta, GA 30303, tel:

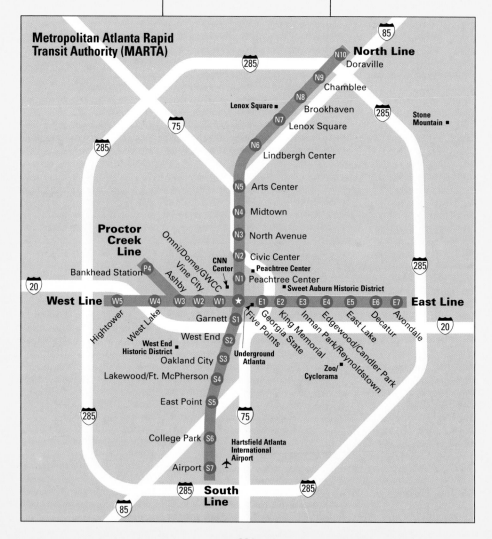

659-0400; fax: 688-0400. Old World opulence, with fine antiques decorating the plush public areas of this 447-unit hotel. Like its sister Ritz in Buckhead, this is the city's most prestigious temporary address. No pets.

The Suite Hotel Underground, 54 Peachtree Street, Atlanta, GA 30303, tel: 223-5555; fax: 223-0467. One hundred and fifty-six of the finest suites in town, located directly at Underground Atlanta. No worries about drinking and driving home from Dantes Down The Hatch.

Westin Peachtree Plaza, 210 Peachtree Street, Atlanta, GA 30343. Tel: 659-1400; fax: 589-7424. With its 1,068 pie-shaped rooms, this 72-story, circular high rise is an Atlanta landmark, and the tallest hotel in America to date. Designed by famed architect John Portman, the structure is a must-see for visitors, whether checking in or not. Small pets allowed.

Expensive
Hyatt Regency Atlanta, 265 Peachtree Street NE, Atlanta, GA 30303, tel: 577-1234; fax: 588-4137. Part of the Peachtree Center shopping and office complex, this 1,279-unit hotel offers a senior discount and weekly rates. Peachtree Center Athletic Club available for a fee. No pets.

Marriott Atlanta Marquis, 265 Peachtree Center Avenue, Atlanta, GA 30303, tel: 521-0000; fax: 586-6299. This whale of a hotel is another John Portman beauty: the atrium lobby has a volume of 9.5 million cu. ft (269,010 cu. meters), and visitors feel they've entered the rib cage of some mythical beast. Pool, sauna, whirlpool, steamroom, health club – all the perks. No pets.

Omni Hotel, 100 CNN Center, Atlanta, GA 30335, tel: 659-0000; fax: 525-5050. Part of the huge Omni complex, this is the place to see CNN or games/concerts at the Georgia Dome. Senior discounts, health club privileges, no pets.

Moderate
Days Inn Downtown, 166 Finley Street, Atlanta, GA 30601, tel: (706) 369-7000; fax: (706) 548-4224. This 105-unit member of the reliable Days Inn chain offers weekly and monthly rates and a senior discount. Pets, extra charge.

The Inn at the Peachtrees, 330 West Peachtree Street NW, Atlanta, GA 30308, tel: 577-6970; fax: 659-3244. This 101-unit motel offers AAA special rates. Fee for health club privileges. No pets.

Quality Inn Habersham, 330 Peachtree Street NE, Atlanta, GA 30308, tel: 577-1980; fax: 688-3706. A senior discount is available at this 91-unit small hotel. Pets allowed. $100 deposit.

Travelodge-Downtown, 311 Courtland Street NE, Atlanta, GA 30303, tel: 659-4545; fax: 659-5934. A 71-unit member of a reliable chain, this motel offers a senior discount. No pets.

Buckhead

Expensive
Ritz-Carlton, Buckhead, 3434 Peachtree Road NE, Atlanta, GA 30326, tel: 237-2700; fax: 239-0078. Architects have made this 22-story hotel intimate and welcoming. Adjacent to Phipps Plaza mall, the Ritz's 18th- and 19th-century art collection has its own self-guided tours. Rooms feature marble baths. Ritzy!

Hotel Nikko Atlanta. 2964 Peachtree Road NW, Atlanta, GA 30305, tel: 365-8100; fax: 233-5686. This neo-Georgian hotel features 440 rooms, health club, sauna and outdoor pool, French and Japanese restaurants, marble bathrooms and a 9,000 sq. ft (840 sq. meter) Japanese garden. No pets.

Swissôtel Atlanta, 3391 Peachtree Road NE, Atlanta, GA 30326, tel: 365-0065; fax: 365-8787. Adjacent to the Lenox Square mall, its aluminum and black granite exterior which echoes the Midtown High Museum of Art. Biedermeier-style furniture, marble bathrooms, a health club, sauna, weight room, art collections, two fine restaurants. 348 rooms.

JW Marriott Hotel, 3300 Lenox Road, Atlanta, GA 30326, tel: 262-3344; fax: 262-8603. This is the most convenient Buckhead location for those dependent on the rapid-rail or addicted to shopping – the Marriott connects directly to Lenox Square mall. This ultramodern high rise offers 371 rooms, complimentary robes, dedicated modem jacks.

Moderate
Embassy Suites Hotel, 3285

Peachtree Road NE, Atlanta, GA 30305, tel: 261-7733; fax: 262-0522. This gem may be Buckhead's best-kept secret for families. All 328 rooms are suites with bedroom and a separate sitting room. Kitchens, work area, twin TVs. Complimentary, cooked-to-order buffet breakfast; two hours of free cocktails in evenings. If you are not satisfied, you do not pay. Indoor and outdoor pools, sauna, steam room.

Terrace Garden Inn, 3405 Lenox Road NE, Atlanta, GA 30326, tel: 261-9250; fax: 848-7301. Southern hospitality comes to mind here, especially towards guests. 364 newly-renovated rooms and suites, a health & racquet center, three dining venues, MARTA and Lenox Square just across the street.

Budget
Holiday Inn at Lenox, 3377 Peachtree Road, Atlanta, GA 30326, tel: 264-1111; fax: 231-3497. Dwarfed by adjacent high rises, this modest hotel has cool views of Lenox Square and suburban greenery. 300 rooms with in-room cable and HBO films on TV, in-room safes, coffee-makers (but the coffee is on you).

Airport

Visitors to cultural and dining destinations in Atlanta proper will find the drive from airport hotels rather long to negotiate twice a day, but for some, especially business travelers, convenience to the airport can have its advantages.

Atlanta Airport Hilton, 1031 Virginia Avenue, Atlanta, GA 30354, tel: 767-9000; fax: 767-0844. There are special weekend and monthly rates at this 501-room mega-hotel, complete with two heated pools, health club and lighted tennis court.

Hyatt Atlanta Airport, 1900 Sullivan Road, College Park, GA 30337, tel: 991-1234; fax: 991-5906. A 397-unit hotel featuring an indoor/outdoor pool and sauna. Senior discounts and airport transportation. No pets.

Marriott Atlanta Airport, 4711 Best Road, College Park, GA 30337, tel: 766-7900; fax: 762-6355. This 642-unit hotel offers a senior discount, raquetball courts, saunas, lighted tennis courts, pool, health club and airport transportation. Pets allowed.

Bed & Breakfast

Throughout the south, there are bed-and-breakfast places, country inns and lodgings of historical interest available. The best reference is the Georgia/North Carolina/South Carolina TourBook, published by the American Automobile Association (AAA).

Atlanta: AAA Auto Club South, 454B Roswell Road, Atlanta, GA 30342, tel: 843-4500.

Savannah: AAA Auto Club South, 712 Mall Boulevard, Savannah, GA 31406, tel: (912) 352-8222. Bed & Breakfast Atlanta, at 1801 Piedmont Avenue NE, Suite 208, tel: 875-0525, or toll free (800) 967-3224, is a service which lists accommodation in private homes and inns in the greater Atlanta area.

Campgrounds

Most camping sites in state parks are on a first-come, first-serve basis. Two-week limit; some sites may be reserved. More than 20 state parks also offer housekeeping cabins. For camping and recreation information: Dept. of Natural Resources Communications Office, 205 Butler Street SE, Suite 1258, Atlanta, GA 30334, tel: 656-3530, or toll free (800) 542-PARK. Also, the US Forest Service, 1720 Peachtree Road NW, Atlanta, GA 30367, tel: 347-2384. The Automobile Association of America publishes an AAA Southeastern CampBook which lists all camping and trailering areas, public and private.

Youth Hostels

Foreign students with valid student IDs, contact the Atlanta Convention and Visitors Bureau, tel: 521-6600.

Athens

Moderate
Best Western Colonial Inn, 170 North Milledge Avenue, Athens, GA 30601. A 69-unit motel with refrigerators, movies, a bed-and-breakfast special. Small pets only, tel: (706) 546-7311; fax: (706) 546-7959.
Days Inn-Downtown, 166 Finley Street, Athens, GA 30601, tel: (706) 369-7000; fax: (706) 548-4224. A 105-unit motel. Pets, $5 charge.

Holiday Inn, PO Box 1666, Athens, GA 30603, tel: (706) 549-4433; fax: (706) 548-3031. Adjacent the University of Georgia, this 238-unit motor inn features a heated indoor pool, whirlpool and exercise room. Pets, in kennels only.

Antebellum Trail

MACON

Expensive
1842 Inn, 353 College Street, Macon, GA 31201, tel: (912) 741-1842; fax: (912) 741-1842. A historic bed-and-breakfast, features 19th-century ambience with some 20th-century perks. Some of the 21 units have fireplaces and whirlpool baths.

Moderate
Best Western-Riverside, 2400 Riverside Drive, Macon, GA 31204, tel: (912) 743-6311; fax: (912) 743-9420. A 123-unit motor inn with pool, health club privileges. No pets.
Courtyard by Marriott, 3990 Sheraton Drive, Macon, GA 31201, tel: (912) 477-8899; fax: (912) 477-4684. Pay movies, heated pool, whirlpool baths, exercise room. 108 units. No pets.

Madison

Ramada Inn Antebellum, 2020 Eatonton Highway, Madison, GA 30650, tel: 342-2121; fax: 342-2865. Formerly the Holiday Inn, this 121-unit motor inn features a pool, steam baths. Pets allowed.

Milledgeville

Holiday Inn, Highway 441 North, Milledgeville, GA 31061, tel: (912) 452-3502; fax: (912) 453-3591. A reliable member of the Atlanta-based chain, this 169-unit motel has a pool, pay movies. Small pets only.

Savannah

Expensive
The Gastonian, 220 East Gaston Street, Savannah, GA 31401, tel: (912) 232-2869; fax: (912) 234-0006. This 13-unit historic bed-and-breakfast consists of restored, connected late-1800s houses. Six rooms with whirlpool bath. No pets allowed.
Hyatt Regency Savannah, 2 West Bay Street, Savannah, GA 31401, tel: (912) 238-1234; fax: (912) 944-3673. This sumptuous member of the Hyatt chain is adjacent to City Hall and features amenities such as pay movies, a heated indoor pool, rental bicycles and airport transfers. Pets allowed.
Magnolia Place Inn, 503 Whitaker Street, Savannah, GA 31401, tel: (912) 236-7674. A 13-unit restored Victorian mansion, this historic bed-and-breakfast has a hot tub in the courtyard and whirlpools and fireplaces in some rooms. No pets.
President's Quarters, 225 East President Street, Savannah, GA 31401, tel: (912) 233-1600; fax: (912) 238-0849. Another bed-and-breakfast in the city's historic district, this restored mansion with a walled garden features 13 rooms and suites with whirlpool baths, refrigerators and movies. No pets.

Moderate
De Soto Hilton, 15 East Liberty Street, Savannah, GA 31412, tel: (912) 232-9000; fax: (912) 232-6018. In the historic district, this 250-unit hotel has a heated pool, health club privileges, pay movies. No pets.
East Bay Inn, 225 East Bay Street, Savannah, GA 31401, tel: (912) 238-1225; fax: (912) 232-2709. An historic bed-and-breakfast, this 28-unit restored 1853 warehouse features large, Georgian-style rooms.
Olde Harbour Inn, 508 East Factors Walk, Savannah, GA 31401, tel: (912) 234-4100; fax: (912) 233-5979. A 24-unit historic bed-and-breakfast in the historic riverfront district. River-view suites with fully-equipped kitchens.

Eating Out

The Atlanta poet James Dickey states boldly that "Southern cooking is the best that's ever been developed...in the world." And to Dickey, the perfect meal is fried chicken drumsticks and okra. Other southern specialties are grits (a porridge of ground hominy corn), cornbread, peach cobbler, fried catfish or crawfish, and country ham smothered in Red Eye Gravy.

But visitors squeamish about grits and crawfish needn't worry: in the last 20 years, the New South has undergone a culinary renaissance, and from the mountains to the coast, Georgia's restaurants reflect a new affluence and sophistication.

Atlanta

If for some reason you were to randomly parachute into Atlanta, odds are you would land on a restaurant – and a *good* restaurant at that.

The following list is nothing if not extremely limited and idiosyncratic. You should not leave Atlanta without stopping in at The Varsity on Spring Street (the world's largest drive-in), or that Jimmy Dean-Ford Fairlane dream of a diner on Ponce de Leon Avenue, the Majestic. Don't miss that other paean to junk food, on "Ponce" as well, the Krispy Kreme donut shop. But the following list should be one to keep body and southern soul together. Other restaurant listings are glossed in the text, and ethnic eateries are covered in *Atlanta Magazine* and *Creative Loafing* listings. For those interested in the up-to-the-minute southern best, the magazine *Southern Living* is a great reference.

Up-Market
Anthony's, 3109 Piedmont Road NE, tel: 262-7379; fax: 261-6009. This is surely Atlanta's "Belle of the Ball," from the first cocktail on the verandah through "Roasts Carved From Our Silver Chariot," and on to a chocolate soufflé. The setting is a 1797 antebellum plantation home, and the service is Anglo-Atlantan. (Yes, one of the owners *does* have a Sheffield accent.) Reservations urged.
Chops, One Buckhead Plaza, 3060 Peachtree Road NW, Suite 150, tel: 262-2675. Anyone mention the word "steakhouse"? This is a beef emporium of the first order, featuring aged prime beef and seafood. The menu's distinctly American and nothing but the best, from the Long Island Blue Point Oysters and Large Live Maine Lobsters, to the Fresh Raspberry Tart.
The Dining Room, Ritz-Carlton Hotel,

Buckhead, 3434 Peachtree Road, tel: 237-2700. Atlanta's best restaurant, presided over by Atlanta's best chef, Guenter Seeger. Four-course masterpieces, Monday–Saturday evenings, paired with appropriate wines. This is a once-in-a-lifetime dining pleasure.
Kamogawa Japanese Restaurant, Hotel Nikko, 3300 Peachtree Road, tel: 841-0314. This three-peach jewel is said to be Elton John's favorite. Stunningly authentic Japanese cuisine in four unique settings: the sushi bar; white-linen-draped tables overlooking the Nikko's splendid Japanese garden; the *teppanyaki* grill; private *tatami* rooms. Reservations urged.
Veni Vidi Vici, 41 14th Street, tel: 875-8424. Rustic Italian cuisine in a decidedly theater district setting. A showcase for the work of third-generation Chef Emilio DiCarlo. Antipasti Piccoli (18 daily specialty starters), handmade pastas, roasted whole lamb and duck, suckling pig with chive mashed potatoes, other pleasures.

Affordable
Buckhead Diner, 3073 Piedmont Road (at East Paces Ferry Road), tel: 262-3336. If Anthony's represents the Old South, the Buckhead Diner represents the New. See and be seen here, and enjoy the glorified pizza, hamburgers, soft-shell crabs, onion rings and tarted-up southern icons such as Banana Cream Pie. It's all "down home" – if home has a pair of BMWs parked out back.
Dante's Down the Hatch. Two locations: 3380 Peachtree Road NE, Buckhead, tel: 266-1600, and 86 Lower Alabama Street, Underground Atlanta, tel: 577-1800. Twenty-three years in Atlanta, Dante Stephensen's fine fondue cuisine (using only Australian beef), 18th-century-sailing-vessel decor, live jazz (and live crocodiles in the moat) have been turning heads and returning patrons such as Jimmy and Rosalyn Carter, Burt Reynolds and William Buckley. Keep your strawberry frozen daiquiri glass as a souvenir. Reservations urged.
Peasant Uptown, 3350 Peachtree Road NE, Buckhead, tel: 261-6341. This mall-side member of the excellent Peasant group looks like the verandah of a colonial plantation – piano music, a cool and laid-back atmosphere, and scrumptious filets of beef or fish.

The Public House, 605 South Atlanta Street, Roswell, tel: 992-4646. An early 19th-century Victorian storefront in the heart of historic Roswell, this restaurant features charming decor, impeccable service, and the superb Kahlua Cheesecake. Peach Pecan Rack of Lamb or Lump Crab Cakes first, though.

Very Reasonable
Goldberg and Son Bagel Bakery-Delicatessen, 4383 Roswell Road NE, tel: 256-3751. Since 1972, the Goldbergs have been serving up award-winning bagels and bialys baked on the premises, Kosher hot dogs, Reubens, pastrami sandwiches. South of New York, this is it. Heading for a concert at Chastain? This is a good place to pick up your picnic.
Mick's, Lenox Square Mall, tel: 262-6425. This neo-Fifties-style chainlet of diners has nine locations in the city. Hamburgers, super salads and pasta prevail, plus killer Oreo cheesecake.
Original House of Pancakes, 4330 Peachtree Road NE (and other locations), tel: 237-4116. Please do not confuse this restaurant chainlet with that other pancake house chain – there's no comparison. The concept of sourdough pancake batters, mixed by hand using premium ingredients, comes from Oregon; the idea lives on in Atlanta. Try their apple pancake, sourdough french Toast or Dutch Baby – and loosen your belt.
Rocky's Brick Oven Pizzeria, 1770 Peachtree Street, tel: 876-1111. It's a pizza joint. But it's a great pizza joint. Wood-fired brick oven pizzas, calzones, antipasta and salads – everything you'd expect. Fun, young, and 50 years of getting it right.
The Majestic Food Shop, 1031 Ponce de Leon Avenue, tel: 875-0276. The diner at the end of the world. By all means come here for the sensory overload of Americana, and eat if you must.
Krispy Kreme (donuts), 295 Ponce de Leon Avenue, tel: 876-7307. *Creative Loafing*'s Cliff Bostock phrases it best: "Swill coffee and eat 'em so hot they're semi-solid with cops, the homeless, hookers, yuppies and make-believe leather boys from the Eagle."
R Thomas Deluxe Grill, 1812 Peachtree Road, tel: 872-2942. This patio-style restaurant with the spray-

Atlanta Cyclorama, Georgia and Cherokee avenues SE, tel: 658-7625. An immense depiction of the Civil War's 1864 Battle of Atlanta in the round. Daily 9.30am–5.30pm.

Atlanta State Farmers' Market, 16 Forest Parkway, Forest Park, tel: 366-6910. Nearly 150 acres (61 hectares) of fresh regional produce, meats, eggs. Daily 8am–5pm.

Carter Library and Museum, 1 Copenhill, tel: 331-0296. Films, videos and displays relating to the life and presidency of Jimmy Carter. Cafe. Monday–Saturday 9am–4.45pm, Sunday noon–4.45pm.

CNN Studio Tours, 1 CNN Center, tel: 827-2491. An inside view of Turner Broadcasting and CNN – home for CNN, Headline News and CNN International. Specialty shops, cinema and restaurants. Tours daily 9am–5pm.

Fox Theatre, 660 Peachtree Street NE, tel: 876-2041. On the National Regiser of Historic Places. A 1929 Egyptian/Art Deco building that remains the venue for live performances and a summer movie series. Tours on Monday, Thursday, Saturday.

Georgia State Capitol, Capitol Hill at Washington Street Tel: 656-2844. Inside this 1889 capitol building are a Hall of Flags and natural science displays. Monday–Friday 8am–5pm. Tours available on the hour, 10am–2pm, except noon.

Governor's Mansion, 391 West Paces Ferry Road NW, tel: 261-1776. Greek Revival style including a collection of Federal Period furniture. Tuesday–Thursday 10–11.30am for tours.

Herndon Home, 587 University Place, tel: 581-9813. Formerly the home of a life insurance mogul, this 1910 building is an African-American house museum. Tuesday–Saturday tours on the hour, 10am–4pm.

Kennesaw Mountain National Battlefield Park. Old Highway 41 and Stilesboro Road, PO Box 1610, Marietta, GA 30061, tel: 427-4686. Civil War battle site in the 1864 Battle of Atlanta. Museum, picnic and hiking sites. Daily 8.30am–5pm.

Martin Luther King, Jr. Historic District, Auburn Avenue between Jackson and Randolph streets, tel: 524-1956. King Center for Nonviolent Social Change, Dr King's birth home and grave, and Ebenezer Baptist Church, where he preached. Several different tours. Daily 9am–5pm, 9am–8pm in summer.

Nexus Contemporary Art Center, 535 Means Street, off Marietta Street, downtown, tel: 688-1970. Tuesday–Saturday, 11am–5pm.

Six Flags Over Georgia, 7561 Six Flags Road SW at I-20, Mableton, GA, tel: 984-9290. Large 331-acre (134-hectare) theme and amusement park, with rides, shows, roller coasters. Open weekends in spring and fall, daily in summer.

Stone Mountain Park, Highway 78, tel: 498-5600. A 3,200-acre (1,295-hectare) park surrounding the world's largest exposed mass of granite. Swimming, golf, fishing. Attractions open June–August, 10am–9pm; September–May, 10am–5.30pm.

Underground Atlanta, Peachtree Street at Upper Alabama Street, tel: 523-2311. Specialty shops, restaurants and entertainment in a six-block urban marketplace. Monday–Saturday 10am–9.30pm, Sunday noon–6pm.

Victorian Birth Home, 501 Auburn Avenue, tel: 331-3919. Daily June–September, 10am–4.30pm; September–May, 10am–3.30pm.

The World of Coca-Cola Pavilion, 55 Martin Luther King Jr Drive, tel: 676-5151. What else – the world of Coca-Cola and the story of Coca-Cola until one drops. Monday–Saturday 10am–9.30pm, Sunday noon–6pm.

Yellow River Wildlife Game Ranch, 4525 Highway 78, Lilburn, tel: 972-6643. Wildlife reserve with 600 native Georgia animals which can be photographed, fed and petted. Open daily 9.30am–dusk.

Zoo Atlanta, Grant Park, 800 Cherokee Avenue SE, tel: 624-5678. Lots of animals in natural habitats without bars. Daily 10am–4.30pm.

Art Galleries

ATLANTA

Once gallery-poor, Atlanta has moved up in the art world. The best source of up-to-the-date information about openings and traveling exhibits is *Creative Loafing*, the free newspaper. The paper's regular "Happenings" section covers not only galleries, but Atlanta arts festivals and their times, telephones, and admission costs.

Abstein Gallery, 558 14th Street, Midtown, tel: 872-8020. Monday–Friday 8.30am–5.30pm, Saturday 10am–4pm.

Ann Jacob Gallery, 3500 Peachtree Road, Phipps Plaza, Buckhead, tel: 262-3399. Monday–Saturday 10am–9pm, Sunday noon–6pm.

Axis Twenty, 200 Peachtree Hills Avenue, near Buckhead, tel: 261-4022. Monday–Friday, 9am–5.30pm, Saturday 10.30am–1.30pm (Saturday hours from September–April only).

Berman Gallery, 3261 Roswell Road, Buckhead, tel: 261-3858. Tuesday–Saturday 10am–5pm.

Camille Love Gallery, 681 Whitehall Street, Suite 2, downtown, tel: 522-5683. Thursday, Friday, Saturday noon–5pm, and by appointment.

Fay Gold Gallery, 247 Buckhead Avenue, East Village Square, Buckhead, tel: 233-2843. Tuesday–Friday 9.30am–5.30pm, Saturday 10am–6pm.

Geode, 3393 Peachtree Road, Plaza Level, Lenox Square, Buckhead, tel: 261-9346. Monday–Saturday 10am–9.30pm, Sunday 12.30–5.30pm.

Illumina, 3500 Peachtree Road, Phipps Plaza, Buckhead, tel: 233-3010. Monday–Saturday 10am–9pm, Sunday noon–5.30pm.

Jackson Fine Art, 3115 E Shadowlawn Avenue, Buckhead, tel: 233-3739. Tuesday–Saturday 10am–5.30pm.

Modern Primitive Gallery, 1402 N Highland Avenue, Virginia/Highland, tel: 892-0556.

Out of the Woods, 22-B Bennett Street, Buckhead, tel: 351-0446. Monday–Friday 10.30am–5.30pm, Saturday 11am–5pm, Sunday 11am–4pm.

Ray's Indian Originals, 90 N Avondale Road, Avondale Estates, tel: 292-4999. Monday–Saturday 10am–6pm. Call to verify.

The Signature Shop and Gallery, 3267 Roswell Road, Buckhead, tel: 237-4426. Monday–Saturday 10am–5pm.

Yanzum-Village Art, 1285 Peachtree Street NE, tel: 874-8063. Across the street from the High Museum.

Vespermann Gallery, 2140 Peachtree Road, Brookwood Square, Buckhead, tel: 350-9545. Monday–Saturday, 10am–6pm.

Music

Classical

Atlanta Opera, 1800 Peachtree Street, Suite 620, tel: 355-3311. Symphony Hall at Woodruff Arts Center. Atlanta's opera season is spring to fall.

Atlanta Symphony Orchestra, 1293 Peachtree Street, Suite 300, Robert W. Woodruff Arts Center, Midtown, tel: 892 2414 (box office), or tel: 733-4200 (information). A wide array of programs – paid and free – including the Summer Pops Series at Chastain Park, augment the regular season.

Onyx Opera Atlanta, PO Box 90486, Atlanta, GA 30364, tel: 762-1194. Onyx was established to celebrate African-American composers and performers.

Southeastern Savoyards, Center Stage Theater, 1274 West Peachtree Street, tel: 233-7002. Light operetta, October–May, especially Gilbert and Sullivan.

Spivey Hall, 900 N Lee Street, Clayton State College, Morrow, tel: 961-3683 (box office). Monday–Friday 8am–5pm.

There are numerous other bands, orchestras and choral guilds in Atlanta. See the *Atlanta Journal/Constitution*, *Creative Loafing* and *Atlanta Magazine* for information on performances.

JAZZ

Cafe 290, 290 Hilderbrand Drive, Balconies Shopping Center, Sandy Springs, tel: 256-3942. Hours for music: Monday–Sunday 8.30pm–2.30am. No cover.

Dante's Down the Hatch, 3380 Peachtree Road, Buckhead, tel: 266-1600. Hours of music: Tuesday–Thursday 7.30–11.30pm, Friday–Saturday, 7.30pm–12.30am, Sunday 7.30–11pm and 60 Upper Alabama Street, Underground Atlanta, Downtown, tel: 577-1800. Hours of music: Monday–Thursday 7–11.30pm, Friday–Saturday 6.30pm–12.30am, Sunday 6–11pm.

La Carrousel Lounge, 830 Martin Luther King Jr Drive, Paschal's Motor Lodge, near West End, tel: 577-3150. Hours of music: Friday–Saturday 9pm–2am. No cover.

Red Light Cafe, 553 Amsterdam Avenue, tel: 874-7828.

Blues

Blind Willie's, 828 N Highland Avenue, Virginia-Highland, tel: 873-2583. Monday–Sunday 8pm–2am.

Country

Miss Kitty's Saloon & Dance Hall, 1038 Franklin Road, Marietta, tel: 426-9077. Monday–Thursday 7pm–1am, Friday–Saturday 7–2pm. Texas Line Dancing, Two Step and Swing are taught Monday and Tuesday from 8–10pm.

Lanierland, 6115 Jot 'Em Down Road, Cumming, tel: 681-1596.

Local Acoustic Music

Eddie's Attic, 515 McDonough Street, Decatur, tel: 377-4976.

Piano Bar

Jellyrolls in Buckhead, 295 East Paces Ferry Road, tel: 261-6866.

Alternative Music

Dottie's Food & Spirits, 307 Memorial Drive, tel: 523-3444.

Dance

Atlanta Ballet, 477 Peachtree Street, tel: 873-5811, or tel: 892-3303 (tickets). Performances are at the Civic Center, 395 Piedmont Avenue.

Georgia Ballet, 999 Whitlock Avenue, Marietta, tel: 425-0258.

Lee Harper & Dancers, 721 Miami Cir, Suite 106, tel: 261-7416.

There are numerous other ballet and dance troupes in the city. See local newspaper listings for performance schedules.

Theater

Atlanta

The Academy Theatre, PO Box 191306, Atlanta, GA 31119, tel: 365-8088. Georgia's oldest resident professional company.

Agatha's A Taste of Mystery Dinner Theater, 693 Peachtree Street, tel: 875-1610. A five-course dinner plus a light, participatory mystery.

Alliance Theatre Company, 1280 Peachtree Street, Woodruff Arts Center, tel: 898-2414. Classic and contemporary productions, plus the Alliance Children's Theatre.

Center for Puppetry Arts, 1404 Spring Street, tel: 873-3391. Adult and children's performances. Monday–Friday 9am–5pm, Saturday 9am–4pm.

Georgia Shakespeare Festival, 4484 Peachtree Road, north Atlanta, tel: 688-8008. Grounds open for picnics at 6.30pm; performance at 8pm.

Jomandi Productions, 1444 Mayson Street, tel: 876-6346. The state's oldest African-American theater company.

Just Us, PO Box 42271, Atlanta, GA 30311-0271, tel: 753-2399. Performance art by writers Pearl Cleage and Zaron Burnett, Jr.

The Shakespeare Tavern, 499 Peachtree Street, downtown, 874-5299. Hours for performances of the **Atlanta Shakespeare Company**, Thursday–Saturday 7.30pm, Sunday 6.30pm. Food service, priced separately, begins 45 minutes prior to curtain.

Movies

The *Atlanta Journal/Constitution* lists movie houses throughout the city, but there are some special film venues that stand out for their film selections and ambiance.

Cinefest, 66 Collins Street, Suite 218, tel: 651-3565. Films that otherwise would not make it to Atlanta are shown here.

IMAGE Film/Video Center, 75 Bennett Street, Suite M-1, tel: 352-4225. Public screenings of non-commercial films and videos. Don't miss the annual Atlanta Film and Video Festival here.

Lefont Garden Hills Cinema, 2835 Peachtree Road, tel: 266-2202. First-run fine films.

Lefont Screening Room, 2581 Piedmont Road, Lindbergh Plaza, tel: 231-2009. Art and classic films.

North Springs Cinema and Draft House, 7270 Roswell Road, North Springs Shopping Center, Sandy Springs, tel: 395-0724. Beer, wine, snacks and cheaper second-run films.

Silent Film Society, 1968 Peachtree Road, tel: 231-1258. Friday evening, Building 77, Piedmont Hospital Complex.

Architectural Tours

American Institute of Architects, Atlanta Chapter, 231 Peachtree Street, Suite B-04, Peachtree Center, downtown, tel: 222-0099. Monday–Friday 8am–5pm. Offers a tour on the second Sunday of each month to a single architectural site of interest, sometimes historical, sometimes modern, sometimes undergoing renovation. Also will arrange custom tours for groups.

Atlanta Preservation Center, 156 7th Street, Ste 3, Midtown, tel: 876-2040 (recorded tour information). Monday–Friday 9am–5pm. Several walking tours daily at various times, mostly historical points of interest.

Guided Sightseeing Tours

Access Atlanta Tours, 231 Peachtree Street, Atlanta 30303, tel: 523-1325.
Antiquity Tours of the Old South, 20 Willow Lane, Newnan 30263, tel: (800) 251-6343.
Atlanta Heritage Tours, 3404 Falling Brook Drive, Suite B, Marietta 30062, tel: 971-8874.
Artlanta Tours, 25 Ridgemore Trace, Atlanta 30328, tel: 252-0682.
Capital City Coach Lines, 933-F Lee Street, Atlanta 30310, tel: 756-0600.
Eventz Over Georgia, 1219 Oakdale Road, Atlanta 30307, tel: 378-1146.
Gray Line of Atlanta, 3745 Zip Industrial Boulevard, Atlanta 30354, tel: 767-0594.
Historic Air Tours, 1954 Airport Road, Chamblee 30341, tel: 457-5217.
Mansions & Magnolias, 4039 Roscoe Road, Newnan 30263, tel: 251-2109.
Travel Care, 699 Roundtree Road, Riverdale 30296, tel: 994-0485.

Nightlife

Atlanta

To see why nearly every Southerner under the age of 40 wants to live near Atlanta, if not in it, open the "Living" section of Saturday's *Atlanta Constitution* or the weekly free newspaper *Creative Loafing*. Classical and pop music concerts, art exhibits, ballet, dance and theater performances, fes-

tivals, performance artists, stand-up comedy acts, film openings, sports. There is so much going on in Atlanta that it is almost impossible to stay abreast of the listings, let alone attend everything.

Individual interests and tastes dictate one's nightlife ambitions, whether it's an evening spent with wild and wacky Georgia Renaissance Festival devotees dressed up in 16th-century outfits, or an evening down at the Roxy in Buckhead, listening to Leonard Cohen, or perhaps over at the Center For Puppetry Arts, watching *Aesop's Tortoise & The Hare & Other Fables*.

The "Happenings" section of *Creative Loafing* contains comprehensive listings for gay and lesbian activities, events, meetings, picnics, rodeos, and religious services.

Clubs, Pubs, Taverns and Other Watering Holes

Agatha's A Taste of Mystery, 693 Peachtree Street NE, œ block north of the Fox Theatre, tel: 875-1610. Pricey. Features "a five-course dinner with wine and murder," and audience participation between courses. Emphasis is on comedy, the dress is casual. Daily 7.30pm, Sunday 7pm. Three hours.

Backstreet Atlanta, 845 Peachtree Street NE, tel: 873-1986. A four-level complex with X-rated cabaret shows, hard-core dancing, dance lessons, talent nights. Cash required; 21 and over. Weekdays 11am–7am, weekends 24 hours.

Berlin, 5920 Roswell Road NW, just outside the Perimeter, tel: 255-4471. European-style dance club with DJ-hosted music. Predominately straight, with a low cover charge, phenomenal sound and lighting, custom-designed pool tables, large outdoor deck, and a "bubbling water wall." Thursday–Saturday 8.30pm–4am.

Café 290, 290 Hilderbrand Drive NE, Sandy Springs, tel: 256-3942. Live jazz nightly, with reasonable steak, seafood, chicken and pasta entrées. Free parking, no cover. Bar opens 4pm, restaurant 6pm; until 2am week nights, 3am weekends.

Comedy Act Theatre, 917 Peachtree Street, midtown, tel: 875-3550. Originally in Los Angeles, Atlanta's African-American comedians have their own

venue.

County Cork, The Prado, 5600 Roswell Road, tel: 303-1976. Live performances, sometimes with traditional instruments. Irish stew and fried oysters. Monday-Saturday 3pm–2am

Danté's Down the Hatch Jazz Nightclub, 3380 Peachtree Road NE, Buckhead, tel: 266-1600. Jazz by the Paul Mitchell Trio, Tuesday–Sunday. Folk music and guitar, Monday night, Also at 86 Lower Alabama Street, Underground Atlanta, tel: 577-1800, featuring a jazz pianist and The Brothers Three. Monday–Saturday 4pm, Sunday 5pm. Dinner served late at both locations. Reservations urged.

Dark Horse Tavern, 816 North Highland Avenue, Virginia/Highlands, tel: 873-3607. A young, casual crowd gathers upstairs for dinner and drinks, then moves downstairs for live music nightly.

Dave's & Buster's, 2215 D&B Drive SE, Marietta, tel: 951-5554. 53,000 sq. ft (5,000 sq. meters) of everything: full-service restaurant, six bars, pocket billiards and shuffle board, video games, virtual reality, live dance bands, karaoke, murder mystery theatre. Monday–Friday 11am, Saturday and Sunday 11.30am. Closes after midnight.

Eddie's Attic Restaurant & Tavern, 515 North McDonough Street, Decatur, tel: 377-4976. Downtown Decatur, a no-frills tavern fare and mostly acoustic pop folk or contemporary folk music. A great, down-home atmosphere with a young crowd. Daily 4pm–2am.

Good Ol' Days, 3013 Peachtree Road, Buckhead, tel: 266-2597 and at 5841 Roswell Road, Sandy Springs, tel: 257-9183. Successful, casual eateries with good, light fare, acoustic music.

Jellyrolls in Buckhead, 295 East Paces Ferry Road, tel: 261-6866. Piano sing-along bar where your request is their command.

Limerick Junction, 824 N Highland Avenue, Virginia-Highland, tel: 874-7147. Monday–Wednesday 5pm–1am, Thursday–Saturday 5pm–2am, Sunday 5pm–12 midnight.

Mama's Country Showcase, 3952 Covington Highway, tel: 288-MAMA. Have to have a 3,000-sq. ft (280-sq. meter) dance floor and a mechanical bull with your brew? This is the place.

Manuel's Tavern, 602 North Highland

Avenue, Poncey/Highland, tel: 525-3447. This tavern dates from 1956, and Atlantans of every persuasion rub shoulders here. If in search of *the* Atlanta bar, this might just be it.

The Masquerade, 695 North Avenue NE, tel: 577-8178. Death metal to reggae to alternative rock. This three-level (Heaven, Purgatory and Hell) dance club features disco and dominatrix nights, live bands in Heaven, pool tables and video games in Purgatory. Daily 9pm–3am.

Miss Kitty's Saloon & Dancehall, 1038 Franklin Road SE, Marietta, tel: 424-6556. Tight-fitting-jeans/bikini-dance/best-chest-in-the-West competitions, karaoke, line-dance contests with cash prizes. Urban cowboys, belly up to this bar.

The Prince of Wales, 1144 Piedmont Avenue NE, tel: 876-0227. A real English pub for homesick British visitors.

The Punch Line, 280 Hilderbrand Drive NE, Sandy Springs, tel: 252-5233. Stand-up comedy. Jay Leno, Robin Williams and Eddie Murphy have hung their hats here. Generally three comics nightly, 2-hour shows. Thursday and Friday shows are nonsmokers only.

Red Light Café, 553 Amsterdam Avenue, tel: 874-7828. Jazz on Sunday at dusk, and acoustic music other nights.

Rupert's Nightclub, 3330 Piedmont Road NE, tel: 266-9834. No jeans, T-shirts and tennis shoes allowed. A Happy Hour Buffet served Tueday, Thursday and Friday. This 28,000-sq. ft (2,600-sq. meter) venue features the 12-piece Rupert's Orchestra: Top 40 tunes, Big Band tunes, and DJ-hosted music between the four nightly sets. Seven full-service bars.

The Star Community Bar, 437 Moreland Avenue NE, tel: 681-9018. Across the street from acoustic-café.

Eat Your Vegetables, this former bank building features rhythm & blues and alternative rock. It has received awards for best local music and is a cheap, safe place. Order from either The Elvis or The Elvez (Tex-Mex) menu.

Taco Mac, 5830 Roswell Road NW, Sandy Springs, tel: 257-0735. According to *Atlanta Magazine*, this bar has Atlanta's best draft beer selection with over 100 brews.

Velvet, 89 Park Place, downtown, tel: 681-9978. Whether it's "Techno Rave," Miami/Latin Dance, "Aphro-dite's Nite-Out," or "Disco Hell," Velvet's theme nights are baroque, gender-blurring, and hot. Not for nothing did U2 hang out here when in town.

The Vortex, 1041 West Peachtree Street NE, tel: 875-1667. Midtown's down-home neighborhood bar.

Gay & Lesbian Atlanta

Atlanta's large and outspoken gay and lesbian community has an excellent newspaper covering international, national, Atlanta and community news – *Southern Voice: Taking Pride In Our Culture*, available throughout the city, tel: 876-1819 for information. The "Out & About" section includes a calendar of events which covers performances, exhibits, picnics, parties, outings, festivals, etc. A listings section details AIDS, cultural, political, professional and service organizations, as well as bars, spiritual groups, sports clubs and student and alumni organizations. *Creative Loafing* is also a good paper for the gay population, as is the free publication *Etcetera*.

Savannah

The Bottom Line, 206 West Julian Street, City Market, tel: (912) 232-0812. Live jazz, swing, and big band music enliven dancing here.

Comedy House Theatre, 711 Mall Boulevard, tel: (912) 356-1045. Live comedy accompanied by dining.

The Cross Roads, 219 West Julian Street, City Market, tel: (912) 234-5438. Blues, live music, dancing.

Hannah's Live Jazz at Trustee's Garden, 20 East Broad Street, The Pirate's House, tel: (912) 233-5757. Jazz, live music, dining.

Slickers, 9 West Bay Street, tel: (912) 233-6999. Top 40 popular hits plus dancing.

Wet Willies, 101 East River Street, tel: (912) 233-5650. Rock and karaoke, dancing, dining.

Festivals

Atlanta

The single best source of information about scheduled and impromptu events in Atlanta is *Atlanta Now: The Official Visitor Guide of the Atlanta Convention & Visitors Bureau*, published bimonthly. 233 Peachtree Street, Suite 2000, Atlanta, GA 30303, tel: 521-6600. In an average two-month period, the *Guide* lists over 100 scheduled events, an indication of the wealth of cultural, sporting and civic activities offered in Atlanta.

Ticket agencies for concerts and other events:
Atlantix, tel: 455-7141.
Ticketmaster, tel: 249-6400.

Athens

Athens Welcome Center, 280 East Dougherty Street, tel: (706) 353-1820.

Savannah

Savannah Visitors Center, 301 Martin Luther King Jr Boulevard, tel: (912) 944-0455.

Diary of Regular Events

Atlanta

January/February

The Peach Bowl, the post-season collegiate football play-off game is played at the Georgia Dome, usually scheduled for late December/early January. Parade. Tel: 586-8500.

Martin Luther King Jr Week is celebrated the second week in January, commemorating Dr King's birthday. A host of activities, performances and gatherings culminate in a "March of Celebration." The third Monday in January is a national holiday for Dr King's birthday. The Martin Luther King Jr Center for Nonviolent Social Change, tel: 524-1956.

Atlanta's **Mardi Gras Parade** is the Friday before Fat Tuesday in February. An after-dark event featuring fancy dress, floats and marching bands, the cavalcade proceeds through downtown Atlanta to Underground, tel: 392-1272.

The Atlanta Flower Show, February/early March, is a massive exhibition of flower, vegetable and other gardens, including gardening demonstrations and products plus special events. Atlanta Apparel Mart, tel: 220-2115.

March/April

Easter falls in March or April, and non-denominational sunrise services are celebrated on the summit of Stone Mountain. Stone Mountain Park, tel: 498-5600.

Atlanta Boat Show features watercraft – from dinghies to cabin cruisers and watersporting gear. Early March, tel: 998-9800.

St Patrick's Day Parade, March 17, begins at the intersection of Peachtree Street and Ralph McGill Boulevard, and winds up at Underground Atlanta. Bands, bagpipes and beer. Attire is informal, but green. Another St Patrick's Day Parade is in Buckhead, setting out from around East Paces Ferry Road and Bolling Way, proceeding to Pharr Road.

The **Atlanta Steeplechase**, featuring the races, of course, but also antique autos. Benefits the Atlanta Speech School. Tickets for this event, usually the first Saturday in April, are by mail only. Atlanta Steeplechase, 3160 Northside Parkway, Atlanta, GA 30327, tel: 237-7436.

The Atlanta Dogwood Festival is Atlanta's premier annual event, over a two-week period in April. House and garden tours, sporting and musical events in Piedmont Park culminate in a weekend fest in the park, usually mid-April. 1360 Powers Ferry Road, Marietta, tel: 952-9151.

The Atlanta Ballet spring performances are scheduled from March–May at the Atlanta Civic Center, 477 Peachtree Street, tel: 873-5811 for information, tel: 892-3303 for tickets. Stone Mountain Park is the site of the **Antebellum Jubilee**, held the first two weekends in April. Civil War encampment, concerts using period instruments, and late 19th-century arts and crafts, tel: 498-5702.

Inman Park Spring Festival and Tour of Homes, is held on the last weekend in April, a benefit which furthers restoration work in Inman Park, a Victorian residential area established after the Civil War. Historic home tours, guided walks, musical events, crafts and a parade. Inman Park, Atlanta, tel: 242-4895.

Georgia Renaissance Festival, held over a seven-week period from April–June, it recreates a balmy, ersatz 18th-century encampment in Fairburn. Craftspeople, "fools," knights and their ladies, even Henry VIII attend in period costume, or a reasonable imitation, tel: 242-4895.

A Taste of Atlanta is held over three days, usually at CNN Center, to benefit the Kidney Foundation. Atlanta restaurants participate, and strolling diners may sample their edible wares for a fraction of menu prices. Fireworks displays and live music accompany grazing, tel: 248-1315.

The **Atlanta Braves** baseball season runs April to October at the Atlanta/Fulton County Stadium, tel: 577-9100 for tickets.

May/June

The **Atlanta Storytelling Festival** is sponsored in May by the Southern Order of Storytellers and the Atlanta Historical Society. The Atlanta History Center, tel: 261-1837.

The **Atlanta Film and Video Festival** held in May for five days, is a juried show of independent works. IMAGE Film and Video Center, tel: 352-4225.

The **Bell South Classic** is a major golf tournament at the Atlanta Country Club staged to benefit Egleston Children's Hospital and attended by some 125,000 annually. Call for tickets well in advance, tel: 951-8777.

Atlanta's **Gay Pride Parade** proceeds from the Civic Center to Piedmont Park on a Sunday in June, National Gay Pride Month, tel: 662-4533.

The **Atlanta Jazz Festival** is a major event in June, sponsored by Atlanta's Bureau of Cultural Affairs and with free events and performances by local and internationally-known musicians. Grant Park. Bureau of Cultural Affairs, City of Atlanta, tel: 653-7160.

The **Atlanta Symphony Orchestra's Summer Concert Series** is held June–August at the Chastain Park Amphitheatre, tel: 892-2414 (box office), or tel: 898-1182 (administrative offices). The **Georgia Shakespeare Festival** is held on the grounds of Oglethorpe University, June–August. Al fresco performances and other events, tel: 264-0020.

July/August

Independence Day events and parades abound in Atlanta on or about the Fourth of July. Major events include the **Fantastic Fourth Celebration** at Georgia's Stone Mountain Park, tel: 498-5702; **Independence Day at Lenox Square** mall, tel: 233-6767; the **WSB Salute 2 America Parade**, tel: 897-7385; and *the* big event for run-

ners, the **Peachtree Road Race**, run by some 45,000 participants who pound the course from Lenox Square to Piedmont Park. Includes a Wheelchair Division and Master's Division. Atlanta Track Club, tel: 231-9065.

The **Civil War Encampment** at the Atlanta History Centre, featuring living-history interpreters in authentic period dress, relives the lives of soldiers and their families, both Union and Confederate. Tel: 814-4000.

The **National Black Arts Festival** celebrates the skills and talents of African-American artists, even-numbered years only, in August, tel: 730-7315.

Atlanta International Food and Wine Festival, hosted at Buckhead hotels and includes wine tastings and seminars, early in August, tel: 873-4482.

The **Atlanta Falcons football** season runs from August to December; home games at the Georgia Dome, tel: 261-5400.

September/October

Around Labor Day, the six-day-long **Montreaux Atlanta International Music Festival** is held in Piedmont Park, and free concerts feature nationally- and internationally-known artists. Paid concerts in Atlanta theatres and other venues are also scheduled. Tel: 653-7160.

Yellow Daisy Festival, hosted at Stone Mountain Park during September, to celebrate the blooming of the Confederate Yellow Daisy with a massive outdoor arts and crafts show, flower show, live entertainment and more. Tel: 498-5702.

Arts Festival of Atlanta in Piedmont Park is a huge outdoor event lasting nine days in mid-September and attracting some two million visitors. Art for sale, performing arts, food and children's events. Tel: 885-1125.

Atlanta Greek Festival highlights modern Hellenic culture and cuisine – primarily the latter – at the Orthodox Cathedral of the Annunciation, tel: 633-5870.

Atlanta Hawks basketball lasts October–March, games at the Omni Coliseum, tel: 681-2100.

The **Atlanta Symphony Orchestra Winter Pops** (Tel: 892-2414) and the **Atlanta Ballet** (Tel: 873-5011) perform during autumn and winter.

Scottish Festival and Highland Games is October's big draw, and held at

Stone Mountain Park. Kilted clans competing in myriad ways, pipe bands, folk dancing, traditional foods, sales of Scottish and Celtic books, tapes and tartans, as well as lots of fiddling and sword dancing. Tel: 634-7402.

Atlanta's Great Miller Lite Chili Cookoff is another October highlight at Stone Mountain for those with stomachs of iron. Chili dogs, Brunswick Stew, hot peppers and lots of silly fun are the side orders, but chili, dished up by competing cook-off teams from around the south, is the main course.

The **Decatur Heritage Festival**, scheduled for early October on Decatur's Courthouse Square, features the work of regional craftspeople as well as down-home music. Dekalb Historical Society, tel: 373-1088.

November/December

Veterans' Day Parade winds its way November 11th from Peachtree & West Peachtree streets to Woodruff Park, complete with all the time-honored American trappings: floats, marching bands, drill teams and patriotic pomp and circumstance.

The **Atlanta Marathon and Half-Marathon** are run on Thanksgiving Day, from Lithonia to Piedmont Park. Atlanta Track Club, tel: 231-9065.

The **Lighting of the Great Tree** happens on Thanksgiving night at Underground Atlanta's Peachtree Fountains, tel: 523-2311.

Christmas at Callanwolde, scheduled at the Callanwolde Fine Arts Center, is a children's, consumers' and spectators' delight. For two weeks in December, this Tudor home fills with specialty shops, carollers, merrymakers and Santa. 980 Briarcliff Road NE, tel: 872-5338.

The **Annual Candlelight Tour of Bulloch Hall**, Roswell, treats visitors to a re-enactment of the marriage of Mittie Bulloch to Cornelius Van Schaak Roosevelt, solemnized in 1853. For **Christmas at Bulloch Hall**, tel: 992-1731.

The **Egleston Children's Christmas Parade and Festival of Trees** is a major Atlanta event, staged to benefit Egleston Children's Hospital. Features Christmas trees decorated by area artists and donated for auction. Georgia World Congress Center, tel: 325-NOEL. The parade, Atlanta's most sumptuous, proceeds from Marietta and

Spring streets to West Peachtree Street and Ralph McGill Boulevard. Tel: 264-9348.

Athens

Contact the Athens Convention and Visitors Bureau for a schedule of events and a valuable Visitors Value Package. PO Box 948, Athens, GA 30603, tel: (706) 546-1805, (800) 653-0603. For an Antebellum Trail brochure, write Antebellum Trail, PO Box 219, Milledgeville, GA 31061.

Savannah

February
1st Saturday Festival.
Georgia Heritage Celebration, tel: (912) 233-7787.
Savannah Irish Festival, tel: (800) 436-3746.
American Traditions Competition, tel: (912) 236-5745.

March
Savannah Onstage, tel: (912) 236-5745.
Tara Feis, Irish Festival, tel: (912) 651-6417.
St Patrick's Day Parade and Celebration, tel: (912) 233-4804.
Annual Savannah Tour of Homes and Gardens, tel: (912) 233-7706.

April
Seafood Festival.
The Hidden Gardens of Historic Savannah, tel: (912) 238-0248.
Siege and Reduction (of Fort Pulaski) Weekend.
Blessing of the Fleet.
Sidewalk Arts Festival.

May
International Day/1st Saturday Festival.
Arts-on-the-River Weekend.
Scottish Games and Highland Gathering, tel: (912) 964-4951.
The War of Jenkins' Ear at Wormsloe Historic Site, commemorating the first official war fought by Georgians.

June
1st Saturday Festival.
Downtown Saturday Night.

July
Great American Fourth of July, tel: (912) 234-0295.

Fireworks on the Beach.
Thunderbolt Seafood Harvest Festival.
Savannah Maritime Festival, tel: (912) 238-4434.

August
Maritime 1st Saturday Festival.

September
1st Saturday Festival.
Savannah Jazz Festival.
Open House at Skidaway Marine Science Complex.

October
Octoberfest on the River.
Jewish Food Festival, tel: (912) 233-1547.
Savannah Greek Festival, tel: (912) 236-8256.

November
1st Saturday Festival.
Christmas Made in the South, tel: (704) 847-9480.

December
Holiday Ice Skating.
Christmas Tour of Inns.
Holiday Tour of Homes, tel: (912) 236-TDNA.
Christmas on the River. Parades, tree lighting, Santa.

Others

Cotton Pickin' Country Fair, Gay, GA, tel: (706) 538-6814. May and October.
Powers Crossroads Country Fair and Arts Festival, near Newnan, tel: 253-2011. Labor Day weekend. September.
Stone Mountain Park, Highway 78, Stone Mountain, tel: 498-5600 (switchboard); 498-5702 (information). Daily 6am–midnight.

Atlanta

It could just be that the entire south comes to Atlanta to shop. Whether wholesale buyers from the hinterlands or affluent homeowners cruising Bennett Street antique stores, Atlanta is a mecca for consumers.

Where to start? Whether here for two days or two weeks, most head for the malls: Lenox Square, Phipps Plaza,

Perimeter and The Galleria, among others. More specific suggestions are sprinkled throughout this book. Museum gift shops, such as those at the High Museum of Art or Fernbank, are also good places to begin.

Size Chart

Women's Dresses/Suits

American	Continental	British
6	38/34N	8/30
8	40/36N	10/32
10	42/38N	12/34
12	44/40N	14/36
14	46/42N	16/38
16	48/44N	18/40

Women's Shoes

American	Continental	British
4½	36	3
5½	37	4
6½	38	5
7½	39	6
8½	40	7
9½	4	18
10½	4	29

Men's Suits

American	Continental	British
34	44	34
—	46	36
38	48	38
—	50	40
42	52	42
—	54	44
46	56	46

Men's Shirts

American	Continental	British
14	36	14
14½	37	14½
15	38	15
15½	39	15½
16	40	16
16½	41	16½
17	42	17

Men's Shoes

American	Continental	British
6½	—	6
7½	40	7
8½	41	8
9½	42	9
10½	43	10
11½	44	11

WOMEN'S RETAIL CLOTHING
UP-MARKET
Bebe, Phipps Plaza, tel: 261-8345.
Neiman Marcus, Lenox Square Mall, tel: 266-8200.

Parisian (department store), Phipps Plaza, Buckhead, tel: 814-3310.
CASUAL
The Snappy Turtle, 110 East Andrews Drive, tel: 237-8341.
BARGAINS
Lana's Discount Designer Apparel, 3019 Peachtree Road NE, tel: 237-4225.
AJS Shoe Warehouse, 1788 Ellsworth Industrial Boulevard, tel: 355-1760.

MEN'S RETAIL CLOTHING
H Stockton Atlanta, 210 Peachtree Street NW, tel: 523-7741.
Mark Shale, Lenox Square, tel: 231-0600.
Sebastian's Closet, 3222 Peachtree Road NE, tel: 365-9033.

FOLK AND AFRICAN ART
See Galleries *above.*

CARDS
Maddix Deluxe, 1034 North Highland Avenue, tel: 892-9337. Cards, candies, garden accessories, bath and bed accoutrements.

TOYS
The Toy School, 5517 Chamblee Dunwoody Road, Dunwoody, tel: 399-5350.

BOOKS
Oxford Books, 360 Pharr Road, tel: 262-3333. Bargain books.
Book Warehouse, 1831 Peachtree Road, tel: 352-8000.

ELECTRONICS
Best Buy, Cumberland Mall, tel: 859-9266.
SPORTS SHOES
Nike Town, Phipps Plaza, tel: 841-6444.

Travel Accessories & Guides

The Civilized Traveller, Phipps Plaza, tel: 264-1252.

CD's, Videos and Cassettes
Turtle's Rhythm and Views, 2099 Peachtree Road NE, tel: 606-7131.

GROCERIES
Kroger Store, 3330 Piedmont Road NE, Buckhead, tel: 237-8022. Open 24 hrs a day.

Sevananda Natural Foods, 1111 Euclid Avenue NE, Little Five Points, tel: 681-2831.

RETRO HABERDASHERY
The Junkman's Daughter, 1130 Euclid Avenue NE, Little Five Points, tel: 577-3188.

ATHENS
CLOTHING
Almanac, 333 East Broad Street, tel: (706) 543-8038.
Heery's, 195 College Avenue, tel: (706) 543-0702.
Moonshine, 265 East Clayton Street, tel: (706) 208-1997.
Recollections, 255 East Clayton Street, tel: (706) 549-9680.
The Traffic Light, Beechwood Shopping Center, tel: (706) 546-5313.

JEWELRY
Aurum Studios Ltd, 125 East Clayton Street, tel: (706) 546-8826.

SPORTS SHOES & CLOTHING
Sports Appeal, Beechwood Shopping Center, tel: (706) 354-0278.

SAVANNAH
Oglethorpe Mall, 7804 Abercorn Street, tel: (912) 354-7038.
Savannah Festival Factory Stores, 11 Gateway Boulevard, South, tel: (912) 925-3089.
Savannah Mall, Rio Road and Abercorn Ext, tel: (912) 927-SHOP.

Sports

Atlanta is sports-crazed, a city in motion. The following is only a smattering of listings. Once again, consult *Creative Loafing* or your hotel concierge regarding your favorite sport. Whether kayaking or boxing or even "disc" golf, chances are someone is doing it.

ATLANTA
PARTICIPANT
Archery
Buckskin Archery, 2396 Cobb Parkway, Kennesaw, tel: 425-2697.

Baseball
Cherokee Batting Range, 711 Bascomb Commercial Park, North. Bell's Ferry Road, Woodstock, tel: 591-4778.

McDivot's Driving Range, 1360 Upper Hembree Road, Roswell, tel: 740-1674. Also for golf.
Softball Country Club, 3500 North Decatur Road, Clarkston, tel: 299-3588.

Boating
Lake Lanier Islands, 6950 Holiday Road, Lake Lanier Islands, Buford, tel: 932-7255.
Lake Lanier Sailing Academy, 6950 Holiday Road, Lake Lanier Islands, tel: 945-8810.

Canoeing
Chattahoochee Nature Center, 9135 Willeo Road, Roswell, tel: 992-2055. April–September, early evening trips.
Southeastern Expeditions, 2936-H Druid Hills Road NE, tel: 329-0433. Rafting, canoeing and kayaking expeditions, April–October.

Cricket
Atlanta Cricket Association, 4660 Bush Road, Duluth, GA 30136, tel: 263-6460.

Cycling
Cycle South, 7210 Highway 85, Riverdale, tel: 991-6642.
Free Flite Bicycles, 1950 Canton Road, Marietta, tel: 422-5237.
My Champ, 3522 Clairmont Road, NE, tel: 633-6023.
Roswell Bicycles, 670 Houze Way, Roswell, tel: 642-4057.

Equestrian
Lake Lanier Islands Stables, 6950 Holiday Road, Lake Lanier Islands, tel: 932-7233. Daily trail rides.

Fishing
Bill Vanderford's Guide Service, 2224 Pine Point Drive, Lawrenceville, tel: 962-1241.
Chattahoochee Fishing Guide Service, PO Box 1563, Gainesville, GA 30503, tel: (706) 536-7986.

Golf
Bobby Jones Golf Course, 384 Woodward Way, Atlanta Memorial Park NW, tel: 355-1009 or tel: 355-1833.
Eagle Watch Country Club, 3055 Eagle Watch Drive, Woodstock, tel: 591-1000.
Lake Lanier Islands Golf Club, 7000 Holiday Road, Lake Lanier Islands, tel:

945-8787.
The Links Golf Club, 340 Howell Mill Road, Jonesboro, tel: 461-5100.
Orchard Hills Golf Club, 600 East Highway 16, Newnan. Exit 8 on I-85 South, tel: 880-9414.
Southerness Golf Club, 4871 Flat Bridge Road, Stockbridge, tel: 808-6000.
Stone Mountain Park Golf Course, Stone Mountain, tel: 498-5717.
Stouffer Pineisle Resort, 9000 Holiday Road, Lake Lanier Islands, tel: 945-8922.
Sugar Creek Golf Course, 2706 Bouldercrest Road SE, tel: 241-7671.

Hiking
Chattahoochee River National Recreation Area, 1978 Island Ford Parkway, Dunwoody, tel: 394-8324, 399-8070.

Rafting
Wildwater Rafting, PO Box 309, Long Creek, SC 29658, tel: (800) 451-9972.

Rock Climbing
High Country, 595 Piedmont Avenue, RIO Shopping Center, tel: 892-0909.

Rowing
Atlanta Rowing Club, 500 Azalea Drive. Roswell, tel: 993-1870.

Running
Atlanta Track Club, 3097 East Shadowlawn Avenue, Buckhead, tel: 231-9064.

Skiing
Atlanta Ski Club, 6303 Barfield Road, Sandy Springs, tel: 255-4800.

Tennis
Atlanta Lawn Tennis Association, 1140 Hammond Drive, Sandy Springs, tel: 399-5788.
Peachtree World of Tennis, 6200 Peachtree Corners Circle, Norcross, tel: 449-6060.

SPECTATOR
Baseball
Atlanta Braves, Atlanta Fulton County Stadium, 521 Capitol Avenue, downtown. Single tickets are best purchased (and most conveniently) through Ticketmaster, tel: 249-6400. Group/season tickets and information, tel: 577-9100.

Basketball
Atlanta Hawks, Omni Coliseum, 100 Techwood Drive. Single tickets are best purchased (and most conveniently) through Ticketmaster, tel: 249-6400. Group tickets/information, tel: 827-3865. Omni Coliseum, tel: 681-2100.

Football
Atlanta Falcons, The Georgia Dome, downtown. Single tickets are best purchased through Ticketmaster, 249-6400. Group tickets and information, tel: 223-8400.

Tennis
Atlanta Thunder, 1720 Peachtree Street, Suite 1022, Atlanta 30309. Part of the professional World Team Tennis. Matches held in July and August. Group tickets and information, tel: 881-8811. Individual tickets must be bought through Ticketmaster, tel: 249-6400.

Other
Atlanta Knights (hockey), 100 Techwood Drive, downtown, tel: 525-5800.
Atlanta Motor Speedway, Highway 19-41, Hampton, tel: 946-4211.
Georgia Institute of Technology, 225 North Avenue, midtown, tel: 894-5400 (athletic information), 894-5447 (tickets).
Road Atlanta, 5300 Winder Way, Braselton, tel: 881-8233.

THE 1996 OLYMPICS
Eight million tickets for the 1996 Summer Olympic Games in Atlanta – the XXXVI Olympiad – went on the market in 1995. The events, scheduled from 20 July–4 August 1996, will be held within "The Olympic Ring," an imaginary circle with a radius of 1½ miles (2.5 km) extending from the Georgia World Congress Center through the heart of the city. Six events will be held at the 3,200-acre (1,300-hectares) Olympic Park at Stone Mountain. Yachting events will be held off the coast of Savannah.

More information about ticketing and availability may be obtained from the Georgia Department of Industry, Trade and Tourism, PO Box 1776, Atlanta, GA 30301-1776, tel: 656-2566; fax 651-9063. (In fact, just about everything one might want to know about the State of Georgia is contained in department's official travel guide, *Georgia On My Mind*, published jointly with Publication Concepts Inc, 1240 Johnson Ferry Place, Suite E-10, Marietta, GA 30068, tel: 578-0778, or toll free (800) 875-0778; fax: 578-0676.

ATHENS
Collegiate Baseball, Basketball and Football
University of Georgia Bulldogs, PO Box 1472, Athens, GA 30613, tel: (706) 542-1231.

SAVANNAH
Savannah has major recreation parks that provide everything from tennis courts and soccer fields to a Fragrant Garden for the Blind (Forsyth Park). There are fishing piers, campgrounds and golf courses, bowling centers and a water park. Deep-sea fishing, sightseeing and dolphin feeding charters may be booked from a number of marinas.

Recreation Parks
Bacon Park, Skidaway Road and Bacon Park Drive. Tennis, archery, baseball, golf, softball.

Daffin Park, 1500 East Victory Drive. Baseball, soccer, basketball, tennis, playgrounds, swimming pool, picnic area, Grayson Stadium.

Forsyth Park, Gaston and Whitaker streets. Tennis, softball, playgrounds, scenic fountain, Fragrant Garden for the Blind.

Kings Ferry, Highway 17 South on Ogeechee River. Boating, swimming, fishing, water skiing, picnic area, playground, overnight camping.

Lake Mayer, Montgomery Crossroad and Sallie Mood Drive. Playground, basketball, tennis, lighted jogging and cycling trail, motorcross bike course, volleyball, baseball, fishing, pedal boats, wheelchair fitness court.

Louis Scott Stell Park, off Bush Road SW. Tennis, basketball, model airplane flying area, motorcross, picnic area, boat rentals, tent camping, trails, sports complex.

For hunting and fishing licenses, contact Wildlife Resources Division, Route 2, Box 219R, Richmond Hill, GA 31324.

Following Up
Films on Video

A wide array of American films dealing with or filmed on location in Georgia are available on video. The following films offer a moving introduction to Atlanta and environs, past and present.

The Big Chill, 1983
Yuppies – former 1960s hippies and activists – meet for the funeral of one of their friends, coming to terms with change and alienation at the South Carolina home of another member of the tribe (Kevin Kline). Writer-director Lawrence Kasdan directs Tom Berenger, Glenn Close, Jeff Goldblum, JoBeth Williams and Mary Kay Place.

The Color Purple, 1985
Directed by Steven Spielberg, starring Danny Glover, Whoopi Goldberg, Margaret Avery and Oprah Winfrey, this is Alice Walker's Pulitzer Prize-winning story of life in rural poverty, and escape from same, in rural Georgia, 1906-37.

Driving Miss Daisy, 1989
Alfred Uhry's stage play was the basis for this film set in Atlanta, and centers on racial prejudice and anti-Semitism in mid-20th century America, in general, and Druid Hills, in particular. Jessica Tandy, Morgan Freeman and Dan Akroyd, directed by Bruce Beresford.

Fried Green Tomatoes, 1991
Based on Fannie Flagg's *Fried Green Tomatoes at the Whistle Stop Cafe*. Set in rural 1930s Alabama, the story deals with racism, homophobia and the importance of the South's oral tradition in providing a sense of history and belonging. Directed by John Avnet, starring Kathy Bates, Jessica Tandy, Mary Stuart Masterson and Mary-Louise Parker.

Glory, 1989
Edward Zwick directed this glorious tribute to the Union Army's African-American soldiers. Set in South Caro-

lina, the film stars Matthew Broderick, Denzel Washington and Morgan Freeman.

Gone With The Wind, 1939
This classic was based on Atlanta journalist Margaret Mitchell's novel about the Civil War and Reconstruction in Georgia. Vivien Leigh as Scarlett O'Hara, Clark Gable as Rhett Butler. Directed by Victor Fleming.

Rambling Rose, 1991
Precocious 19-year-old housekeeper Rose (Laura Dern) seduces an entire family of respectable 1930s Georgians, altering their lives forever. Based on an autobiographical novel by Atlanta-born author Calder Willingham, the film also stars Robert Duvall, Diane Ladd and Lukas Haas. Martha Coolidge directed.

Steel Magnolias, 1989
Herbert Ross directed this melodrama about the unity of southern women through triumph and tears. Sally Field, Dolly Parton, Shirley MacLaine, Daryl Hannah, Olympia Dukakis, Julia Roberts, Sam Shepard and Tom Skerritt.

Books

Many of these books are available at Oxford Books, 2345 Peachtree Road NE, tel: 364-2700; Oxford Books at Buckhead, 360 Pharr Road NE, tel: 262-3333.

General

A City of Neighborhoods, photography by Joseph F. Thompson, narrative by Robert Isbell. University of South Carolina Press, Columbia, SC, 1993.
A Selection of Nineteenth Century Homes in Historic Marietta, Georgia, by Elizabeth Atherton and Meredith Rambo. Marietta GA, 1976.
A Walking Tour of the University of Georgia, by F.N. Boney. University of Georgia Press, Athens, 1989.
Across Atlanta: A Resident's Guide, by Jane Schneider and Marge McDonald. Peachtree Publishers, Ltd, Atlanta, 1992.
AIA Guide to the Architecture of Atlanta, by Isabelle Gournay with photographs by Paul G. Beswick. The University of Georgia Press, Athens,

Georgia, and London, 1993.

American Classicist – The Architecture of Philip Trammell Shutze, by Elizabeth M. Dowling. Rizzoli International, New York, 1989.

Architecture of Neel Reid in Georgia, by James Grady. University of Georgia Press, Athens, 1973.

Atlanta and Environs, A Chronicle of its People and Events, Vols I and II, by Franklin M. Garrett. University of Georgia Press, Athens, 1954.

Atlanta and Environs, A Chronicle of Its People and Events, Vol III, by Harold H. Martin. University of Georgia Press, Athens, 1987.

Atlanta Architecture, the Victorian Heritage: 1837–1918, by Elizabeth A. Lyon. Atlanta Historical Society, 1976.

Atlanta City Directory, by Atlanta City Directory Company. Various publishers, 1870–1992.

Atlanta Walks: A Guide to Walking, Running, and Bicycling Historic and Scenic Atlanta, by Ren and Helen Davis. Peachtree Publishers Ltd, Atlanta, 1993.

Atlanta's Lasting Landmarks. Atlanta Urban Design Commission, Atlanta, 1987.

Atlanta, 1847–1890, City Building in the Old South and the New, by James Michael Russell. Louisiana State University Press, 1988.

Atlanta, A City of the Modern South, by Writers Program of the Work Projects Administration. Smith and Durrell, 1942.

Atlanta, Triumph of a People, by Norman Shavin and Bruce Galphin. Capricorn Corporation, Atlanta, 1982.

Automobile Age Atlanta, The Making of a Southern Metropolis 1900–1935, by Howard L. Preston. University of Georgia Press, Athens, 1979.

Classic Atlanta, by Van Jones Martin and William R Mitchell, Jr. St Martin Publishing, New Orleans, 1991.

Emory University 1915–1965, A Semicentennial History, by Thomas H. English. Higgins-McArthur and Co., Atlanta, 1966.

Engineering the New South, Georgia Tech 1885–1985, by Ronald H. Bayor and others. University of Georgia Press, Athens, 1985.

From Plantation to Peachtree, by Robert M. Craig and others. Haas Publishing Co., Atlanta, 1987.

Gardens of Georgia, by William R. Mitchell and Richard J. Moore.

Peachtree Publishers, Atlanta, 1987.

Geologic Guide to Panola Mountain State Park – Rock Outcrop Trail, by Robert L. Atkins and Martha M. Griffin. State of Georgia Dept. of Natural Resources, 1977.

Georgia's Stone Mountain, by Willard Neal. Stone Mountain Memorial Association, Atlanta, 1970.

Henry Grady's New South: Atlanta, A Brave and Beautiful City, by Harold E. Davis. University of Alabama Press, 1990.

Historical Guide for Kennesaw Mountain National Battlefield Park and Marietta, Georgia, by Bowling C. Yates. Kennesaw Mountain Historical Association, Marietta GA, 1976.

Identifying American Architecture, A Pictorial Guide to Styles and Terms, 1600–1945, by John J.G. Blumenson. American Association for State and Local History, Nashville TN, 1981.

Inside Buckhead: Special 150th Anniversary Edition. Inside Publishing, Atlanta, Summer 1988.

Insight Pocket Guide: Atlanta, by Elizabeth Boleman-Herring. Apa Publications, Singapore, 1994.

Landmark Homes of Georgia 1783–1983, Two Hundred Years of Architecture, Interiors and Gardens, by Van Jones Martin and William R. Mitchell, Jr. Golden Coast Publishing, Savannah, 1982.

Living Atlanta, An Oral History of the City, 1914–1948, by Clifford M. Kuhn and others. University of Georgia Press, Athens, 1990.

Morris Brown College, The First Hundred Years, by George A. Sewell and Cornelieus V. Troup. Morris Brown College, Atlanta, 1981.

New Men, New Cities, New South: Atlanta, Nashville, Charleston, Mobile, 1860–1910, by Don H. Doyle. University of North Carolina Press, 1990.

Oakland Cemetery: Atlanta's Most Tangible Link. Oakland Cemetery, Inc., Atlanta, 1977.

Olmsted South: Old South Critic/New South Planner, edited by Dana F. White and Victor A. Kramer. Greenwood Press, 1979.

Sojourn in Savannah, An Official Guidebook of Savannah and the Surrounding Countryside. Franklin S. Traub Trust, 1990.

The Antebellum Plantation at Georgia's Stone Mountain Park, by Nor-

man Shavin. Capricorn Corporation, Atlanta, 1985.

The Battle of Atlanta and the Georgia Campaign, by William Key. Peachtree Publishers, Atlanta, 1981.

The Georgia Catalogue – Historic American Building Survey, A Guide to the Architecture of the State, by John Linley. University of Georgia Press, Athens, 1982.

The Guide to the Architecture of Georgia, by Tom Spector and Susan Owings. University of South Carolina Press, Columbia, 1993.

The Old in New Atlanta, A Directory of Houses, Buildings and Churches Built Prior to 1915 Still Standing in the Mid-1970s in Atlanta and Environs, by Jane F. Matthews and Elizabeth M Sawyer. JEMS Publications, Atlanta, 1978.

The Story of Atlanta University 1865–1965, by Clarence A. Bacote. Princeton University Press, Princeton NJ, 1969.

The Story of Decatur, 1823–1899, by Caroline McKinney Clarke. Higgins-McArthur/Longino and Porter, Atlanta, 1973.

The Story of Spelman College, by Florence M. Read. Princeton University Press, Princeton NJ, 1961.

Vanishing DeKalb: A Pictorial History. DeKalb Historical Society, Decatur GA, 1985.

Walk Together Children, The Story of the Birth and Growth of the Interdenominational Theological Center, by Harry V. Richardson. Interdenominational Theological Center Press, Atlanta, 1981.

War So Terrible, Sherman and Atlanta, by James P. Jones and James L. McDonough. WW Norton and Co., New York, 1987.

William Berry Hartsfield, Mayor of Atlanta, by Harold H. Martin. University of Georgia Press, Athens, 1978.

Fiction

Gone With The Wind, by Margaret Mitchell. MacMillan, New York, 1936 (still in print).

Midnight in the Garden of Good and Evil, by John Berendt, Random House, New York, 1994.

Check also for recent editions of works by Pat Conroy (**The Prince of Tides, The Lords of Discipline**), Fanny Flagg (**Fried Green Tomatoes at the**

Whistlestop Café), Flannery O'Connor (*A Good Man Is Hard to Find and Others, Everything That Rises Must Converge*), Ferrol Sams, Anne River Siddons, and collected columns by the late *Atlanta Journal/Constitution* humorist Lewis Grizzard.

Other Insight Guides

The 190-title *Insight Guides* series covers every continent, marrying high-quality text with stunning photography as in the present book. A complementary series of more than 100 *Insight Pocket Guides* provides carefully-timed itineraries and personal recommendations from local experts and are designed for the reader with limited time to spare.

Among other Insight titles which cover this region are:

Insight Guide: New Orleans captures the essence of this alluring city, in the process explaining the origins of jazz, giving the best tips on places to eat, and delving into the Mardi Gras.

Insight Guide: Miami focuses on Florida's most visited city, capturing its pungent past and its vibrant present, and illustrating its art deco architecture with top-class photography.

Insight Pocket Guide: Atlanta provides full-day and half-day itineraries which include all the key attractions, plus personal recommendations for dining, shopping and nightlife.

Insight Guide: Florida has comprehensive coverage of the Sunshine State, from the luxury of Palm Beach to the wonders of the Everglades, from the "Last Frontier" of Florida's northern territory to the legendary Daytona Speedway.

Insight Guide: Crossing America is for those restless souls who want to experience America by driving across it. The book documents three routes, vividly portraying the people and places you'll encounter on the way.

A
B
C
D
E
F
G
H
I
J
a
b
c
d
e
f
g
h
i
j
k
l